Industry, the State, and
Public Policy in Mexico

Latin American Monographs, No. 66
Institute of Latin American Studies
The University of Texas at Austin

INDUSTRY, THE STATE, AND PUBLIC POLICY IN MEXICO

By Dale Story

WITHDRAWN

 University of Texas Press, Austin

Library of Congress Cataloging in Publication Data

Story, Dale, 1950–
  Industry, the state, and public policy in Mexico

  (Latin American monographs / Institute of Latin
  American Studies, the University of Texas at Austin ; no. 66)
  Bibliography: p.
  Includes index.
  1. Industry and state—Mexico. 2. Industrialists—Mexico.
  I. Title. II. Series: Latin American monographs (University of Texas
  at Austin. Institute of Latin American Studies) ; no. 66
  HD3616.M43S76   1986   338.972   85–13363
  ISBN 0-292-73837-4

First edition, 1986
Requests for permission to reproduce material from
this work should be sent to
  Permissions
  University of Texas Press
  P.O. Box 7819
  Austin, Texas 78713

To my parents

Contents

viii   Contents

Figures

Tables

Preface

Many of the ideas for this book were developed several years ago while I was conducting a comparative study of industrialization and political change in Latin America. Among other findings, this early research convinced me that more case-study analysis would be extremely useful in exposing the richness and validity of concepts and the importance and completeness of theories in this area.

I selected Mexico for this case study for a number of reasons. First, it is becoming an increasingly significant nation from both a political and an economic perspective. Thus, a better understanding of the political interactions involving its industrial sector could be quite beneficial. Second, scholarly research on Mexico has been reevaluating a number of traditional concepts (including authoritarianism and dependency) as they apply to the country. Analysis of the role of industrialists could contribute to this rethinking of previous notions of Mexico's development. Finally, Mexico presents some significant differences in terms of the major variables that are the focus of this book. Substantiating these differences is a major function of this research. These variations demonstrate that the principal concepts of economic and political development are continuous variables rather than general categorizations, and the Mexican distinctions help uncover important linkages among the variables.

I use two original data sets in this book: industrial production data from 1929 to 1981, disaggregated by twelve industrial branches, and a survey of the political attitudes of industrial leaders from the two most important industrial organizations in Mexico (with a survey of Venezuelan industrial leaders also included for comparison). The industrialization data come principally from primary Mexican government sources, and the survey is a mail questionnaire administered in the summer of 1980. I gathered additional information during research trips to Mexico in the summers of 1979 and 1980 and in the first half of 1983. I interviewed industrial leaders and conducted archival research in public and private libraries in Mexico (particularly those at the Banco de México, Nacional Financiera, and the Centro de Investigación y Docencia Económicas). Sources at a number of U.S. libraries were also utilized, including the Indiana University Library, the Benson Latin American Collection at the University of Texas, the Columbus Memorial Library of the Organization of American States, the Library of Congress, and the U.S. Department of State Library. The librarians at all of these institutions were quite generous with their services and their resources. An extended stay at the Nettie Lee Benson Collection at the University of Texas at Austin in the summer of 1981 was particularly helpful. Throughout the project, I have attempted to utilize as many Mexican sources as possible, including newspapers, magazines, journals, industrial sector publications, government documents, and monographs.

I am grateful to a number of institutions for financial assistance in bringing this research to fruition. Two grants from the Organized Research Fund of the University of Texas at Arlington supported the field research in Mexico in 1979 and 1980 as well as a trip to Washington, D.C., to utilize sources there. A National Endowment for the Humanities summer stipend provided the opportunity to devote full time one summer to writing a major portion of this book, and a grant from the Mellon Foundation financed the research at the Benson Latin American Collection in Austin. Finally, a Fulbright research grant provided an invaluable six-month stay in Mexico in 1983.

During the Fulbright grant, I was fortunate to be affiliated with the Centro de Investigación y Docencia Económicas (CIDE) in Mexico City. CIDE provided excellent resources and a conducive environment for refining the analysis in the latter stages of this research. Colleagues there who were particularly helpful in providing comments, data sources, and insights were María Amparo Casar, Gabriel Díaz Rivera, Eduardo Jacobs, Wilson Peres, and Francisco Valdés.

I am also indebted to a number of other scholars who offered their comments on various parts of this manuscript. David Collier, the late John Gillespie, Paul Kuznets, Philippe Schmitter, and Richard Stryker contributed immensely to the early formulations of these ideas in the context of the comparative research. After the focus switched to a case study of Mexico, several knowledgeable colleagues provided their useful insights and opinions on various chapters: Roderic Camp, William Glade, Daniel Levy, John F. H. Purcell, Karl Schmitt, Evelyn Stevens, Gabriel Székely, and Van Whiting. Of course, none of these individuals are responsible for the flaws that remain.

Finally, personal thanks are owed to Anita, whose patience seldom wore thin, to Arian and Alejandro, who are too young to understand but nonetheless contributed in their special way, and to my parents, who made it all possible.

Industry, the State, and
Public Policy in Mexico

1. Introduction

Mexico's industrial sector has a long history of affecting economic, and even political, outcomes in that nation. Though the Industrial Revolution in Mexico is usually described as beginning in the 1940s, the industrialization process made significant progress in the decades prior to World War II. In fact, industrial development in Mexico can be dated as far back as 1840, when small factories devoted to fabrics, paper, ironworks, and the like, initiated the transition from artisan to modern industry. But the earliest major advances in industrial development were made in the late 1800s, particularly with the construction of railroads and the establishment of metallurgical factories. One of the outstanding accomplishments of this era was the founding in 1903 of the first steel mill in Latin America —the Compañía de Fierro y Acero de Monterrey. Thus, as described in a well-known economic history of Latin America, by the turn of the century "the pace of manufacturing development was sufficiently rapid to place Mexico at the forefront of Latin American manufacturing nations" (Glade 1969:337).

Mexican industrialists also played an important role in political development at an early stage, beginning with the Mexican Revolution of 1910–1920. The incipient industrial sector, both entrepreneurs and labor, supported the Revolution and benefited from it. Many revolutionary leaders, including Francisco Madero, José María Maytorena, Aarón Sáenz, and Venustiano Carranza, came from entrepreneurial backgrounds and had ties to the industrial sector.[1] Also, the first organized industrial groups were formed during the Revolution. In 1917 the Mexican Industrial Center of Puebla took the initiative of asking the government to help establish a national industrial organization to promote the specific interests of industry. As a result, the Congress of Industrialists was arranged in November 1917 to deal with the formation of industrial chambers and means of promoting industrial development (Shafer 1973:25–29). This congress shortly became the Confederation of Industrial Chambers (Confederación de Cámaras Industriales, CONCAMIN), which continues to be the national organization representing industrialists before the state.

The policy initiatives in the revolutionary period that benefited industry included protectionist tariffs in 1916 and tax relief in 1920 (Ross and Christensen 1959:29–31; Glade 1963:85). Finally, the Revolution and its aftermath (especially the reforms of the 1930s) essentially eliminated the large, traditional landowners (the export-oriented oligarchy) as a potent economic and political force and paved the way for industrial dominance in the postwar period.

In the present era, the significance of the Mexican industrial sector has been enhanced by its reemergence as a powerful petroleum-exporting nation combined with its newly acquired status as an advanced developing country (ADC). Though Mexico achieved considerable prominence as a source of petroleum in the 1970s, its history as an international petroleum power is not restricted to recent times. It first emerged as one of the world's major exporters of oil in the initial decades of this century. By 1921 it was second only to the United States as a producer of petroleum. Production peaked at 500,000 barrels per day (or almost 200 million barrels annually) in that year. However, domestic and international factors combined to inhibit oil exploitation in Mexico after that. In particular, the clashes between the foreign oil companies and the Mexican government in the 1930s, which led to the expropriation of all foreign petroleum interests in 1938, caused substantial disruptions in petroleum output.[2]

Though the situation stabilized in the postwar period, the energy picture was bleak for Mexico as it entered the 1970s. Mexico recorded its first overall petroleum trade deficit in 1970, and the imbalance increased to over $250 million in 1974.[3] But new oil deposits were soon discovered, and the Mexican petroleum industry experienced a drastic turnaround in the mid-1970s. By 1981 Mexico was the world's fourth-largest producer of petroleum, and the petroleum wealth was being discussed as the catalyst for rapid industrial development. In probably the major initiative of these years, the 1979 National Industrial Development Plan proposed utilizing petroleum revenues to promote industrial growth.[4] Though economic growth supported by the petroleum boom ended in 1982, the 1983 *Informe* of the general director of the Mexican Petroleum Company (Petróleos Mexicanos, PEMEX) stated that proven reserves of hydrocarbons were 72 billion barrels and that 1982 production of crude oil increased 19 percent over 1981, to 2.746 million barrels per day (*Informe del Director General de Petróleos Mexicanos*, 18 March 1983, pp. 2–3).

Primarily because of the dynamism of its industrial sector, Mexico was also emerging in the 1970s as a member of that elite set of Third World nations labeled the advanced developing countries.[5] One author defines ADCs by four characteristics: (1) relatively advanced levels of economic development, based on rapid and sustained rates of economic growth; (2) relatively large, sophisticated, and diverse industrial sectors; (3) the acquisition of substantial international influence through economic transactions such as trade and capital inflows; and (4) the implementation of effective, outward-oriented development strategies (Mathieson 1979:5–6). Despite the difficulties encountered in the early 1980s, Mexico essentially possesses all of these characteristics. Since the Second World War its economic growth has been rapid, fairly continuous, and reasonably balanced among economic sectors. Yet industry has clearly been the dominant sector, with the highest growth rates and expansion into fairly complex methods of production. Even before the recent petroleum discoveries, Mexico had attained some international stature on the basis of its economic significance in trade and capital transactions. And, despite some high protectionist barriers in certain industries, its development strategy has been increasingly concerned with growth in the external sector. Thus, fueled by Mexico's dual status as an oil-exporting nation and an ADC, the private industrial sector has assumed an even more important part in the country's overall development in recent years.

Mexican industry faces a number of important challenges in the 1980s, especially given the near economic collapse in 1982. Largely because of an enormous external debt and erratic economic policies (especially the devaluations of February and August and the imposition of exchange controls for some four months), real economic growth decreased 0.2 percent in 1982 (with the manufacturing sector the most affected), inflation approached 100 percent, real investment fell over 15 percent, unemployment doubled, and thousands of firms faced bankruptcy. To improve the situation over the long term, the Mexican economy will need to reduce the disequilibriums in the external sector, that is, the dominance of petroleum exports, rapid increases in manufacturing imports, and over-reliance on external financing. For its part, the goals of the private sector will be to diminish the burden of some $25 billion in foreign debt, increase nonpetroleum exports substantially, and attempt to finance its own imports. The economic crisis of 1982 does not necessarily mark the end of Mexico's successful economic development in the postwar period. But the nation faces several years of sacrifice and austerity, and the responses of the private industrial sector will be crucial to overcoming the crisis.

Objectives of This Study

Recognizing the apparent significance of the Mexican industrial sector in the past and at present, the principal objective of this book is to analyze the political and economic roles of industrial entrepreneurs in postwar Mexico. My underlying assumption is that the political and economic activities of the industrial sector are closely intertwined in the mixed economic setting of Mexico.[6] Industrialists have performed important functions not only in accumulating capital and organizing economic enterprises but also by bringing together the forces of social change that have aided in the displacement of traditional elites and by stimulating political and economic modernization. Specifically, industrial entrepreneurs have emerged as a major force influencing the politics of industrial growth. The public-policy arena has become a primary focus of attention for industrialists, whose political role either in organized groups or as individual actors has been significant since the end of World War II.

Despite their importance, few studies have stressed the interrelations of the economic and political functions of industrial entrepreneurs in Mexico.[7] In particular, the political impact of the industrial sector has not been adequately explored. Hence, one of my main objectives is to examine the significance of the political and economic roles of Mexican industrialists. In addition, this book aims to present the principal factors in the industrialization process in Mexico and to analyze the political system in terms of state-industry relations and the impact of industry on public policy.

One of the key relationships this study explores is the influence of the development of industrial entrepreneurship on industrial growth. A rich literature emphasizes the contribution of industrial entrepreneurs to economic progress, industrialization, and various aspects of economic and social change.[8] In the context of Latin America, the general conclusion has been that a strong group of private, domestic entrepreneurs has failed to emerge and assume a significant role in economic progress.[9]

A host of factors have been used to explain this lack of entrepreneurial development: the international division of labor (involving the existence of dependent and monocultural economies in Latin America); increases in the rate of population growth; a high propensity to consume and to invest speculatively; sociocultural deterrents, such as the lack of a "Protestant ethic"; the relative importance of immigrant entrepreneurs and state enterprise as opposed to "national" private entrepreneurs; the permeability of traditional elites in relation to newer elite groups and the overall rigidity of the class structure; and continual political instability. I shall examine critically the conclusion that Latin American industrialists have not been a major force in development and determine whether Mexico represents any significant differences from traditional generalizations about the role of industrial entrepreneurs in Latin American countries.

In addition to their crucial economic functions, industrialists also have become influential political actors. Robert Dahl (1959) has emphasized the importance of the political role of entrepreneurs and has criticized the discipline of political science for failing to examine the relation of business to politics. Since the time of Dahl's critique, awareness of the political significance of entrepreneurs has increased, but few studies before this one have specifically focused on this topic.

The increasing role of the state in the realm of private industrial entrepreneurship, especially in the developing nations, has heightened the relevance of politics to industrial entrepreneurs.[10] Entrepreneurs have always depended on the state for military security, the protection of property rights, the maintenance of political stability, and the impartial administration of laws. But in recent decades, industrial entrepreneurs have come increasingly to rely on the state for important economic assistance, including broadened access to public credit, various incentives for production, protection from external competition, and the provision of adequate infrastructural facilities.

The state's increased role in the economy has led in turn to a greater emphasis on political participation among industrial entrepreneurs.[11] Industrialists have become aware of the need for political influence in order to secure economic advantages, and strategies to achieve political influence have become crucial to them. In many cases, their influence has become especially noticeable in the political parties, in the regulatory agencies, and in the selection of political leaders. A particular concern of Latin American industrialists has been to achieve greater input into the economic planning process.

A number of studies have stressed the importance of organized business or industrial associations as political pressure groups.[12] Particularly in Western European countries like Italy, France, Spain, and West Germany, business associations have become influential power brokers. The Italian industrial association has been described at times as the most successful interest group in that nation, and one author has said that the German business association has been "among the major determinants of Germany's future" (Hartmann 1959:217). The business associations in these Western European countries have important contacts and influence in the political parties, the legislature, and various agencies in the executive branch. In contrast to the organized business groups in Western Europe, those in the United States have at times been much weaker in the political arena and certainly have preferred to cultivate a more apolitical image.[13] As this study will show, industrial associations in Mexico tend to approximate the European model of high levels of political participation and political influence.[14]

In sum, this book will focus on the economic and political roles of Mexican industrialists through several different viewpoints. Utilizing the industrial censuses of Mexico and other official sources, this study will document the pattern of industrial growth (its progress and problems) and the contributions of the private sector to the industrial process. An evaluation of relations between the state and industry in Mexico will lead to a rethinking of the nature of the Mexican state, especially with regard to elite sectors. Finally, the role of the private sector in some recent policy decisions will be examined, and new directions in planning industrial development in the "petroleum era" will be explored.

Theoretical Perspectives and Principal Thesis

This book addresses two major theoretical arguments relating to Latin American development: the meaning of late and dependent development, and the nature of the authoritarian state. I accept the general relevance of these themes to Mexico, but the principal thesis here is that Mexico is an important variant of both.

The concept of late and dependent development describes two related phenomena: (1) industrialization did not become significant in most Latin American countries until the twentieth century; and (2) industrial progress has been generally dependent on a variety of forces external to those countries.[15] Latin American economies began their modernization process after most aspects of a modern society had already been acquired in the advanced industrial countries. The existence of a previous model for modernization produced pressures in Latin America that tended to alter and destabilize its developmental process. The "demonstration effect" gave rise to ever-increasing demands for rapid growth, higher standards of living, greater political and economic equality, advanced technology, and so forth.

But the developing economies were not able to meet all these expectations. Attempts to develop too rapidly produced problems of capital absorption, sectoral disequilibrium, monetary instability, and inappropriate technology. Also, labor and lower-class claims for political influence and more equitable income distribution (no matter how just or warranted) did interfere with the process of capital accumulation. Hence, many aspects of late development presented obstacles to the economic progress of Latin America and served to destabilize political development in the region.

Dependent development has been theoretically and empirically linked to the concept of late development in Latin America, since both are seen as functions of advancement in the industrial nations. The most common definition of dependence states that it is "a situation in which the economy of certain countries is conditioned by the development and expansion of another economy to which the former is subjected" (Dos Santos 1968:26). Dependent relations are said to exist between peripheral nations and center nations, with the economic development of the former plagued by constraints, lack of autonomy, and inequalities (international and domestic). More concretely, economic dependency in Latin America is usually viewed in two dimensions: as trade dependency (commodity or geographic concentration), and as capital dependency (public and private). In terms of the impact of these unequal relations, one of the most frequently cited outcomes (with special relevance to this study) has been the lack of development of a class of private, domestic entrepreneurs.

As previously stated, one of the central themes of this study is that Mexico represents significant variance from absolute interpretations of late and dependent development. First, the timing of development is relative within Latin America, and Mexico experienced certain aspects of modernization quite early. Second, dependency is a continuous variable, and its impact differs according to the degree of dependency and the existence of other, intervening variables. In certain areas Mexico has managed economic dependency with some success, but it also has had to endure certain other aspects of dependency, especially its proximity to the United States. These distinctive characteristics of late and dependent development in Mexico have been reflected in the pattern of industrial growth.

Partly due to its late and dependent development, Latin American industrialization has been posited as having a unique impact on political outcomes. One argument, developed in the context of Western Europe and the United States, states that industrial growth has contributed to political democratization. This theory has been substantiated by considerable empirical evidence. Probably the most influential work in a long line of cross-national studies on this topic is Seymour Martin Lipset's (1959).[16]

However, this theory has been put into question in Latin America by the turn toward authoritarianism in the most industrialized countries of the region. A revised theory, as developed by Guillermo O'Donnell (1973), argues that numerous economic difficulties (trade imbalances, foreign exchange shortages, inflation, and others) are associated with advanced stages of import-substituting industrialization (in intermediate and capital goods). These economic problems create a political environment conducive to the establishment of "bureaucratic-authoritarian" regimes in which the military along with economic technocrats and the "internationalized bourgeoisie" gain dominant political status.[17] These regimes promote advanced industrialization while they favor transnational corporations and exclude the popular sectors (labor and peasants) from economic benefits and political power.[18]

This theory of authoritarian development would appear to fit Mexico in a number of ways. Principally, Mexico is one of the most advanced nations in Latin America, and its political system has usually been depicted as authoritarian. However, this book will argue that Mexico represents an important variant of the authoritarian framework. Especially with regard to state-industry relations, Mexico does not perfectly fit the model of an authoritarian state. The Mexican industrial sector has considerable, independent influence on many policy decisions.

In relating these theoretical perspectives to the objectives of this study, the following chapters critically examine two opposing interpretations of the role of entrepreneurs vis-à-vis the state. One view, labeled the "narrower" conceptualization of entrepreneurs by Frits Wils (1979:15–17), describes the private sector in Latin America as a weak class dominated by foreign interests and by an all-powerful state.[19] Another perspective posits that influential economic elites dominate the state and severely limit the autonomy of state actions (Hamilton 1982:26–39, 282–286). These two perspectives represent antithetical ideal types, which form a continuum along which cases can be arrayed. On the one hand, this book explores how and to what extent the Mexican case deviates from the "narrow" conceptualization of Latin American entrepreneurs entirely subordinate to the state and foreign capital. On the other hand, it analyzes the argument of limited state autonomy by testing a plausible corollary: that the private sector exercises considerable independence from state control. The thesis to be examined here is that Mexico is an important variant from these ideal types, with enviable industrial success due in great part to domestic forces, relative autonomy for elite sectors, and noticeable industrial influence on policy.

Data and Sources

Much of my analysis relies on compilations of data—both quantitative and qualitative—gathered from original sources in Mexico. The quantitative data principally include the measures of industrialization in chapter 2, the information on foreign investment, public enterprises, and government expenditures in chapter 3, and the survey data on industrial entrepreneurs in chapter 5. The industrial data cover the years 1929 to 1983 and are disaggregated into twelve industrial branches. As much as possible, the figures for each industrial branch have been deflated by the price indices for that branch. The principal sources are the comparable industrial censuses since 1929 and Banco de México data. Appendix A discusses the improvements that these data represent in terms of disaggregation and comparability as well as the methods used to calculate the longitudinal, value-added data.

The figures on government expenditures and public firms in chapter 3 come primarily from the publications of government agencies, including the Secretaría de Programación y Presupuesto, the Dirección General de Estadística, Nacional Financiera, and the Banco de México. The public sector spending data extend from 1895 to 1980 and are disaggregated into several different categories. Most of the foreign investment data in chapter 3 (including total foreign investment, manufacturing share, U.S. share, and foreign participation and Mexicanizations by branch) are from published and unpublished documents of the Dirección General de Inversiones Extranjeras, the Secretaría de Comercio y Fomento Industrial (and its precursors), and the Banco de México. Finally, data on individual firms are aggregated in a comparison of the one hundred largest enterprises in the Mexican economy.

The survey data in chapter 5 were collected in 1980 with responses from 109 Mexican industrialists and 32 Venezuelan industrialists who are leaders of the major industrial trade associations in their respective countries. I use the Venezuelan sample as a point of comparison to represent a strong private sector in a more competitive political system. The survey primarily involves fixed-response measures concerning political ideology and perceptions of political influence and is the first survey research to focus on the political orientations of industrial elites in Mexico.

Chapters 4, 6, and 7 largely employ qualitative information on the activities of industrial organizations in Mexico, state-industry relations, certain economic policies and industrial influence, and national plans and development strategies. In addition to the secondary sources available in the literature on these topics, I have utilized publications of private sector groups and government offices, Mexican newspapers and periodicals, and correspondence with some principal political and economic actors in Mexico. Finally, I conducted personal interviews with various Mexican industrialists, government officials, and other individuals on three visits to Mexico (in 1979, 1980, and 1983).

Organization of the Book

This book analyzes the major themes in three parts. The first focuses on the progress of industrialization in the Mexican situation of late and dependent development. In this context, chapter 2 focuses on the pattern of industrial growth in Mexico as it has evolved in the present century, and the third chapter depicts the characteristics of the mixed economic setting in Mexico and compares the relative contributions of state, private domestic, and foreign capital. The second part of the book discusses the political role and ideology of Mexican industrialists and their interest associations. Here, chapter 4 examines state-industry relations in the context of three characteristics of authoritarianism: limited political pluralism, low subject-mobilization, and hierarchical ordering of relationships. And to gain a comparative perspective, the ideology of industrial elites in Mexico and Venezuela is contrasted in chapter 5, especially as that ideology relates to sectoral consciousness, nationalism, and attitudes toward the state and organized labor. Finally, Part 3 emphasizes the role of industrialists in the policy process. In this part, the sixth chapter presents a typology of the policy process and analyzes the Mexican decision not to join the General Agreement on Trade and Tariffs (with a brief contrast with the decision to nationalize the banks); and chapter 7 explores the policy initiatives of the López Portillo administration and early de la Madrid government, especially regarding the development of economic plans relating petroleum policy to industrialization. The Conclusion summarizes the major findings of the book, stresses the linkages among key variables, and discusses future implications of these findings.

Part 1. Industrial Progress under Late and Dependent Development

2. The Pattern of Industrial Growth in Mexico

Industrial growth in Latin America has been among the region's most important socioeconomic phenomena in the twentieth century. Shortly after the 1930 Depression, the more advanced Latin American nations (particularly Argentina, Brazil, Chile, and Mexico) began their "Industrial Revolutions," involving the emergence of a dynamic and self-sufficient industrial sector. To varying degrees, public policymakers and private entrepreneurs began to concentrate on achieving rapid industrial growth. Mexico in particular became one of the few success stories. I use a wide range of data from many different sources to describe the initial emergence of the Mexican industrial sector, the creation of new firms across time, aggregate and disaggregate rates of growth, and the timing of different aspects of industrialization. In some instances, to provide a basis of comparison, I present the Mexican data with similar data from other advanced nations in the region. I use data collected primarily from early industrial censuses to assess the timing of the emergence of a significant industrial sector. Industrial censuses from later years and other sources then provide data on expanding industrial capacity as exhibited in the creation of new industrial firms. I have calculated aggregate and disaggregate growth rates from 1929 to 1983 from the industrial production data described and presented in appendix A. These data have been collected from a wide variety of sources using the following criteria for selection: (1) disaggregate price indices to deflate current values; (2) a "base year" for valuing output that does not have any disproportionately high prices in any industrial category; and (3) the most comparable data available. These data are more comprehensive than any previous compilations and their quality represents a substantial improvement. (The criteria and the actual methods and sources I utilized to ensure the quality of the data are described in detail in appendix A.) Finally, I have used data on import substitution to evaluate the timing of different aspects or phases of industrialization.

In addition to overall industrial growth, the internal structure of the industrial sector and the growth rates of different parts of that sector are important features of industrialization. Thus, this chapter examines not only aggregate levels of industrial output but also industrialization data disaggregated according to different industrial categories. The growth patterns within and among these categories are then explored.

In disaggregate analyses of industrialization, most interpretations agree that industrialization in Latin America is not unique in generally proceeding from concentration on small, labor-intensive firms producing simple, consumer goods to concentration on large, capital-intensive firms employing complex technology and manufacturing capital or producer goods.[1] However, any deviations from this pattern will be uncovered here using the data on disaggregate growth rates and on the structure of the industrial sector. The major industrial categories I use are consumer goods, intermediate goods, and capital goods.

Adjectives used to describe types of industries such as consumer, intermediate, capital, traditional, and dynamic have often been indiscriminately applied. For the sake of clarity, in this study they will be defined according to the classifications of the "old" International Standard Industrial Classification (ISIC):[2]

20 = foodstuffs	30 = rubber products
21 = beverages	31 = chemical products
22 = tobacco	32 = petroleum products
23 = textiles	33 = nonmetallic mineral products
24 = footwear, clothing	34 = basic metal products
25 = wood and wood products	35 = metal products
26 = furniture	36 = machinery
27 = paper and paper products	37 = electrical machinery
28 = printing and publishing	38 = transport equipment
29 = leather	39 = other

The classifications corresponding to various adjectives used in this study to describe types of industries are as follows:[3]

consumer = 20–26	traditional (or light) = 20–29
intermediate = 27–32	
capital = 33–39	dynamic (or heavy) = 30–39

Some disaggregate analyses have stressed the existence of chronological "stages" of industrial growth in Latin America.[4] But, since these stages actually tend to vary from country to country, this study will focus instead on the timing of three aspects or types of industrialization: (1) industrialization that is concentrated in the processing of export products; (2) import-substituting industrialization (ISI) that is concentrated in the substitution of imports of consumer goods, especially nondurables (often termed horizontal ISI);[5] and (3) ISI that is concentrated in the substitution of imports of intermediate goods and capital goods (often termed "vertical" and "backward-linking" ISI).[6] Differences in the timing of these aspects of industrialization reflect important differences in patterns of industrial growth.

Emergence of Industry

Of all the nations in Latin America, only Argentina established an industrial base earlier than Mexico. Even Brazilian industry lagged slightly behind that of Mexico during the early stages of industrialization. All three countries had the early advantages of large market size and urban concentration, though per capita income was somewhat lower in Mexico (United Nations Economic Commission for Latin America 1966:8). Industrialization in these three countries began in earnest in the 1880s, and growth in Mexico was especially rapid from 1894 to 1901.[7] During this period, wealthy Mexicans and immigrants formed the core of an emerging group of industrialists. One private report in 1883 claims some 3,000 industrial establishments in existence, and an official survey shows a total of 6,234 industrial establishments in 1902.[8] The most comparable data for Argentina and Brazil show 32,000 industrial firms in Argentina by 1908 and about 4,000 industrial enterprises in Brazil by 1909.[9]

After the rapid growth up to the turn of the century, Mexico's industrial production slowed somewhat in the next two decades, and most industrial indices declined in absolute terms from 1911 to 1920, during the Revolution (Wythe 1949:276; Rosenzweig 1965:318, 328–331). But in the 1920s Mexican industry expanded tremendously, even though it had not yet achieved parity with Argentine industry. The first Mexican industrial census, in 1930, lists a total of 48,850 establishments with almost 320,000 employees and close to one billion pesos in total capital invested.[10]

Another measure of the timing of initial industrialization is the industrial share of the gross domestic product. The data in table 1 confirm the respective rankings of Argentina, Mexico, and Brazil in the emergence of

Table 1
Industrial Share of GDP, Argentina, Brazil, Mexico
(Percentages)

	Share of GDP		
	Argentina	**Brazil**	**Mexico**
1900	18.1	—	12.6
1908	18.7	—	12.5
1929	22.8	11.7	14.2
1936	25.9	11.8	16.8
1945	28.9	16.2	20.9

Source: United Nations Economic Commission for Latin America (1966), Statistical Annex, p. 2.

Note: — means no data available.

the industrial sector. By this indicator, Argentine industry had progressed enormously by 1900, whereas Mexican industry did not reach this level until around 1940. Yet, the industrial share in Mexico remained larger than that in Brazil through 1945, and, as will be seen below, in the postwar period both nations have surpassed Argentina.

Timing of Creation of New Industrial Firms

One of the difficulties in evaluating the creation of new industrial enterprises across time in Mexico is the lack of comparability of certain of the industrial censuses. The 1930 census includes almost all industrial firms, but the 1935, 1940, and 1945 censuses only cover those establishments producing over ten thousand pesos in total output. The more recent censuses ostensibly cover all establishments, but apparent differences do exist among these, especially between the 1950 and 1955 censuses, on the one hand, and the 1960, 1965, 1970, and 1975 censuses, on the other. Thus, one cannot be sure what the trends in the establishment of new industries were between 1945 and 1950 and between 1955 and 1960.

The figures for the number of establishments and the average number of employees per establishment for the industrial censuses from 1935 to 1975 are given in table 2. Though the 1930 industrial census reports over forty-eight thousand industrial firms, 91.8 percent of these had a total production less than twenty thousand pesos. Taking into consideration the differences in coverage between the 1930 and the 1935 censuses, the

Table 2
Mexican Industrial Census Data

	Total No. of Establishments	Avg. No. of Workers/ Establishment	% of Total Establishments in Traditional Industries
1935	7,619	41.7	82.6
1940	13,510	28.9	89.8
1945	31,195	18.4	82.4
1950	74,252	10.9	75.9
1955	75,770	28.7	74.4
1960	83,207	9.7	77.4
1965	119,563	12.9	73.7
1975	119,212	14.3	73.5

Sources: **1935–55**: Comparative data published in Dirección General de Estadística, *Sexto Censo Industrial 1956*, Vol. 1; **1960–75**: *VII Censo Industrial 1961, VIII Censo Industrial 1966, IX Censo Industrial 1971,* and *X Censo Industrial 1976.*

number of establishments probably increased slightly in those five years. In the next ten years the pace of new-firm foundings quickened, and the number of establishments rose 77 percent from 1935 to 1940 and 131 percent from 1940 to 1945. This decade produced the largest proportional increase in the number of industrial enterprises, since the growth of new industries was much slower from 1950 to 1955 and from 1960 to 1975. Hence, the greatest expansion in the number of industrial enterprises occurred between 1935 and 1945.

Some of the largest industrial enterprises also appear to have been created relatively early in Mexico. The greatest average number of workers per firm is recorded in the 1935 census, though the elimination of the smallest establishments in this census may partially account for this large number. The average size of industrial firms as measured by the average number of workers then decreased from 1935 to 1945, since much of the increase in numbers of firms was apparently in very small establishments. This trend reversed itself after 1950, when there was a large increase in the average number of workers. From 1955 to 1960, even considering the differences in coverage of the two censuses, the number of workers per establishment probably declined, but this average began to increase again in the 1960s. Overall, most of the industrial establishments have always been small, and in 1975 establishments with five or fewer employees still constituted over 80 percent of the total.

The timing of the creation of new industrial firms can also be examined according to the type of industries being formed. In addition to the early expansion of industrial enterprises, these data demonstrate the early modernization of the Mexican industrial sector. Table 2 also shows the percentage of industrial firms devoted to the traditional industries. Though these firms have always constituted a majority, their share began to decrease after 1940. In fact, the greatest decline in the proportion of traditional industries occurred from 1940 to 1950. Of course, the corollary is that the dynamic industries were making their greatest strides in this decade in terms of new establishments.

Aggregate Growth Rates

The most common indicator of industrialization is the aggregate growth rates of industrial output, and this composite measure gives another view of the relative success of Mexican industrialization across time. Table 3 provides the comparative average annual growth rates in industry for the five most advanced economies in Latin America: Argentina, Brazil, Chile, Mexico, and Venezuela. The overall average industrial growth rate in Mexico is 6.9 percent annually. This ranks behind only the rapid industrialization of Venezuela, which has used petroleum revenues to fuel progress in manufacturing for decades. The Mexican data also reiterate the early successes in that country. Mexico had its highest rates of growth in the 1940s, though growth rates since that time have also been high (figure 1).

Disaggregate Growth Rates and Industrial Structure

These aggregate data reveal only part of the picture of industrial development in Mexico. The growth pattern of different branches within the industrial sector and the relative importance of those branches provide important details on the strengths and weaknesses within the industrial sector. The disaggregate data here have been grouped according to consumer-goods, intermediate-goods, and capital-goods industries (table 4 and figure 2). The basic hypothesis that the emphasis of *growth* shifts chronologically from consumer to intermediate to capital-goods industries does not really fit the Mexican experience. No consistent periods of increase in growth rates for intermediate or capital goods industries are detected, and the growth rates in consumer-goods industries have not steadily decreased (except from 1940 to 1955). But the data do present a distinct difference in the *total* average growth rates for capital and intermediate goods industries, on the one hand, and those for consumer-goods industries, on the

Table 3
Average Annual Industrial Growth Rates
(Percentages)

	Average Annual Industrial Growth Rate				
	Argentina	Brazil	Chile	Mexico	Venezuela
1900–10	7.3	—	—	—	—
1910–20	2.9	—	6.7[a]	—	—
1920–30	7.4	3.9	2.1	—	—
1930–35	0.8	8.0	5.6	−0.5[b]	—
1935–40	4.9	8.3	3.6	8.4	—
1940–45	5.0	8.5	3.1	13.1	5.4[c]
1945–50	7.2	10.7	4.1	11.9	17.0[d]
1950–55	6.8	5.1	3.4	5.0	18.6
1955–60	3.6	9.5	5.7	7.6	11.6
1960–65	5.0	4.2	6.5	9.8	9.8
1965–70	5.1	11.5	1.9	8.9	4.6
1970–75	5.0	7.2	−3.2	6.2	9.0
1975–80	−1.0	5.8	7.6	6.8	5.0
1980–83	−4.5	−5.5	−6.1	−2.4	−0.6
Overall average	4.4	6.4	3.6	6.9	7.7

Sources: The sources for Mexico are described in appendix A. The data for the other nations have been collected using the same criteria and methodology as the data for Mexico. For those sources up to 1975, see Story (1978:426–447), and after 1975, see Inter-American Development Bank, *Economic and Social Progress in Latin America.*

Notes: — means no data available.
[a]For 1914–20
[b]For 1929–35
[c]For 1936–48
[d]For 1948–50

other hand. The capital and intermediate-goods industries have developed at almost twice the rate of the consumer-goods industries.

These differential growth rates have produced the changes in the structure of the industrial sector shown in table 5. Consumer goods have continually decreased their share of industrial output, and intermediate and capital goods have steadily expanded their proportions (except during the economic crisis of the early 1980s, when capital-goods industries in

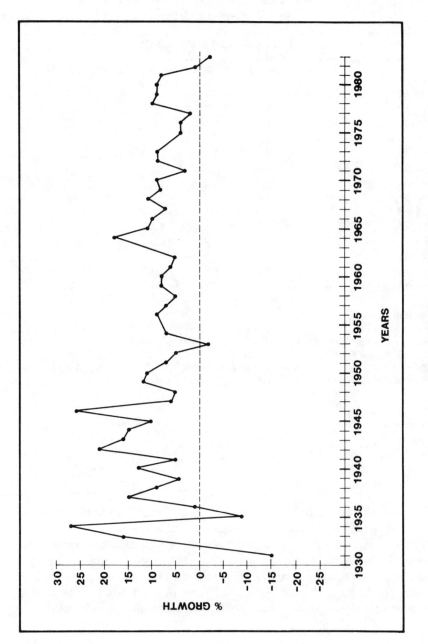

Figure 1: Annual Industrial Growth Rates, Mexico

Table 4
Average Annual Disaggregate Industrial Growth Rates, Mexico
(Percentages)

| | Average Annual Disaggregate Growth Rate | | |
	Consumer Goods	Intermediate Goods	Capital Goods
1929–35	−0.2	−2.6	0.5
1935–40	4.5	13.6	22.9
1940–45	14.4	10.6	10.6
1945–50	8.0	14.7	21.3
1950–55	3.0	12.2	4.6
1955–60	4.4	11.6	9.8
1960–65	6.8	10.4	13.3
1965–70	6.3	10.7	10.2
1970–75	2.1	6.7	9.0
1975–80	5.0	5.2	9.0
1980–83	1.4	1.9	−7.2
Overall average	5.0	8.5	9.6

Sources: See appendix A.

particular performed poorly). In 1930, over three-fourths of all industrial production was concentrated in the consumer-goods industries. Their percentage dropped below 50 percent in 1956, and capital goods finally surpassed consumer goods in relative proportions in 1968. Actually, the capital-goods industries achieved their most successful growth decades earlier. After stagnating along with the rest of industry in the early 1930s, their highest growth rates came between 1935 and 1950 (table 4 and figure 2). This again substantiates the early modernization of industry in Mexico.

Timing of Different Aspects of Industrialization

These data on disaggregate growth rates and the composition of the industrial sector can be combined with data on import substitution to delineate the timing of three different stages of industrialization: (1) export-oriented industrialization; (2) horizontal ISI, stressing the substitution of nondurable consumer goods (generally light or traditional industries); and (3) vertical ISI, stressing the substitution of intermediate and capital goods (generally heavy or dynamic industries). Once again the

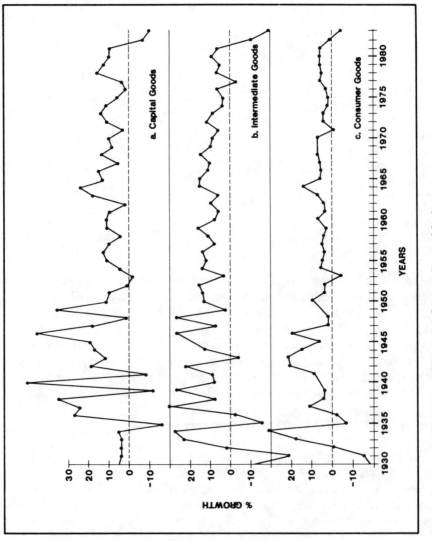

Figure 2: Annual Disaggregate Industrial Growth Rates, Mexico

findings demonstrate the successful industrial growth in Mexico and the relatively early development of the more advanced industrial branches.

Table 5
Composition of Mexican Industry
(Percentages)

	Consumer Goods	Intermediate Goods	Capital Goods
1929	76.0	13.5	10.5
1935	77.0	11.9	11.1
1940	64.2	15.0	20.8
1945	67.9	13.5	18.6
1950	56.9	15.2	27.9
1955	51.8	20.8	27.4
1960	44.7	25.0	30.3
1965	38.8	25.7	35.5
1970	34.4	27.9	37.7
1975	31.5	29.1	39.4
1980	26.0	26.4	47.6
1983	29.1	30.1	40.8

Sources: See appendix A.

The Porfirian era (1876–1910) was the golden age for export-oriented growth.[11] Economic policies favored the agricultural and mineral export sectors by encouraging foreign investment and land concentration and by providing for the integration of the market through improved internal transportation and communication facilities. Growth in the export sector was astounding, as the value of exports rose 600 percent in thirty-five years. Exports also became diversified, since gold and silver were declining while industrial minerals such as lead and copper were increasing in importance and new agricultural exports were being introduced, including coffee, cattle, cotton, and sugar (King 1970:4; Hansen 1971:13–14).

Though exports of primary products dominated the economy, they nonetheless stimulated the emergence of modern industry. The export boom required greater industrial inputs and, by creating a larger domestic market, led to increased consumption of manufactured goods. Other factors favoring industrial growth included improved domestic transportation, the abolition of taxes on internal transactions (*alcabalas*), peso depreciation from 1876 to 1905, and stability in the prices of imported goods and the costs of labor (Rosenzweig 1965:318, 326–337, 330; Hansen 1974:19).

The leading industries established in the Porfiriato were primarily in areas related either to exports or to agricultural production (cotton and wool mills, jute factories, paper mills, sugar refineries, breweries, cigarette factories), and many of these have remained the most important enterprises in their respective areas (Wythe 1949:275–276). Yet, in Mexico industrialization was linked to the export sector to a lesser degree than in many other Latin American countries (Rosenzweig 1965:319). For example, all leather products were exported without tanning, and many fibers (most notably henequen) left the country without elaboration.

The end of the period of export-led industrialization can best be set as 1929, when the creation of the National Revolutionary party (Partido Nacional Revolucionario, PNR) ended the era of "*caudillismo*" in Mexican politics and the Depression diminished Mexico's foreign trade by half.[12] Of course, the Revolution began the dismantling of the traditional export economy, and the agrarian reform and nationalizations of railroads and petroleum companies under Cárdenas (1934–1940) were also key factors in the demise of export-sector hegemony. But the events surrounding 1929 marked the most crucial turning point from export domination to domestic industrialization and import substitution.

Horizontal ISI in Mexico was stressed between 1930 and 1955. The data in table 6 show that imports of traditional industrial goods as a proportion of total supply dropped from 26.8 percent to 14.2 percent in this period.[13] The only time ISI in these goods was not achieved was from 1939 to 1944. Thus, rapid growth in all industrial sectors in the early forties was not due to import substitution but rather to vastly increased domestic demand (King 1970:24). Both domestic production and imports of manufactured goods increased in the war years.

Of course, import substitution was first completed in *finished* consumer goods (those that are imported as final, complete products as opposed to those that must be assembled). Data show that by 1939 imports of these goods were only a negligible part (2.7 percent) of total expenditures for consumption (King 1970:135–136). Then, by 1945 imports were less than 10 percent of *all* consumer goods, and most of these imports were in durable consumer goods. The import share of total supply of consumer goods increased from 1946 to 1947 and again from 1950 to 1953 to 13 to 14 percent, but devaluations in the 1948–1949 period and in 1954 plus other industrialization policies apparently contributed to lowering this proportion below 10 percent each time. The greatest decreases were in consumer durables (United Nations Economic Commission for Latin America 1957, pt. II:143ff). By 1960, data on individual categories show that only in automobiles (24.8 percent) did imports provide more than 10 percent of domestic consumption of finished consumer goods, and most of these automobile imports went only into the United States border areas of Mexico (King 1970:139).

Table 6
Import Coefficients, Mexican Industry
(Percentages)

	Import Coefficient			Import Coefficient	
	Traditional Industries	Dynamic Industries		Traditional Industries	Dynamic Industries
1929	26.8	73.6	1955	14.2	40.4
1934	23.5	70.2	1960	9.7	46.4
1939	20.4	51.5	1965	10.4	39.2
1944	21.6	53.9	1970	10.8	34.7
1950	17.1	51.0	1981	10.0	38.5

Sources: Trade data are from Dirección General de Estadística (DGE), *Anuario estadístico del comercio exterior, Anuario estadístico, Compendio estadístico*, and Instituto Mexicano de Comercio Exterior, *Boletín Mensual*. Industrialization data prior to 1981 are from the results of various industrial censuses published by the DGE and by the United Nations, Department of Economic and Social Affairs, Statistical Office, *Growth of World Industry*. Industrial data for 1981 are from Banco de México (1982a).

Note: The import coefficient equals imports as a percentage of total supply (domestic value-added plus imports).

The early development of heavy industry in Mexico is shown by the substantial progress achieved in vertical ISI in the late 1930s (see tables 4 and 6). Imports as a percentage of total supply in the dynamic industries fell from 70.2 percent in 1934 to 51.5 percent in 1939, which represents the largest drop in any five-year period. Average annual growth rates in capital goods also reached their peak between 1935 and 1940 (22.9 percent *annually*). Though vertical ISI slowed significantly in the 1940s, it picked up again after 1950. And since 1960 import substitution has concentrated exclusively on dynamic industries. Yet, there is still progress to be made in the substitution of consumer durable, intermediate, and capital goods. As of 1966, over 55 percent of all investment in machinery and equipment was spent on imports (King 1970:140), and in 1970 over one-third of the total supply of goods in dynamic industries was still being imported (table

6). The late 1970s actually saw increases in the import coefficients of some critical industries, and by 1980 around half the total supply in a number of heavy industries was being imported: basic chemicals (62.3 percent), machinery (59.5 percent), automobile (47.9 percent), and electrical appliances (47.6 percent—see Schatán 1981:86–87; Casar 1982:94). Even so, one economist says that "Mexico appears to have import-substituted more effectively than many other developing countries of similar size and wealth" (Reynolds 1970:212).

Conclusion: Industrial Strengths and Weaknesses

Certainly this chapter has emphasized the industrial successes in Mexico —both in an absolute sense and relative to other Latin American nations. Aggregate industrial growth from 1929 to 1983 averaged 6.9 percent annually, second only to Venezuela among the more developed Latin American countries. The most rapid growth has been in the intermediate- and capital-goods industries, which have averaged 8.5 and 9.6 percent annual growth rates, respectively. Thus, Mexico has achieved integrated industrialization in that industrial expansion has moved beyond the light, consumer goods into the basic, heavy industries.

The timing of industrial progress provides further evidence that Mexico has been in the forefront of industrial development in Latin America. Only Argentina created its industrial base earlier than Mexico. By 1930 almost fifty thousand industrial firms existed in Mexico (though many were fairly small), and manufacture's share of GDP was around 15 percent. The shift to heavier industries also appeared quite early in Mexico. The most rapid establishment of new firms, especially in the dynamic industries, occurred from 1935 to 1945. And the decade and a half between 1935 and 1950 produced an extremely fast-paced development of capital-goods industries as well as substantial import substitution in these industries. Since that time industrialization in all areas has continued to advance at high rates.

However, at the same time that this industrial success has vaulted Mexico into the exclusive company of the advanced developing countries, significant problem areas have arisen. In the first place, Mexico has not been immune to cycles of industrial growth, that is, successive periods of ascent and descent in annual growth rates. The decade of the 1970s is a good example.[14] After peak years in 1972 and 1973, industrial growth slowed substantially in the mid-1970s. Growth rates decreased from 9 percent in 1973 to 3 percent in 1975 and stayed at modest levels for the next two years (4 percent in 1976 and 3 percent in 1977). These figures were considerably below expectations. But the period from 1978 to 1981 saw industrial growth rebound to about 10 percent in both 1978 and 1979 and around 7 percent for both 1980 and 1981. The economic crisis of 1982 then abruptly began another downward cycle, as manufacturing production in real terms actually fell 2.4 percent in that year and declined over 7 percent in 1983.[15]

Another serious problem, relating to the structure of the Mexican industrial sector, has been the existence of certain "dualities," especially in terms of location and firm size. The first dualism is seen between the major urban centers (Mexico City and its immediate surroundings, Guadalajara, and Monterrey) and the rest of the country. Most of the national industrial capacity is concentrated in these three metropolitan areas. Data from the 1975 industrial census show that they provided about two-thirds of total value-added in the manufacturing sector. The other dualism exists between an abundance of small and inefficient industrial establishments and a few large and dynamic firms that dominate the sector. In the 1975 industrial census over 80 percent of all industrial firms were classified as "artisan" (less than five employees), yet these provided less than 3 percent of total value-added. Small enterprises, with between six and one hundred employees, provided the remaining 20 percent of the total value-added. On the other hand, the medium and large enterprises were only 2.6 percent of the total number of manufacturing establishments but they contributed 77 percent of the total value-added in industry (Secretaría de Programación y Presupuesto 1980a). These concentrations in terms of size and location have had negative social effects (unemployment, urban congestion, and the like) and have stymied the development of a more diversified national industrial plant.

The enormous deficits and disequilibriums in the external sector represent another problem area for Mexico's manufacturing industries. Though Mexico has achieved considerable success in import substitution, especially in consumer goods, overall levels of imports have continued to rise. In fact, between 1977 and 1980 the total import coefficient of imports to internal demand increased from 10 percent to 17 percent (Casar 1982:87). In particular, Mexican industries greatly depend on the importation of capital goods and raw materials. This dependence is partially a legacy of an overvalued peso, but has been exacerbated by the trade liberalization of recent years. Manufactured imports have increased noticeably in the last few years, and the industrial sector has been the major contributor, in terms of economic sectors, to the country's trade deficit.

Government policies certainly have contributed to this external deficit for industry. Overprotection in certain areas has made many industries uncompetitive in international markets and encouraged them to focus solely on the domestic market. And the overvalued peso has promoted the dependence on cheap imports of parts and supplies. In addition, the industrial firms themselves have not looked toward external markets. One 1978 government study of a representative sample of private industrial enterprises showed that only 39 percent had exported any of their products in 1977 and that these exports represented only 9 percent of their total sales (Oficina de Asesores del C. Presidente de la República 1978:125). Hence, as a result of both government policies and the inward-oriented attitudes of the industrial firms, manufactured exports have been stagnating in recent years and actually declined in real terms in 1979 and 1980. Manufactured exports were over one-third of total exports in the mid-1970s but had declined to below 15 percent by 1982.

Due to their overreliance on foreign borrowing and external sources of inputs, the foreign exchange problems of 1982 especially affected the industrial enterprises. Many private companies found themselves unable either to service their foreign debt or to import the necessary goods and raw materials. Successive devaluations had greatly increased their already enormous debt burdens, and the dollar shortage left them without any foreign exchange to make interest payments or to buy foreign goods. The classic example of these difficulties is Grupo Alfa, the largest private conglomerate in Mexico, which had to appeal to the government for an emergency loan in the fall of 1981 and suspended its principal payments on some $2.3 billion in foreign debt in April 1982.

The Mexican economy appears particularly weak in comparison with the other ADCs. One of the reasons could be the increasing dominance of petroleum. Mexico's advantages as an oil exporter may actually be a threat to its status among the rapidly industrializing Third World countries. The expansion of manufactured exports, which are the most important aspect of ADCs, can be stymied in a petroleum-dependent economy with an overvalued currency. Whatever the actual impact of petroleum wealth in Mexico, that country's economy has not performed as ably in recent years as the economies of the other five ADCs.

The data in table 7 show Mexico's inferior position among the ADCs. It has the slowest growth rates in real GDP and surpassed only Hong Kong in industrial growth, indicating that its domestic economy has not functioned comparably with the others. The absolute value of Mexico's exports has been less than that of the other ADCs, and growth rates in Mexican exports were also the lowest in the period 1967–1977. Mexico's relative position in export growth improved in the late 1970s, but only because its exports did not slow down as much as those in the other countries, largely

because of foreign sales of Mexican petroleum. Of course, these economies are the elite within the Third World; almost all other developing
countries remain envious even of Mexico's accomplishments.

Table 7
Economic Data for Advanced Developing Countries

Economic Indicator	Hong Kong	Singapore	South Korea	Taiwan	Brazil	Mexico
Average annual real GDP growth, 1970–81 (%)	9.9	8.5	9.1	7.2[b]	8.4[a]	6.5
Average annual growth in industrial production, 1970–81 (%)	4.3[a]	9.0	14.4	12.2[c]	9.1[a]	7.4
Average annual growth in value of exports (%)						
1967–77	20.2	21.9	41.2	30.7	22.1	13.5
1970–81	9.7	12.0[a]	22.0	28.2	8.7	15.3
1981 value of exports (million $)	21,737	20,967	21,254	23,065	23,172	20,033

Sources: Mathieson (1979:10, 13, 15); World Bank, *World Development Report*, various
years; and *Europa Year Book 1983.*

Notes: [a]1970–80

[b]1970–79

[c]1970–77

In sum, Mexico has achieved general postwar success in industrialization, though it has shown some signs of weakness, especially in relation to
other advanced developing nations. Besides industry's vulnerability to
cyclical growth, dualisms in size and location, and external deficits, the
nation's increasing concentration on petroleum production poses a potential threat to industrial expansion, especially in manufactured exports.
These weaknesses are the greatest challenges for Mexican industry in the
1980s.

3. Dependent Industrialization in a Mixed Economy

A recurring theme in both the dependency literature and the research on entrepreneurship in Latin America is that private domestic entrepreneurs have not fulfilled their function as a leading force in national development. Unlike in the industrial nations, in which private domestic capital is overwhelmingly dominant, most economies in Latin America rely significantly on two additional sources of investment and entrepreneurship: the state (or the public sector), and subsidiaries of multinational corporations (MNCs). The state assists economic development through public policies designed to promote the private sector and through direct public investment in various enterprises. It may try to bolster private firms through various incentives and advantages, or it may simply decide to assume the role of owner itself.[1] Foreign investment also may displace domestic capital in some of the most advanced industrial branches.

Though it is difficult to determine cause and effect, the linkages between a weak and dependent private sector and stronger roles for both the state and MNCs are clearly posited in the literature. In cases of "associated-dependent development," substantial if not miraculous rates of economic growth are said to be achieved largely through the impetus of foreign investment in conjunction with government intervention in the economy.[2] In contrast, private firms that are wholly owned by national capital are described as the smallest, least efficient, and most marginal enterprises. The previous chapter established the existence of a pattern of relatively successful industrialization in Mexico, but that analysis did not reveal how much of that success could be attributed to the efforts of private domestic entrepreneurs. This chapter begins to answer that question by assessing the relative positions of the two "rivals" of Mexican industrialists: the public sector, and foreign capital.[3]

The Evolution of State Intervention in the Economy

The concept of a mixed economy as applied to Mexico indicates that the state has assumed a much more important economic role than in the purer capitalist economies, such as the United States. The government plays a crucial part in a mixed economy through a wide range of policies, including regulation, social services, artificial incentives, and public investment. This analysis concentrates on those aspects of government economic involvement most pertinent to the industrial sector, beginning with public policies of industrial protectionism and promotion.[4]

The import-substitution strategy adopted in postwar Mexico has aimed at aiding industrial development with selective economic policies while protecting domestic production from external competition (imports). Protectionist policies have included foreign-exchange regulations, tariff rates, and import licenses, whereas promotion policies have primarily embodied credit manipulation and tax exemptions.

In most cases, three periods in the evolution of protectionist policies can be identified: (1) a period when such policies are intended either as temporary responses to balance-of-payments crises or as revenue measures; (2) a period when such policies are specifically designed to encourage industrialization; and (3) a period when protectionism is deemphasized in favor of efficiency. As might be expected, most promotion policies are instituted during the second phase of protectionist policies, the phase in which government economic policies are most deliberately employed to aid industrial growth.

Some tariffs were granted to the incipient industrial sector in the nineteenth century. In fact, these tariffs, which primarily applied to textiles, provided 60 percent of all federal government revenues in 1868 (De la Peña 1945:190). But tariffs did not become relevant to other industrial branches until 1916, when a new protectionist tariff was granted to jute and malt manufacturers.[5] By this time the first phase of industrialization policies was in full swing. The state had begun selectively to consult with interested private parties over tariff revisions, but had not adopted a policy of encouraging industry in general through higher tariffs. The 1930 tariff law was the basis for all future tariff legislation, and it placed the highest levies (ranging from 40 to 100 percent) on textiles. However, in the 1930s most tariffs were still levied primarily for revenue purposes. Thus, the Great Depression did not lead to major qualitative changes in economic policies in Mexico, partly because of the continued preoccupation with consolidating political power after the Revolution.

The first industrial-promotion policies were initiated in the 1920s. The government announced tax relief for certain new industrial ventures in 1920, and additional tax exemptions for some industries were decreed in 1927 and 1932. Yet, these had little effect until they were extended considerably, around 1940. Credit policies acquired some importance in the 1930s with the expansion of public credit institutions and the financing of public works that were beneficial to industry. Nacional Financiera (NAFINSA, the national Development Bank) was created in December 1933 to engage in a wide variety of financial operations, including industrial loans. Also, in 1937 the Industrial Development Bank (Banco Nacional Obrery y de Fomento Industrial) was established. Still, these credit policies benefited industry only in a minor way.

The second phase of industrialization policies, in which economic policies are deliberately used to protect and promote industry, began in the 1940s. Promotion of industry through tax exemptions and credit policies became especially significant between 1939 and 1941, and foreign-trade policies became overtly protectionist in the four-year period from 1944 to 1947.

Tax exemptions have been an important part of industrial promotion law in Mexico. A 1939 decree and the 1941 Law of Manufacturing Industries granted five-year exemptions from virtually all federal taxes to "new and necessary" industries (defined in note 6). The 1946 Law for the Development of Manufacturing Industries extended exemptions to more industries and granted exemptions for up to ten years, though eligibility requirements became more precise and fewer taxes were covered. Due to changes in the administration of this law in 1948, even fewer taxes were included in the exemption program, and restrictions were applied to the qualifying firms, such as requiring a certain amount of inputs to be bought in Mexico and fixing price ceilings. The Law for the Development of New and Necessary Industries in 1955 codified these restrictions. Though the number of qualified firms and the amount of the exemptions were being reduced, the government was furthering its effort to promote import substitution by aiding those industries with the potential for replacing imports.[6]

Public credit became a significant factor in industrial development in December 1940, when a new charter reorganized NAFINSA to concentrate on industrial development.[7] From then until 1946, NAFINSA's principal assets were in iron and steel, electrical appliances, sugar, paper, and fertilizers. One of its most notable accomplishments was the Altos Hornos de México iron and steel plant at Monclova in the northern state of Coahuila. This project was initiated by private capital during the Second

World War, but NAFINSA had become the majority stockholder by 1947, since private investment proved inadequate. After 1947 NAFINSA's promotional efforts became particularly concentrated in infrastructure and heavy industry. Throughout most of the postwar period it reflected Mexico's commitment to import substitution, since a major criterion for assistance was the potential for import replacement (Blair 1964:225–226). Most recently its emphasis has been on the capital-goods industry. By 1981 the NAFINSA industrial group included eighty-one enterprises of which nineteen were created in the 1977–1981 period. These included firms to manufacture steam turbines, heavy steel castings, petrochemicals, electrical equipment, tractors, and the like (Nacional Financiera, *1981 Annual Report*, pp. 6, 47–52).

Protectionist policies have been more important in achieving industrial growth in Mexico than the credit or tax-exemption policies, and the quantitative control of imports through a licensing system as well as *ad valorem* tariffs have been the mainstays of this protectionist system since 1947. Before 1947 the only instrument for protecting domestic industries from foreign competition was the specific tariff, and this was used mostly for purposes of revenue. In 1930 trade duties and tariffs represented 37 percent of total federal revenues, and in 1940 they were still 23 percent (De la Peña 1945:190). Some tariffs were high enough to be considered protective in the 1930s (mostly for textile and food products: see Mosk 1950: 68), but in general even the tariff increases were implemented to raise revenues.[8] That the tariff was assigned according to weight or volume (a specific tariff) was also a detriment to its protectionist purposes, since the effect of the tariff was reduced as the price of imported goods increased. Finally, in December 1942 the United States and Mexico signed a trade agreement in which both countries agreed not to increase certain tariff rates (ibid.:72; Izquierdo 1964:251–252, 264–265). This further inhibited any attempts to increase the protectionist nature of Mexican tariffs.

The protectionist era in Mexico's trade policy was ushered in by two dramatic decrees in July 1947: the creation of import controls, and a change in the tariff system.[9] The officially declared purpose of these measures was to correct the balance-of-payments deficits incurred after World War II, but the actual intent (as demonstrated in the size of the tariff increases and the types of goods subjected to controls) was to protect many Mexican industries from foreign competition. The tariff decree increased a number of duties, and in November 1947 the method of levying duties was changed from specific to compound (a combination of specific and *ad valorem* methods), which halted the erosion of the effectiveness of the specific rate. Most of the items selected for the tariff increases, which were as much as 100 to 200 percent, were essential consumer goods, thus strongly suggesting a protectionist purpose behind the new tariffs (Mosk 1950: 75).

The import-control system had actually been created in 1944 under an emergency war powers act, but it was not applied until 1947. The type of goods subjected to import licensing under the 1944 decree suggests that an underlying purpose was protectionism for import-substituting industries. Up to the summer of 1947 the government had one general list and several minor lists of goods requiring permits, and the majority of these goods were semimanufactured or finished products that were competing with domestic output (Mosk 1950:80–81; Strassman 1968:289). The controls were not applied, however, until July 1947, when a group of luxury goods representing some 18 percent of total imports in 1946 were prevented from entering Mexico in order to correct the balance-of-payments deficit. Yet even this ban on luxury goods was adopted with an eye to protectionism. For instance, the ban on automobiles was accompanied by annual quotas on imports of assembly parts, so that between 1946 and 1948 the number of automobiles assembled in Mexico increased from 10,460 to 21,597 (Izquierdo 1964:265).

Thus, the 1944 decree and the 1947 application of import controls, along with the 1947 changes in the tariff system, set up the framework for the protectionist system of postwar Mexico. The import controls were eased in 1951, but reimposed and extended in 1954, when a number of consumer goods were added to the list of controlled imports. Beginning in 1959, industrial integration (or "backward-linking" industrialization) was emphasized as a major objective of protectionist policies (Izquierdo 1964: 273; King 1970:42). Manufacturers were encouraged to buy substantial domestic inputs, especially in electronics and automotives.

During the 1960s the promotion of industrial integration continued to be a major goal of trade policies, though some emphasis was being placed on more efficient production of domestic goods and on the exportation of manufactured goods (Strassman 1968:290–291; Bueno 1971:199–202). No major revisions were made in tariffs, but the proportion of items in the tariff code subject to import controls was increasing, from 44 percent in 1962 to 60 percent in 1966. And the greatest protection was afforded those items with the largest degree of product elaboration in the internal market (Ten Kate et al. 1979:39, 134–135, 153). President Echeverría then reinforced the system of protectionism in the first half of the 1970s through a general tariff rise and the extension of controls to all imports.

Trade liberalization received its first impetus during López Portillo's administration, when the petroleum boom improved the balance-of-payments picture for Mexico and the demand for imports escalated. López Portillo began to replace import licenses with tariffs and to lower tariff levels gradually. In 1979 he initiated a policy of figuring import duties according to the "normal value" of the imported good rather than the "official price." This change was an attempt to produce "economically rational" duties that in most cases would be lower than previous duties. These measures had the greatest effect on increasing the imports of durable consumer and capital goods (Schatán 1981).

The process of trade liberalization has not been a steady one, however. With the deficit in the external sector growing in 1981, new measures were taken in the summer to stem the flow of imports. Tariffs were raised substantially on some three hundred "luxury" goods, and import controls were reestablished on almost all items. Of course, the imposition of foreign-exchange controls and the general lack of foreign exchange in mid-1982 greatly reduced the level of imports. The scarcity of foreign currency continued in 1983, but the new government of Miguel de la Madrid did revive the goal of trade liberalization. The average level of tariffs was reduced from over 20 percent to about 15 percent, and the policy of granting prior permits on imports was eased (*Razones*, 24 January–6 February 1983; and *Unomásuno*, 16 February and 9 May 1983). The secretary of commerce and industrial development, speaking before the National Association of Importers and Exporters, summarized the trade policy of the de la Madrid team when he criticized the "permanent protection" of previous governments and emphasized the goal of making Mexican industries more competitive in international markets (*Excélsior*, 1 January 1983).

Exchange-rate policies in the 1970s were not an instrument of government aid to industry, but rather were more of a burden on the industrial sector. Throughout the postwar period Mexico had maintained a remarkably stable exchange-rate system. But by the 1970s the peso was becoming increasingly overvalued. The overvalued peso generally was a deterrent to more rapid industrial growth in that it discouraged Mexican exports (especially manufactured products that were characterized by price elasticity in demand) while encouraging imports. Though Presidents Echeverría and López Portillo devalued the peso in 1976 and 1982, respectively, these actions were too late and too little. Figuring an equilibrium exchange rate according to a theory of "purchasing power parity," the Mexican peso remained overvalued, in spite of the devaluations. This overvalued peso in turn dampened industrial expansion by increasing the relative prices of manufactured exports and decreasing the relative prices of competing imports. Only with the establishment of a "free" rate of exchange by de la Madrid in December 1982 did Mexican manufactured exports finally become price competitive. But even then, exporters complained that they were forced to exchange their foreign currency at a "controlled" rate, some 33 percent lower than the "free" rate (interview, 16 March 1983).

Of course, the significance of government industrialization policies does not necessarily indicate the subordination of private industrialists to the state as an economic actor (see table 8 for a summary of these policies).

Table 8
Major Industrialization Policies, Mexico

Date	Policy
PHASE I	
1916	Tariff increase
1920	Tax exemptions
1927	Tax exemptions
1930	Tariff law
1932	Tax exemptions
1933–38	NAFINSA (public credit)
	Public works
	Industrial Development Bank (credit expansion)
PHASE II	
1939	Tax exemptions
1940	NAFINSA reorganized (public credit)
1941	Law of Manufacturing Industries (tax exemptions)
1944	Import controls
1946	Law for the Development of Manufacturing Industries (tax exemptions)
1947	Import controls
	Tariff increases and *ad valorem* tariff
1954	Import controls extended
1955	Law for the Development of New and Necessary Industries (tax exemption)
1959	Import controls for industrial integration
1964	Emphasis on more efficient production
1970–75	Tariff increases and extension of import controls
PHASE III	
1976	Import controls replaced
1979	"Normal" valuation for import duties
1981	Import controls reestablished
1983	Tariff reductions and easing of controls

Most of these policies were designed to benefit certain enterprises and activities within the private sector. As such, they could be evidence of the influence of private industrial entrepreneurs (to be explored in detail in parts 2 and 3 here). A more explicit indicator of the direct economic role of the state as a rival to private entrepreneurship, however, is the level of public ownership and investment.

The Growth of the Public Sector

The Mexican state has become a substantial economic power through steadily increasing expenditures in productive capacity. Though most of the early initiatives to expand public control of the economy occurred in the two decades between 1920 and 1940, some government acquisitions actually predated the Revolution. The most significant expansion of the public sector under Porfirio Díaz was the purchase engineered by finance minister José Limantour of 51 percent of the stock in the three largest railroads. These were then integrated into the government-controlled National Railways of Mexico, or Ferrocarriles Nacionales Mexicanos (Wright 1971:51–61). Then during the Revolution, the basis for public ownership was greatly strengthened through Article 27 of the 1917 Constitution. This article granted subsoil rights to the government, allowed private property to be expropriated for public use, and provided for government limitations on the holdings of private individuals (LaCascia 1969: 1–14; Wright 1971:61–71; and Hansen 1974:89–90).

President Plutarco Calles really laid the economic base of the modern state in the 1920s, with the creation in 1925 of the Banco de México (the Central Bank) being most important. This institution provided public control over the money supply and over major financial institutions.[10] The Banco Nacional de Crédito Agrícola was founded by Calles in 1926 to boost investment in the agricultural sector. The presidency of Lázaro Cárdenas brought the establishment of four more public financial bodies: the Banco Nacional Hipotecario Urbano y de Obras Públicas, in 1934, to finance public works and low-cost housing; the Banco Nacional de Comercio Exterior, also in 1934, to grant short-term credits for agricultural exports; the Banco de Crédito Ejidal, in 1935; and the Banco Nacional Obrero y de Fomento Industrial, in 1937. As previously mentioned, the National Development Bank, NAFINSA, was started in 1933. By 1953, all public sector banks provided over half of all bank financing (Glade 1963: 73–74), and in 1982 López Portillo completed state domination of this sector by nationalizing the remainder of the private sector banks, except the one foreign bank (Citibank).

The foundation for government control in mining and in generation of electricity was also established under Calles. Article 27 of the 1917 Constitution rendered the 1884 Mining Law unconstitutional (the law did not recognize state subsoil rights), but substitute legislation was not enacted until the 1926 Mining Law (Wionczek 1971). This law restored the nation's subsoil rights and placed all mining enterprises under government regulation. Also in 1926 Calles promulgated the National Electricity Code, though the law was not implemented until 1928 (Wythe 1949:319–324; Wionczek 1964:41–43). This legislation declared the electricity industry to be a public utility subject to state regulation.

In the late 1930s Cárdenas created the first nationalized industries in railroads and petroleum and formed important public enterprises, such as PEMEX and the Comisión Federal de Electricidad (CFE).[11] He based his actions on the 1936 Expropriations Law, which allowed the state to nationalize private properties for "causes of public utility" (Wythe 1949: 321–322). In 1937 he expropriated the minority foreign interests in the National Railways, and the foreign-owned petroleum companies were nationalized in 1938.[12] In 1937 he also formed the first major public corporation, CFE, with the purpose of "organizing and directing a national system for electrical power generation" (Wionczek 1964:62). This was followed in 1938 by the creation of PEMEX to carry out the exploration, production, refining, and eventually the marketing of Mexican oil. Almost from their inception, these two public corporations have dominated the government's public enterprise portfolio. Numerous industrial plants were also taken over by the state in the late 1930s.

The next major moves to expand public ownership were initiated during the administrations of Adolfo López Mateos (1958–1964) and Gustavo Díaz Ordaz (1964–1970), beginning with the nationalizations of the large, foreign-owned electrical power firms. Though the CFE had greatly increased its ownership of total electrical capacity (up to 40 percent by 1960), one-third of all electricity generated in Mexico in 1960 was still in the hands of two foreign companies: the American and Foreign Power Company, and the Mexican Light and Power Company. The foreign companies claimed they could not obtain sufficient profits in Mexico due to government control over their rates, however, and they began to consider selling their holdings to the state in the late 1950s. The nationalization plans for both companies then were quickly completed in 1960.[13] Though scholars disagree over who was most favored by the terms of compensation, the companies themselves declared that they had been treated equitably.[14]

The mining industry was also the object of nationalization efforts in the

1960s (Wionczek 1967:237–251, 288–294, and 1971:289–292, 304; Baklanoff 1975:48–49). Initially, the 1961 Mining Law promoted the "Mexicanization" of mining firms by stipulating that only firms with a majority of Mexican capital (either public or private) would receive new concessions. Tax incentives for the transfer of control into Mexican hands were added in 1963. These measures resulted in the acquisition of the Mexican affiliates of American Metal Climax and American Smelting and Refining by joint enterprises of Mexican public and private capital. The large sulphur industry in Mexico, which was the world's leading exporter of sulphur in 1964, was also affected by the nationalization measures of the 1960s. Two U.S. firms, Pan American Sulphur and Texas Gulf Sulphur, dominated this sector until the mid-1960s. But in 1967 the Mexican government acquired 34 percent and private Mexican capital 23 percent of Pan American, and Mexican public and private capital evenly divided the purchase of 66 percent of Texas Gulf. The dominance of the state in the sulphur industry was completed in 1972 when the government, acting through NAFINSA, bought the remaining foreign interests in Pan American and thereafter controlled three-fourths of Mexico's sulphur production and one-half of its reserves. Most recently, the copper mining industry (specifically the Mexican subsidiary of Anaconda) was Mexicanized in 1973, when the Mexican government purchased 26 percent ownership and private Mexican interests another 25 percent.

Another economic branch affected by nationalist sentiments was the telephone system (Baklanoff 1975:46). In 1958 majority control of the nation's telephone system, Teléfonos de México, passed from foreign control to private Mexican entrepreneurs. And under the same policies of President Luis Echeverría that brought state ownership to the sulphur and copper mining industries, the public sector assumed control of Teléfonos de México in 1972.

Echeverría (1970–1976) greatly increased the size of the public sector in terms of expenditures as well as of direct ownership. From the revenue side, total government income increased from 8 percent of the gross domestic product in 1970 to 12.5 percent in 1975. But expenditures were growing even faster, as the federal deficit increased sixfold during the Echeverría *sexenio* (six-year term). The most well-known public works were the government-built resorts at Cancún and Ixtapa, but Echeverría also built a new steel mill and hydroelectric plants and financed new oil exploration. Overall, the number of state-owned companies multiplied spectacularly, from 86 to 740 (P. Smith 1979:280–281). In 1974 alone the public sector increased its exports by 76 percent over the previous year and its personnel by 30 percent (*Análisis Político*, 8 November 1976).

Yet, spectacular jumps in government spending and ownership did not begin with Echeverría. Throughout the twentieth century, public-sector expenditures have increased enormously (table 9). The only exceptions are the tumultuous years surrounding the Revolution. Even when expressed in real per capita terms, public sector spending from 1895 to 1980 grew by a factor over eighteen times the original level. The greatest advances have

Table 9
Public Sector Expenditures, Mexico

	Expenditures (millions of 1960 pesos)			Total Public Sector Per Capita Spending	
	A Total Public Sector Spending[a]	B Public Enterprises[b]	B/A (%)	1960 Pesos	% growth 5-Year Intervals
1895	1,622	0.0	0.0	128	
1900	1,924	0.0	0.0	141	10.2
1905	2,093	0.0	0.0	145	2.8
1910	1,782	0.0	0.0	118	−18.6
.					
.					
1925	2,874	296	10.3	189	
1930	3,108	300	9.7	188	−0.5
1935	3,660	320	8.7	202	7.4
1940	5,195	822	15.8	264	30.7
1945	6,392	1,178	18.4	287	8.7
1950	10,305	3,197	31.0	400	39.4
1955	13,551	3,392	25.0	452	13.0
1960	24,097	8,499	35.3	689	52.4
1965	39,948	14,343	35.9	966	40.2
1970	55,378	19,202	34.7	1,128	16.8
1975	98,890	31,241	31.6	1,689	49.7
1980	162,971	69,263	42.5	2,331	38.0

Sources: Mann (1979); Análisis Político, 30 November 1980; Secretaría de Programación y Presupuesto, Información sobre gasto público 1969–1978; Dirección General de Estadística, Anuario estadístico; and Banco de México, Indicadores económicos.

Notes: [a]Includes the federal government, all federal entities (states, municipalities, and the Federal District), and public enterprises.

[b]Also referred to as the decentralized enterprises—includes the capital spending of the "organismos descentralizados" and the "empresas paraestatales" along with the current and capital expenditures of the national social security agencies (IMSS and ISSSTE).

occurred in the postwar period, especially between 1955 and 1965 and again from 1970 to 1980.

Leading the way in these increased expenditures have been the public enterprises—often referred to in English as the "decentralized" enterprises or in Spanish as the "*organismos descentralizados*" and "*empresas paraestatales.*" Beginning with a small expenditure in 1925 (exclusively devoted to Ferrocarriles Nacionales de México), spending on the decentralized enterprises had increased over 200-fold by 1980. In the late 1970s these public sector firms accounted for one-half of the federal government budget (excluding states and municipalities), though projections for the austerity budget of 1983 showed their share reduced to "only" 41 percent of total federal government expenditures (Nacional Financiera 1981:310, 317–318; *Diario Oficial*, 31 December 1982). Of course, these are the expenditures on productive capacity that most closely touch the private sector.

The significance of direct public investment in the industrial sector is evident in data dividing government expenditures between capital and current categories and among administrative, economic, and social spending. Of course, the two categories (which are not mutually exclusive) most relevant to private industrial enterprise are capital expenditures, which create durable assets, and economic spending, which separates outlays on economic sectors such as industry and agriculture from other categories like defense and social welfare. Though current spending still exceeds capital outlays, the latter category grew steadily at the expense of the former between 1925 and 1975 (table 10). Also, economic-category expenditures had surpassed the other two classifications by 1940. Despite somewhat contradictory data in recent years (see note a in table 10), spending in the economic sectors has continued at high levels. In examining the sectoral allocations of public investment since 1940, the greatest increases have come in industry, which by 1979 received close to one-half of the total (table 11). Total public investment in real terms has at least doubled every decade, and almost tripled in the 1970s. And within this growth in investment, industry has been the dominant sector.

Direct state investment has also focused on the largest enterprises in the Mexican economy. In an economy with ownership already heavily concentrated, the Mexican government has increased this tendency by investing in the very largest firms. In comparisons of the six largest Latin American nations in the early 1960s, only Mexico had an ownership structure in which the eleven largest business firms were exclusively owned by the state (Brandenburg 1964:51–66). Those companies, in order of their size in 1964, were Ferrocarriles Nacionales de México, CFE, PEMEX, Compañía de Luz y Fuerza del Centro (electricity), Banco Nacional de Crédito Ejidal, CONASUPO, Ferrocarril del Pacífico, Banco Nacional de Crédito Agrícola, Industrial Eléctrica Mexicana (electricity), NAFINSA, and Ferrocarril Chihuahua al Pacífico. Of the top thirty corporations in 1964, the

Table 10
Total Public Sector Spending, Classified, Mexico
(Percentages)

| | Classification | | | | Classification | | |
	Current	Capital	Total	Admin-istrative	Eco-nomic	Social	Total
1895	93	7	100	86	9	5	100
1925	78	22	100	49	43	8	100
1940	63	37	100	33	49	18	100
1960	61	39	100	21	39	40	100
1975	60	40	100	26[a]	37[a]	37[a]	100
1980	65	35	100	—[a]	—[a]	—[a]	—[a]

Sources: Mann (1979); and Secretaría de Programación y Presupuesto, *Anuario estadístico 1980*.

Notes: [a]FitzGerald (1978a:4) presents different data for 1971 to 1975, which show a greater role for economic expenditures. His respective figures for administrative, economic, and social spending percentages are 17, 60, and 23. Data from Mexican government sources (Dirección General de Estadística) show that by 1979 economic expenditures were 75 percent of the total.

Table 11
Sectorial Allocation of Public Investment, Mexico

| | Public Investment (%) | | | | | |
Sector	1940–49	1950–59	1960–68	1969–72	1973–76	1977–79
Agriculture	18	15	9	13	18	21
Industry	14	30	39	37	34	43
Transportation	54	39	26	22	23	14
Social benefit	12	14	23	26	23	20
Administration & defense	2	2	3	2	2	2
Total (billions 1960 pesos)	2.7	6.0	14.2	22.1	34.6	60.7

Sources: FitzGerald (1978a:6); and Secretaría de Programación y Presupuesto (1980).

Mexican state controlled 82.8 percent of the ownership, compared to 74 percent ownership for the Venezuelan government, 61 percent in Argentina, 59 percent in Brazil, 54 percent in Colombia, and 43 percent in Chile.

The degree of state ownership in the largest Mexican enterprises has declined somewhat recently, but is still substantial. In 1972 the Mexican goverment controlled 42 percent of the largest fifty nonfinancial firms, and by 1978 the twenty-nine largest state enterprises owned 68.3 percent of the total capital in the top one hundred Mexican corporations (Newfarmer and Mueller 1975:53; Lomnitz 1982:61). In terms of sales, state firms provided 32 percent of the sales of the top one hundred industrial corporations in Mexico in 1975 and averaged about 45 percent of the sales of the one hundred largest firms from all sectors between 1974 and 1981, before increasing to over 60 percent in 1983 (see table 23). The 1976 industrial census also indicates the extremely large size of the state enterprises, which were on the average fifty times the size (according to value-added) of the private industrial firms (Secretaría de Programación y Presupuesto 1979a).

At present, the most important state enterprises are PEMEX and the two electric companies (CFE and Compañía de Luz y Fuerza del Centro). In fact, 1975 data show that these three companies received 66 percent of total goverment outlays on public enterprises and produced over 75 percent of total value-added by public firms (table 12; FitzGerald 1978a:11). PEMEX by itself is by far the largest enterprise in Mexico and in recent years has accounted for 20 to 25 percent of the federal government budget.[15]

Yet, state-owned companies still span a wide range of activities. According to the 1976 industrial census, though the foodstuffs branch has the largest number of public firms outside the energy sector, state enterprises are diversified throughout industry and mining (table 12; also see Peres Núñez 1982). Among the total of over eight hundred public corporations (including the so-called auxiliary entities) cited by NAFINSA in 1982 in *El Mercado de Valores*, the most important can be listed in five categories:[16]

1. Basic products for industry and agriculture: PEMEX, Grupo SIDERMEX (steel mills of Altos Hornos de México, Fundidora Monterrey, and Siderúrgica Lázaro Cárdenas), Siderúrgica Nacional (steel), Fomento Industrial SOMEX (automotive, petrochemicals, and metallurgy), Fertilizantes Mexicanos (chemicals), Diesel Nacional (automotives), and Productos Pesqueros Mexicanos (fishing).

2. Electricity: CFE and Compañía de Luz y Fuerza del Centro.

3. Communications and transportation: Teléfonos de México; Aeronaves de México; Ferrocarriles Nacionales Mexicanos and other railroad

Table 12
Production of State Enterprises, by Industrial Branch, 1975, Mexico

Activity	No. of Establishments	Total Product (million pesos)	Value-Added (million pesos)
Industry			
Foodstuffs	70	7,169	2,471
Beverages	2	52	17
Tobacco	24	.2,123	873
Textiles	24	2,473	1,113
Footwear and clothing	1	170	83
Wood and wood products	15	580	288
Furniture	2	11	7
Paper and paper products	10	1,271	484
Printing and publishing	3	76	56
Chemical products	18	3,640	942
Petroleum products	1	253	114
Nonmetallic mineral products	7	716	460
Basic metal products	17	13,363	4,588
Metal products	9	1,586	780
Machinery	6	327	137
Electrical machinery	3	988	414
Transportation equipment	14	8,660	2,768
Other industry	1	41	28
Subtotal[a]	227	43,499	15,623
Mining			
Carbon and graphite	5	624	268
Metallic minerals	10	1,687	999
Nonmetallic minerals	3	1,084	765
Salt	2	2	2
Subtotal[a]	20	3,397	2,034

Sources: Secretaría de Programación y Presupuesto (1979b) and (1980).

Note: [a]The industry and mining subtotals do not include the "auxiliary entities," of which there were 478 in 1975, with a total value-added of 1,384 million pesos.

Table 12—Continued

Activity	No. of Establishments	Total Product (million pesos)	Value-Added (million pesos)
Energy			
Extraction and refining of petroleum and basic petrochemicals	95	65,693	40,217
Electrical energy	32	21,235	15,563
Subtotal	127	86,928	55,780
Total	374	133,824	73,437

companies; Aeroméxico and Mexicana (airlines); Caminos y Puentes Federales de Ingresos (toll roads); Productora e Importadora de Papel (newsprint); and Aeropuertos y Servicios Auxiliares (airport).

4. Commerce: CONASUPO; Instituto Mexicano del Comercio Exterior (foreign trade); and Instituto Mexicano del Café (coffee).

5. Banking: all, except the one foreign bank (Citibank). Prior to the bank nationalizations the most important state financial institutions were the Banco de México and NAFINSA. The largest of the nationalized banks are BANCOMER, BANAMEX, Banco SERFIN, Banco Mexicano SOMEX, and Multibanco COMERMEX.[17]

This suggests that public ownership (by its sheer size) can pose a potential threat in terms of supplanting private enterprise. However, a number of questions about the relative importance of public investments in Mexico can be raised, and any conclusions about the superior and growing size of the Mexican public sector need to be substantially moderated. In the first place, the data show that those segments of the government's budget of most concern to the private sector have not increased their proportional share throughout the last three decades. Outlays on public companies, capital expenditures, economic sectors, and industrial investment have not appreciably increased as a percentage of total public spending since 1950 (tables 9–11). Also, public investment as a proportion of total investment and as a proportion of the gross domestic product has not increased since 1940. Public investment in the forties was almost one-half of the total investment, whereas by the seventies it was only about two-fifths.[18] Finally, the total of governmental exhaustive expenditures (those on productive capacity) plus investment of government enterprises as a percentage of the gross domestic product remained around 10 percent from the 1940s through 1970 (Reynolds 1971:338; Aceituno and Ruprah 1982:60). Though this percentage did increase noticeably during the Echeverría *sexenio*, public expenditures in Mexico have still maintained a fairly low and reasonably constant share of GDP.

The Mexican public sector even appears relatively small in comparative data. In the mid-1960s, Mexican government expenditures as a percentage of GDP were substantially less than the averages for other countries, regardless of the size of the per capita product (Reynolds 1971:343–345). In direct comparisons with eight other Latin American nations in 1966 (ranging in size from Bolivia to Brazil), Mexican government expenditures are by far the smallest percentage of the gross national product. And among twenty-four nations in 1975, total public sector spending as a percentage of GDP in Mexico was 16.7 percent, compared to an average of 29.3 percent for eight industrialized nations and 23.0 percent for sixteen developing countries.[19] Hence, whether compared with other nations in the region or worldwide, government expenditures in Mexico are among the lowest when expressed as a proportion of the total national product.

Finally, private Mexican industrialists benefit from many of these government expenditures, including those on state-owned companies. Government enterprises provide private investors with a relatively adequate infrastructure (roads, airports, railroads, ports) and with many subsidized goods and services (from banking to electricity) at artificially low rates and prices. Of the major public companies listed above, those in most direct competition with private entrepreneurs are probably CONASUPO, the steel mills, the fertilizer company, and the manufacturer of diesel engine products. Others, including the electrical enterprises, the communication and transport companies, and the banking institutions, are generally beneficial to private enterprise. Even the largest public corporation, PEMEX, is not opposed by private business leaders. Though they may criticize inflationary spending by the petroleum company, they do not question the state's ownership of this subsoil resource.

Public Policy toward Foreign Capital

The other potential rivals to private Mexican entrepreneurs are the subsidiaries of multinational corporations operating in Mexico. Foreign investment became a powerful force in Mexico in the late nineteenth century, during the Porfiriato. Despite the antiforeign sentiments of the Mexican Revolution and the nationalist strains that continue to permeate Mexican ideology, foreign investors have retained a prominent position in modern Mexico.

Due to the historical diversification of the Mexican economy, foreign capital has not been concentrated in one or two principal sectors, in contrast to such monocultural economies as Chile's and Venezuela's.[20] But the development of government policies toward foreign enterprise in Mexico follows a similar pattern, of increasing state control as the balance of power shifts to the host government. This process, which has progressed at an uneven pace, has centered around two policy goals, the nationalization of certain basic industries, and the Mexicanization of the remainder. Of course, some of these policies were key aspects of the expansion of the public sector, as discussed above. As will be seen in more detail here, the first goal, nationalization, was advanced significantly in the 1930s, whereas Mexicanization was particularly emphasized in the early 1960s and again in the early 1970s.

Mexico during the administration of Porfirio Díaz was quite attractive to European and U.S. investors. The economy prospered, with mineral exports leading the way,[21] and the development strategy was designed to attract foreign capital to this sector (Wright 1971:51-61). The crucial pieces of legislation were the 1884 Mining Law and the 1901 Petroleum Law—both of which gave subsoil rights to surface owners (usually foreign interests). Even in the early stages of the Revolution, the more moderate leadership saw the need to court foreign enterprise. In his initial revolutionary program, the Plan of San Luis Potosí, Francisco Madero (who ousted Díaz) promised to respect all foreign economic holdings (ibid.: 61-71; Ruiz 1976:29).

The interests of foreign capital were first challenged when Venustiano Carranza (soon to be president) pledged to nullify all foreign contracts and to end all monopolies held by international businesses. And, of course, these nationalist opinions were incorporated into the 1917 Constitution through Article 27. In addition to bestowing subsoil rights on the state and allowing the expropriation of foreign private property, the article included the so-called Calvo Clause, named after the Argentine Dr. Carlos Calvo (Wright 1971:97-101; Ramos Garza 1972:13-19). Essentially, this provision rejects any foreign intervention to collect debts or protect property by making all foreigners subject to the same laws as citizens of the host country. Such intervention had been an embarrassment for Mexico in the past (the Mexican-American War of 1846 and European intervention in 1862); Article 27 aimed to discourage similar occurrences in the future.

For over two decades following the 1917 Constitution, the Mexican state and foreign investors struggled over ownership and management of natural resources (especially petroleum) and essential services (especially electricity). The foreign oil companies had legitimate worries about the security of their investments. The Mexican government under Obregón first tried to reassure them with the 1923 Bucareli Pact, which recognized the rights of foreign owners who had properly acquired their petroleum interests before 1917. Then, President Calles altered the Mexican stance by enacting the 1925 Petroleum Law, which recognized existing petroleum rights for only fifty years, and the 1926 Mining Law, which reaffirmed public ownership of subsoil rights. In the same nationalistic vein, the 1926 Electricity Code established government regulatory control over the electric companies.

Though the 1925 Petroleum Law was amended in 1928 (largely because of the efforts of U.S. Ambassador Dwight Morrow) to confirm in perpetuity oil rights obtained before 1 May 1917, the stage was set for Cárdenas's dramatic expropriations of the foreign oil companies in 1938. The nationalization of petroleum, still celebrated annually in Mexico, together with several other policy initiatives marked the 1930s as a decade that fulfilled much of the nationalism embodied in the 1917 Constitution. The oil expropriation was precipitated by a labor disagreement, and a contributing factor was the 1931 Labor Law, which among other provisions required that 90 percent of all employees (except management) be Mexican (Glade 1963:88). Of course, the takeover of the petroleum companies was preceded by the 1936 Expropriations Law and the 1937 nationalization of the railroads. Finally, the decade saw two pieces of legislation enacted in areas of the economic infrastructure dominated by foreign capital. The 1938 Law of Electrical Industries extended government regulations, limited existing concessions to fifty years, and instituted a policy of no new concessions to foreign companies (Wionczek 1964:59–74), and the 1939 Communications Law reserved communications facilities to Mexican companies. The 1930s were clearly a high point of Mexican nationalism.

However, much more conciliatory policies toward international businesses were pursued over the next decade and a half. President Avila Camacho (1940–1946) immediately set out to soothe the ruffled feelings of the expropriated property owners. Between 1940 and 1942 the claims of all U.S. oil companies were settled, and those of British oil companies were paid by 1946 (Mosk 1950:84; Baklanoff 1975:46). Also, the Mexican-American General Agreement of 1941 was negotiated to settle in full the claims of expropriated U.S. landowners. These accords established the cooperative tone of relations between the state and foreign investment in the immediate postwar period.

From the viewpoint of foreign investors, the only disadvantageous policy during the Avila Camacho *sexenio* was the Emergency Decree of 27 June 1944, which required permission from the Ministry of Foreign Relations for foreign investors to acquire enterprises, to form new Mexican corporations in joint ventures, or to displace Mexican investors (Wright 1971:71–92, 101–113; Ramos Garza 1972:19–33). For the first time the foreign relations minister was empowered to require majority Mexican ownership (Mexicanization). The decree, based on a 1942 law that enabled the president to suspend individual freedoms during the war, was originally intended only as a temporary response to the influx of foreign capital into Mexico during World War II. But when Congress suspended the 1942 law in 1945, it allowed all emergency economic measures to become law. Hence, the Ministry of Foreign Relations continued to follow the 1944 decree, which became the basic legislation regulating foreign investment.

Shortly after the 1944 decree became permanent law, the original list of activities required to be majority Mexican-owned was published. These included broadcasting, the motion picture industry, airlines operating from Mexico, urban and highway transport, fishing companies, carbonated beverage enterprises, and publishers. For fifteen years after this initial list was issued, very few areas were added to the Mexicanization requirements. In fact, President Alemán (1946–1952) began an intentional policy of enforcing the 1944 decree very loosely.

Mexicanization did not become meaningful until the López Mateos administration (1958–1964). A much more significant change than the trivial lists previously published of companies covered by the 1944 decree was López Mateo's selective denials of necessary import licenses and tax exemptions to companies without majority Mexican ownership (Wright 1971:71–92). A series of additional measures from 1958 to 1962 further strengthened the policy of Mexicanization. In 1958 Mexican interests assumed majority ownership in the telephone system. The 1959 Petrochemical Law gave the state control of certain petrochemical activities and the Mexican private sector control of the remainder. This legislation has been described as the "earliest effort to give legislative detail to Mexicanization policy" (Business International Corporation 1979:11). Also in 1959 the government announced that all companies producing raw materials or basic products must have majority Mexican ownership. The electrical power companies were nationalized in 1960, and the new mining law of 1961 disallowed any new concessions to foreign-dominated firms. Finally, a 1962 automotive industry decree began the process of Mexicanizing all inputs to the automobile assembly companies.[22] This plethora of policy changes swung the pendulum significantly toward Mexican control of key sectors and away from foreign dominance.

The Díaz Ordaz government (1964–1970) was more open to foreign investment, but it did not retreat from the initiatives of López Mateos and even enacted the 1970 Mexicanization Decree six months before the presidential succession. This decree required majority Mexican capital in steel, cement, glass, fertilizer, cellulose, and aluminum. Yet, the incoming president, Luis Echeverría still provided a stark contrast with Díaz Ordaz and swung economic nationalism as far to the left as had Cárdenas in the 1930s.

Within Echeverría's populist program stressing income redistribution, an enlarged economic role for the state, and a sometimes openly hostile relationship with private business, probably the most far-reaching initiatives were several laws regulating foreign capital and technology (Aguilar M. et al. 1977:160–182; Blair 1977; Weinert 1977). The most important was the 1973 Law to Promote Mexican Investment and Regulate Foreign Investment, which made 51 percent Mexican ownership the general rule for new ventures, established a Foreign Investment Commission (CNIE, Comisión Nacional de Inversiones Extranjeras) to enforce its provisions, and restricted the use of *prestanombres* ("borrowed names") to circumvent Mexicanization requirements.[23] This law was really a response to demands coming from opposite directions. Its enactment followed a host of criticisms of MNCs in the media as well as pressures from the U.S. government to clarify the "rules of the game" for foreign investors. It replaced previous Mexicanization laws and decrees and became the definitive statement on Mexican policy toward foreign investment.

The CNIE was empowered to approve or reject new foreign investment and to grant exceptions to the Mexicanization requirements. The 1973 law enumerated seventeen factors to be considered by the CNIE in considering applications from foreign investors. These criteria include the contributions of the investment to the national economy and to development goals, its potential multiplier effects, and its impact on local cultural values. Though the 1973 law was a more detailed and concrete statement of official policy toward foreign investment, the policy, as has always been true, was implemented on a case-by-case basis. This flexibility has permitted substantial discretion on the part of the president and his appointed bureaucrats. Under Echeverría, it was applied in a fairly strict manner, discouraging and alienating the international business community.

Other major foreign-investment legislation enacted under Echeverría included the 1973 Law on Transfer of Technology and the 1976 Law on Patents and Trademarks (Business International Corporation 1979:30–35; Whiting 1979:17–18). The technology transfer law required the registration and review of all new contracts through a newly created registry on technology transfer. The objectives of the law were to limit excessive payments or royalties in licenses and contracts and to eliminate any contracts deemed incongruous with Mexican interests. The patents and trademark legislation constrained the use of patents and mandated that foreign trademarks must be linked to a new Mexican trademark (*Latin America Economic Report*, 28 May 1976). This latter provision was a rather novel idea that has proved difficult to enforce because of private sector opposition.[24]

The hostile orientation toward MNCs under Echeverría was changed dramatically by López Portillo, under whom a rapprochement between foreign investors and the Mexican government occurred. This reconciliation was due in part to a lowering of nationalist rhetoric and a desire to court the foreign capital needed for Mexico's economic development and in part to the willingness of foreign investors to accept the rules of the game in Mexico now that oil had been rediscovered. López Portillo first considered altering the 1973 legislation on foreign investment but decided this was too difficult. Instead, he chose to interpret the legislation more loosely.[25] The Mexican government became willing to bend the Mexicanization requirements for acceptable foreign investment that provided modern technology not available in Mexico.

Foreign-investment policy has become even more flexible under de la Madrid, who has allowed more expansion of firms with majority foreign capital and encouraged more foreign investment in priority sectors such as automobiles, steel, and other capital goods.[26] One of his most significant actions was the sale of the two state-owned automobile firms, VAM and Renault, to a private French concern in June 1983. These enterprises had been Mexicanized years earlier by the state, but in an overall reorganiation of the automotive industry were reprivatized by the de la Madrid administration.

The Penetration of Foreign Investment

Prior to the Mexican Revolution, total foreign investment in Mexico had reached astounding heights. The accumulated direct investment from abroad in 1911 has been estimated at 3.4 billion pesos (in current values), or $1.7 billion, and the indirect investment (public debt) at 0.5 billion pesos, or $0.3 billion (Cosío Villegas 1965:1154; Wright 1971:54). The United States was the dominant source, with almost 40 percent of all foreign investment in Mexico. Most of the foreign capital was associated with the export sector, particularly the railroads (whose chief purpose was to transport export products) and mining. These two areas accounted for two-thirds of all direct foreign investment in 1911.

Total foreign investment remained reasonably constant over the next two decades. By 1926, accumulated foreign capital in Mexico was 3.5 billion pesos (Navarrete R. 1967:116). The only increases were in the

Table 13
Total Foreign Investments, Mexico

	Total Foreign Investment (current values in millions U.S.$)	Annual Growth (%)	Industrial Share (%)	U.S. Share (%)
1940	449	—	7.1	61.4
1941	453	0.9	8.5	61.3
1942	477	5.3	9.7	63.9
1943	491	2.9	11.7	65.2
1944	532	8.4	13.2	66.6
1945	569	7.0	17.6	68.7
1946	575	1.1	24.4	73.8
1947	619	7.7	27.2	75.6
1948	609	− 1.6	28.6	70.4
1949	519	− 14.8	28.5	72.6
1950	566	9.1	26.1	68.9
1951	675	19.3	26.8	69.5
1952	729	8.0	30.9	75.7
1953	789	8.2	32.7	73.1
1954	834	5.7	33.3	70.5
1955	953	14.3	34.8	77.4
1956	1,091	14.5	35.4	78.4
1957	1,165	6.8	40.2	83.0
1958	1,170	0.4	42.5	75.7
1959	1,245	6.4	42.8	74.1
1960	1,081	− 13.2	55.7	83.2
1961	1,130	4.5	60.7	85.3
1962	1,286	13.8	60.6	85.0
1963	1,417	10.2	63.1	84.6
1964	1,552	9.5	65.3	83.5
1965	1,745	12.4	68.8	83.5
1966	1,938	11.1	68.7	83.6
1967	2,096	8.2	71.8	80.0
1968	2,316	10.5	73.2	81.1
1969	2,576	11.2	74.0	79.2
1970	2,822	9.5	73.8	79.5
1971	2,997	6.2	75.5	81.0

Sources: Sepúlveda and Chumacero (1973:119–120); Banco de México, *Indicadores del sector externo* (various years); Banco de México (1982b, vol. 2:397–401); and Dirección General de Inversiones Extranjeras y Transferencia de Tecnologia, *Anuario estadístico*; and unpublished data.

Table 13—Continued

	Total Foreign Investment (current values in millions U.S.$)	Annual Growth (%)	Industrial Share (%)	U.S. Share (%)
1972	3,174	5.9	73.5	80.1
1973	3,623	14.1	76.3	76.6
1974	4,275	18.0	76.5	77.5
1975	4,584	7.2	75.1	72.5
1976	3,284	−28.4	76.1	71.1
1977	3,707	12.9	76.0	68.9
1978	4,739	27.8	77.7	69.1
1979	6,645	40.2	77.1	68.0
1980	9,955	49.8	77.5	66.2
1981	11,036	10.9	78.4	68.0
1982	11,499	4.2	77.4	68.0

petroleum sector, as Mexico was becoming one of the world's leading suppliers. U.S. petroleum investment jumped from $20 million in 1911 to $206 million in 1929 (Newfarmer and Mueller 1975:47). However, U.S. investment in other areas decreased substantially.[27]

Foreign investment in Mexico (as elsewhere) experienced a decline after the Depression; this slide was not reversed until 1940. In fact, the 1929 level of total foreign investment ($1.7 billion) was not reached again until the mid-1960s (Wright 1971:61–71). U.S. investment fell from $1.3 billion in 1930 to $0.8 billion in 1940 (in 1953 dollars—U.S. Department of Commerce, *Survey of Current Business*). In addition to the impact of the Depression, the policies of Cárdenas contributed to the drop in foreign capital.

When foreign investment in Mexico began to expand again after 1940, manufacturing was the favored sector (table 13). Foreign investment in Mexican industry tripled from 1940 to 1945 and doubled again by 1952, and direct foreign industrial investment increased from 7.1 percent of the total in 1940 to over one-half by 1960 and to 75 percent by the 1970s. On the other hand, mining, public services, communication, and transportation, which accounted for 87.1 percent of all foreign investment in 1940, were reduced to 5.9 percent by 1970 (Sepúlveda and Chumacero 1973:50).

Another important trend in foreign investment in the postwar period (at least until the early 1960s) was the increasing dominance of U.S. capital. The United States provided two-thirds of all foreign investment in Mexico in 1950, and by 1960 its share had risen to over 80 percent (table 13). West Germany, Japan, and Switzerland increased their proportions of total foreign investment in Mexico in the 1970s, but in 1982 U.S. capital still represented 68 percent. U.S. investment recorded consistent increases from 1950 to 1957 and, along with total foreign investment in Mexico, enjoyed renewed growth throughout the 1960s (figure 3). Total U.S. investment (in 1953 dollars) rose from $839 million in 1963 to $1453 million in 1969, and U.S. investment in manufacturing went from $470 million to $910 million in the same period. The slowest growth occurred during the presidencies of López Mateos (especially from 1958 to 1961) and Echeverría (with the largest postwar decrease in 1976).

The absolute figures show that foreign investment flowed into Mexico in large sums before the Revolution, stagnated from then until 1930, diminished in the 1930s, and finally began to expand again after 1940. However, to understand the relative importance of foreign investment to the economy one must compare foreign investment to total investment and to other aggregate economic indicators. During the Porfiriato foreign capital was certainly the dominant force in the Mexican economy. Foreign investment in the first decade of this century represented 66 percent of all investment in Mexico (Hansen 1974:17). And by the Revolution foreigners owned over half of the total wealth of the country, and foreign enterprise dominated every sector except agriculture and the artisan industries (Wright 1971:53). Specifically, foreign investment controlled 76 percent of all major corporations in 1910—100 percent in oil, 98 percent in mining, and 89 percent in industry (Baird and McCaughan 1979:72–73). Clearly, Porfirio Díaz had sold out to the interests of international capital and was basing economic development on foreign enterprise.

However, the Revolution and its aftermath drastically altered the dominance of foreign investment. By 1939 foreign capital was financing only 15 percent of total investment; from 1939 to 1950 it was reduced to 6 percent of gross fixed investment; and it rebounded just to about 10 percent of total investment in the 1950s.[28] The relative importance of foreign investment in the 1960s was even weaker, as the contributions of foreign enterprises to total fixed-capital formation varied from a high of 6.4 percent in 1966 to a low of 3.1 percent of the total in 1968. In terms of output, the MNCs' share of the total value of production was only 9.8 percent in 1962 and 12.6 percent in 1970.[29] Foreign capital was even less significant in the 1970s, when new foreign investment averaged below 3 percent of total investment and less than one percent of gross domestic product (table 14). Hence, since the Revolution foreign investment has contributed only a minor share of the total capital formation and national economic output.

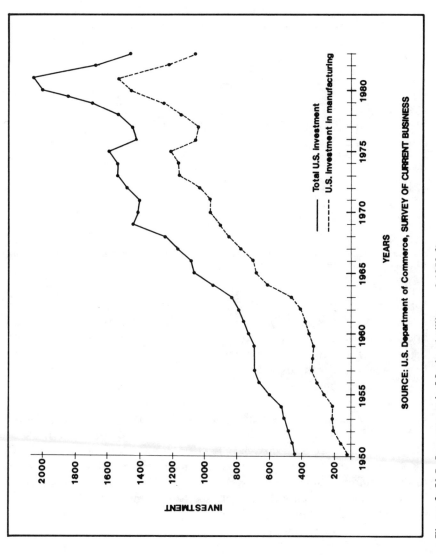

Figure 3: U.S. Investment in Mexico (millions of 1953 $)

Table 14
Direct Foreign Investment Compared to Total Investment and GDP, Mexico

	Direct Foreign Investment as % of Total Investment (annual increments)	New Foreign Investment as % of GDP
1970	3.0	0.60
1971	2.6	0.46
1972	2.4	0.46
1973	2.8	0.58
1974	2.6	0.56
1975	1.7	0.37
1976	1.7	0.38
1977	2.2	0.44
1978	1.8	0.41
1979	2.7	0.67
1980	3.5	1.25
1981	3.1	0.84
1970–1981	2.7	0.58

Sources: Dirección General de Inversiones Extranjeras y Transferencia de Tecnología, *Anuario estadístico 1981*; and unpublished data.

Since the enactment of the 1973 Foreign Investment Law, the Mexicanization process has contributed to the reduced role of foreign capital. Specifically, very few foreign-dominated firms have been established, and many have reverted to Mexican control, either public or private. Foreign firms, whether already existing or newly established, that are to be Mexicanized usually opt for one of three basic types of majority Mexican partners: (1) the large, private sector conglomerates of "groups" (Grupo Alfa, Grupo DESC, Industrias Peñoles); (2) the formerly private sector banks (BANCOMER, BANAMEX, SERFIN, SOMEX, COMERMEX); or (3) the public sector (NAFINSA, DINA, PEMEX).[30] Appendices B and C list a number of the most significant Mexicanized firms, along with their foreign "parent" and their Mexican "partner." Though the plurality of the Mexican partners are the private sector conglomerates, a substantial number of foreign firms also have formed joint enterprises with the banks and with state participation.

The goal of reducing foreign control is evident in the efforts of the Foreign Investment Commission and the available data on Mexicanizations. Of the 789 resolutions approved by the Foreign Investment Commission between 1978 and 1982 (1,222 applications were received), only 6 involved the acquisition of majority foreign ownership and these 6 transactions represented a negligible amount of the total value of the approved resolutions (table 15). Aside from the stock transfers, which involved relatively small dollar amounts, most of the approvals were the creation of new establishments, and very few of these had majority foreign control.

Table 15
Foreign Investment Commission Resolutions, 1978–1982, Mexico

Type of Resolution	No. Approved	Total Value (millions U.S. $)
Stock transfers	296	424.3
Foreigner to foreigner	69	11.3
Foreigner to foreigner (same group)	20	3.8
Mexican to foreigner	82	124.6
By consolidation	16	4.4
Through increases	109	280.2
New establishment	283	1,876.1
New product line	76	642.9
Incorporation	128	261.8
Acquisition of over 49% ownership	6	0.8
Total	789	3,205.9

Source: Comisión Nacional de Inversiones Extranjeras.

From 1973 to 1982 only 44 new enterprises were created with more than 49 percent foreign participation, whereas 1,987 new firms had less than 49 percent foreign investment (table 16). The 240 *maquiladoras* are special cases of "in-bond" industries that are exempted from the foreign-investment legislation. In addition to the small number of new firms with foreign control, 498 existing firms had been Mexicanized by 1982 under the 1973 Foreign Investment Law.

The disaggregate data on Mexicanizations imply that the state has attempted to reduce foreign control within those sectors that MNCs have traditionally dominated. In the lists of Mexicanizations in appendices B and C, almost all are manufacturing industries, particularly in the chemical, electrical, and metallurgical branches. And these are among the areas that have the highest levels of foreign participation and in which most of the foreign firms are located. Of the 5,593 firms with foreign participation in 1981 (table 17), the majority are from the industrial sector, which also

Table 16
Mexicanizations and New Foreign Enterprises

%Foreign Participation	No. New Enterprises with Foreign Participation[a]										Total
	1973	1974	1975	1976	1977	1978	1979	1980	1981	1982	
Less than 49	83	123	140	164	160	169	287	213	330	318	1,987
Greater than 49	2	3	7	0	3	4	16	9	0	0	44
100 (*maquiladoras*)[b]	24	34	6	11	12	34	25	25	39	30	240
Total	109	160	153	175	175	207	328	247	369	348	2,271
Mexicanizations[c]	n.d.	n.d.	9	52	40	47	32	98	220	n.d.	498

Sources: [a]Dirección General de Inversiones Extranjeras y Transferencia de Tecnología, *Anuario estadístico 1981*; and unpublished data.

Notes: [a]Formed under 1973 Foreign Investment Law

[b]The *maquiladoras* (or in-bond industries) with 100 percent foreign ownership have been permitted by Mexican law since 1965, mostly along the U.S.-Mexico border. They are exclusively devoted to the assembly of foreign components (imported duty free from the United States), which are then exported back to the United States (paying duties only on the value-added), and they are exempted from most foreign investment legislation.

[c]Mexicanized operations reduce foreign participation in a firm below the legal maximum of 49 percent.

has the highest percentage of foreign participation (54.6 compared to 50.8 for all sectors combined) and most of the Mexicanizations between 1973 and 1981 (54.5 percent).

Table 17
Foreign Participation and Mexicanizations, by Sector

Sector	No. of Firms[a]	No. with Majority Foreign Participation (% of total)	Avg. % of Foreign Participation	% of Total Firms Mexicanized 1973–81
Agriculture	17	9 (52.9)	48.1	4.9
Mining	241	18 (7.5)	38.0	1.4
Industry	2,899	1,431 (49.4)	54.6	54.5
Commerce	1,222	668 (54.7)	43.7	26.6
Services	1,214	519 (42.8)	38.6	12.6
Total	5,593	2,645 (47.3)	50.8	100.0

Sources: Secretaría de Patrimonio y Fomento Industrial, Dirección General de Informática, unpublished data; and Dirección General de Inversiones Extranjeras y Transferencia de Tecnología, *Anuario estadístico*; and unpublished data.

Note: [a]Firms with foreign participation, as of September 1981.

The same phenomenon exists within the industrial sector (table 18). The greatest number of Mexicanizations have occurred in the electrical and chemical branches, which also have the largest number of firms with foreign participation and high percentages of foreign participation per firm (58.1 percent and 57.8 percent, respectively). Including the machinery and foodstuffs industries, these four branches have 55 percent of the industrial firms with foreign participation (60.5 percent of these with majority foreign participation) as well as 53.7 percent of the cases of Mexicanization. The only exception to this "targeting" of Mexicanizations is the footwear and clothing branch, which has 104 foreign firms with the highest average level of foreign control (80.9 percent) but very few cases of Mexicanized companies. So, at least since the 1973 legislation, the Mexican

Table 18
Foreign Participation and Mexicanizations, by Industrial Branch

Industrial Branch	No. of Firms[a]	No. with Majority Foreign Participation (% of total)	Avg. % of Foreign Participation	% of Total Industrial Firms Mexicanized 1973–81
Food-stuffs (20)	209	94 (45.0)	75.0	11.6
Beverages (21)	58	27 (46.6)	52.1	4.1
Tobacco (22)	9	3 (33.3)	46.6	0.8
Textiles (23)	93	44 (47.3)	53.8	7.4
Footwear, clothing (24)	104	69 (66.4)	80.9	3.3
Wood (25)	22	10 (45.5)	38.5	0.8
Furniture (26)	21	11 (52.4)	44.3	0.0
Paper (27)	44	24 (54.5)	60.7	5.8
Printing (28)	110	36 (32.7)	56.8	2.5
Leather (29)	15	6 (40.0)	49.3	0.0
Rubber (30)	23	11 (47.8)	66.2	0.0
Chemical (31)	564	317 (56.2)	57.8	14.0
Petroleum (32)	23	4 (17.4)	40.7	0.8
Nonmetallic minerals (33)	72	21 (29.2)	52.3	4.1

Sources: Secretaría de Patrimonio y Fomento Industrial, Dirección General de Informática, unpublished data; and Dirección General de Inversiones Extranjeras y Transferencia de Tecnología, *Anuario estadístico*; and unpublished data.

Notes: [a]Firms with foreign participation, as of September 1981.
    Totals may not add to 100 because of rounding.

Table 18—Continued

Industrial Branch	No. of Firms[a]	No. with Majority Foreign Participation (% of total)	Avg. % of Foreign Participation	% of Total Industrial Firms Mexicanized 1973–81
Basic metals (34)	38	11 (28.9)	22.3	1.6
Metal products (35)	226	110 (48.7)	52.1	1.6
Machinery (36)	380	152 (40.0)	51.4	12.4
Electrical (37)	441	303 (68.7)	58.1	15.7
Transportation (38)	144	48 (33.3)	68.6	3.3
Other (39)	303	130 (42.9)	61.9	9.9
Total	2,899	1,431 (49.4)	54.6	100.0

Table 19
Enterprises with Foreign Participation, Mexico

	No. of Enterprises							
	1974	1975	1976	1977	1978	1979	1980	1981
With some foreign participation	4,259	4,406	4,570	4,733	4,906	5,209	5,431	5,731
With majority foreign participation	3,110	3,108	3,056	3,019	2,976	2,960	2,871	2,651
(% of total)	(73.0)	(70.5)	(66.9)	(63.8)	(60.7)	(56.8)	(52.9)	(46.3)

Sources: Dirección General de Inversiones Extranjeras y Transferencia de Tecnología, Anuario estadístico 1981; and unpublished data.

government has generally focused the Mexicanization process on those sectors and branches with the highest concentrations of foreign firms and foreign capital.

These efforts do not represent a total success for the policy aim of achieving majority Mexican control—in fact, as of 1981, 46 percent of the 5,731 enterprises registered with the Foreign Investment Commission still had majority foreign ownership. But at least the number of foreign-dominated firms was being reduced. In 1974, almost three-quarters of the 4,259 firms with foreign participation had majority external ownership (table 19). Also the number of Mexican firms being acquired by MNCs has substantially declined. Studies of pre-1974 data show that acquisition of an existing Mexican firm was the preferred form of market entry for MNCs.[31] But since then the Foreign Investment Commission has approved very few such acquisitions, and most new foreign investment has been directed toward forming a new enterprise in conjunction with majority Mexican capital (either public or private).

Though the overall significance of foreign investment to the Mexican economy is diminishing, two characteristics of MNCs operating in Mexico represent negative trends from a nationalist point of view: deficits in the balance of payments of foreign firms, and their concentrated power within the economy. Between 1971 and 1981 enterprises with foreign participation contributed 58 percent of both the nation's trade deficit and its deficit in current account (which reached a record $11 billion in 1981; see table 20). In 1980 and 1981 the trade deficit of the MNCs was even larger than that for the economy overall. Clearly, the policy goal of having foreign companies export more than they import is far from being achieved, and government officials on various occasions have expressed their concern over the contributions of MNCs to the growing deficits in the external sector (*Unomásuno*, 24 February 1983; and interview, 5 April 1983).

The other major trend, which poses a threat to private national enterprise, is the concentration of MNCs among the largest firms and in the key industries. On the average, foreign firms are substantially larger than domestic firms. One survey concluded that MNCs average twenty-nine times the size of national companies (Fajnzylber and Martínez Tarragó 1976:210). Obviously, the foreign enterprises are disproportionately found among the largest firms. For example, almost one-half of the largest one hundred firms in the 1970s had foreign participation, and foreign enterprises controlled about 50 percent of the assets and capital of the top three hundred industrial firms (see Newfarmer and Mueller 1975:53–55; and Fajnzylber and Martínez Tarragó 1976:165, 389–390).

Though foreign firms contribute a minority of production and capital in the total economy and even within the industrial sector, the MNCs are dominant in the leading industries (especially capital goods) and are much more dynamic than their domestic counterparts. Among the list of the five hundred largest industrial companies in 1970, MNCs controlled 87 percent of the capital in nonelectrical machinery, 82 percent in electrical machinery, 80 percent in rubber, 70 percent in transportation equipment, and 57 percent in chemical products (Fajnzylber and Martínez Tarragó 1976:165,389–390). Futhermore, MNCs in 1970 had 85 percent of total industrial sales in rubber, 79 percent in electrical machinery, 68 percent in chemical products, 62 percent in nonelectrical machinery, and 50 percent in transportation equipment.[32] Data from the 1975 industrial census show that MNCs provided only 28 percent of total industrial production, but they dominated the output in crucial sectors such as chemicals (50.1 percent), rubber (60.1 percent), nonelectrical machinery (54.9 percent), electrical machinery (56.2 percent), and transportation equipment (65.2 percent; see Peres Núñez 1982:135). However, as noted in the discussion of the Mexicanization process, public policy has at least recognized this concentration among sectors and attempted to reduce it through a select policy of diminishing majority foreign control in particular areas.

Because they have been concentrated in these industries, foreign firms

Table 20
Balance in Current Account, Mexico and Foreign Enterprises
(Millions U.S. $)

	Trade Balance			Current Account Balance		
	(1) Mexico	(2) Foreign Enterprises	2/1 (%)	(3) Mexico	(4) Foreign Enterprises	4/3 (%)
1971	− 889.9	− 478.9	53.8	− 928.9	− 782.6	84.3
1972	− 1,095.7	− 545.5	49.8	− 1,005.7	− 902.7	89.8
1973	− 1,820.7	− 682.0	37.5	− 1,528.8	− 1,129.3	73.9
1974	− 3,295.5	− 828.0	25.1	− 3,226.0	− 1,327.0	41.1
1975	− 3,637.0	− 1,033.0	28.4	− 4,442.6	− 1,658.2	37.3
1976	− 2,644.4	− 887.0	33.5	− 3,683.3	− 1,622.1	44.0
1977	− 1,054.7	− 606.3	57.5	− 1,596.4	− 1,220.0	76.4
1978	− 1,854.4	− 800.5	43.2	− 2,693.0	− 1,604.1	59.6
1979	− 3,162.0	− 1,759.6	55.6	− 4,875.8	− 2,733.1	56.1
1980	− 3,178.7	− 3,365.8	105.9	− 6,760.8	− 4,861.9	71.9
1981	− 3,725.3	− 4,338.6	116.5	− 11,704.1	− 6,679.4	57.1
1971–1981	− 26,358.3	− 15,325.2	58.1	− 42,445.4	− 24,520.4	57.8

Sources: Banco de México and Dirección General de Inversiones Extranjeras y Transferencia de Tecnología, unpublished data.

have tended to be more dynamic, growing faster and creating more employment than domestic firms. From 1962 to 1970 average annual growth in industrial production (in current prices) was 11.0 percent for national firms and 17.4 percent for MNCs (Fajnzylber and Martínez Tarragó 1976: 247). Between 1965 and 1970 employment expanded at the average annual rate of 12.1 percent in MNCs and only 1.5 percent in national firms (ibid.: 275).

Finally, MNCs tend to locate in oligopolistic or monopolistic markets. Even without isolating the role of foreign enterprises, the Mexican economy is heavily concentrated and with little competition. For example, only 1.5 percent of the industrial corporations in Mexico in 1965 controlled 77 percent of all industrial capital (Cinta G. 1972:183; Baird and McCaughan 1979:90–91). In the 1970s, 40 percent of the 230 industrial branches in Mexico were oligopolies in which the 4 largest plants controlled at least 50 percent of the market.[33] And MNCs were particularly evident in these oligopolistic branches. Over 60 percent of all foreign enterprises were located in the industries where the top 4 firms had over 50 percent of the market. Also, 47 percent of the industrial branches (producing 55 percent of total industrial output) had at least 2 MNCs among the top 4 plants, and in 10 percent of the industries (representing 18 percent of all industrial production), the top companies were all MNCs. Even the foreign investors recognize themselves as the dominant forces in their areas. In one survey of 239 U.S. firms operating in Mexico, 81 percent considered themselves "leaders" in their market (Robinson and Smith 1976:246). The factors they cited most often were their superior product quality and their edge in technological know-how.

Quantitative Comparisons of Investment Sources

The analysis in this chapter has produced a number of qualified conclusions in regard to the respective roles of the public sector and foreign investment in Mexico. The state certainly appears to have assumed a strongly interventionist role through economic policies and direct investment. Industrialization policies of protection and promotion were most significant between 1939 and 1964, and government expenditures have been steadily growing in all areas, especially in public enterprises and industrial investment.

Yet some signs point to a slight retrenchment by the public sector in recent decades. The proportion of public investment in manufacturing and capital expenditures has not increased significantly since 1960; the share of public investment in total investment has shrunk to about two-fifths; and government expenditures on productive capacity have remained around 10 percent of the GDP. Also in comparisons with other nations in Latin America and throughout the world, the Mexican public sector proves to be relatively small. Finally, many public enterprises, especially those in infrastructure and services, are largely complementary and beneficial to the private sector. So, however significant the public sector may be in Mexico, it is not a tremendous threat to the private sector.

In terms of the influence of foreign investment in the Mexican economy, public policies toward foreign capital show some meaningful attempts to control dependency and manage the MNCs. The state has expropriated certain foreign enterprises operating in basic sectors (the railroads, the petroleum companies, the telephone system, the electric utilities, and the mining companies), and Mexicanization has been the stated policy for the remaining MNCs. These policies have achieved some results in minimizing the role of foreign investment. After being about one-half the total wealth in 1910, foreign investment in the postwar era has amounted to less than 10 percent of all investment in Mexico (and less than 5 percent in the 1970s). Two negative aspects of foreign investment remain—the growing balance-of-payments deficits of foreign firms, and the concentration of MNCs among the largest enterprises in the most dynamic sectors. But, at least in recent years, Mexicanization has focused on reducing the role of foreign capital within those industrial branches where MNCs have been most dominant.

Despite some of the qualifications, these results suggest that the Mexican private sector still enjoys a healthy, and possibly even dominant, position in relation to private foreign and public investment. As further evidence, in most comparisons among these three sources of capital, the domestic private sector has the edge. As one noted Mexican has stated, "One of the great accomplishments of the Revolution has been the financing of national economic development primarily with domestic resources."[34] Data comparing national private, public, and foreign investment confirm this conclusion (table 21). In fact, even before the Revolution, domestic capital provided one-half of all investment, and the major postrevolutionary change was the substitution of public sector investment for foreign. Private domestic capital has always represented at least 50 percent of the total in Mexico and averaged almost 56 percent in the 1970s. In addition, census data from 1965 through the most recently published industrial census in 1975 show that the private national firms have contributed a majority of total industrial production, even though their share has dimin-

Table 21
National Private, Public, and Foreign Investment, Mexico
(Percentages)

	Total Investment	National Private Investment	Public Investment	Foreign Investment
1902–03	100	50.0	5.0	45.0
1939–50	100	54.0	40.0	6.0
1950–59	100	51.0	39.0	10.0
1970	100	62.6	34.4	3.0
1971	100	70.8	26.7	2.5
1972	100	64.4	33.2	2.4
1973	100	58.9	38.3	2.8
1974	100	61.1	36.4	2.5
1975	100	55.9	42.5	1.6
1976	100	58.4	39.9	1.7
1977	100	53.5	44.4	2.1
1978	100	52.1	46.1	1.8
1979	100	53.6	43.8	2.6
1980	100	53.8	42.8	3.4
1981	100	54.6	42.4	3.0
1971–81	100	55.9	41.5	2.6

Sources: Navarrete R. (1967:111, 113); Dirección General de Inversiones Extranjeras y Transferencia de Tecnología, *Anuario estadístico*; and unpublished data. Also see Vernon (1963:199); Goldsmith (1966:76); Fernández Hurtado (1967:55); LaCascia (1969:72–74, 78); and King (1970:63).

ished from 64 percent in 1965 to 55 percent in 1975 (table 22). The proportion of industrial output from the multinational firms is about one-half that of the private nationals, and the state's share is even less.

Analysis that focuses on just the largest enterprises within the Mexican economy provides slightly different results, particularly regarding the contributions of public sector entities, but the private Mexican corporations still prove to have a significant (and growing) role, even among the upper echelons of the Mexican productive plant. Table 23 presents data on the total sales of the largest twenty-five and one hundred firms or conglomerates from 1974 to 1982 and the largest five hundred for 1983. As I stated before, the Mexican economy is concentrated in the hands of a relatively small number of very large corporations. For example, in the late 1970s the one hundred largest enterprises accounted for about one-

Table 22
Contribution to Total Industrial Production, by Enterprise Type, Mexico
(Percentages)

	Enterprise Contribution		
	State	MNCs	Private National
1965	12.4	23.7	63.9
1970	12.2	32.4	55.4
1975	17.1	28.1	54.8

Source: Peres Núñez (1982:135), utilizing Secretaría de Programación y Presupuesto *VIII censo industrial, IX censo industrial, X censo industrial*, Sepúlveda and Chumacero (1973: 173–177), and Fajnzylber and Martínez Tarragó (1976:154).

third of all economic production in Mexico. Concentrated economic power is even evident within the ranks of the largest companies. In 1983 the top one hundred firms provided almost 90 percent of the total sales of the top five hundred, and the top twenty-five contributed more than 75 percent of all sales of the top one hundred. Thus, the data on these large corporations can reveal much about economic power in Mexico.

One of the most striking conclusions about the distribution of sales among the largest firms is the dominance of a few state corporations. Considering all economic sectors, the state has totaled from 55 to 74 percent of the sales of the top twenty-five and from 45 percent to 69 percent for the top one hundred. PEMEX obviously leads the list, and in 1983 the government petroleum company was about fifteen times the size of the second largest Mexican enterprise. Other state firms in the top twenty-five include CFE, SIDERMEX, CONASUPO, Fomento Industrial SOMEX, Teléfonos de México, Fertilizantes Mexicanos, DINA, and Ferrocarriles Nacionales de México. A number of these are in the services and commerce sectors, so the state is not quite as dominant within industry; but even here the government corporations had almost one-third of all sales of the top one hundred in 1974.

The concentration of public enterprises among the very largest is evident in the 1983 data that summarize the distribution of sales for the largest five hundred firms. The number of state firms and their relative importance steadily diminish after the top twenty-five companies. Eight of the first twenty-five are from the public sector (with 74.1 percent of sales), but they number only seventeen among the largest one hundred (61 percent of sales) and thirty-eight of the largest five hundred (54.9 percent of sales). In other words, only thirty government companies are found between no. 26

Table 23
Contribution to Total Sales, by Enterprise Type, Mexico
(Percentages)

Year	State Enterprises (no.)		MNCs (no.)	Private National Enterprises (no.)	Total (no.)
		Majority Foreign[a]	"Mexicanized"[b]		
1974 Industrial sector					
Top 25	43.5	21.1	13.2	22.2	100
	(4)	(7)	(5)	(9)	(25)
Top 100	32.1	24.8	17.4	25.7	100
	(11)	(31)	(22)	(36)	(100)
1974 All sectors					
Top 25	55.9	15.9	11.1	17.1	100
	(7)	(6)	(4)	(8)	(25)
Top 100	44.2	15.9	16.5	23.4	100
	(22)	(18)	(24)	(36)	(100)
1975 All sectors					
Top 25	58.9	12.2	10.2	18.7	100
	(8)	(4)	(4)	(9)	(25)
Top 100	45.3	15.6	14.1	25.0	100
	(21)	(23)	(20)	(36)	(100)
1976 All sectors					
Top 25	63.2	12.0	10.0	14.8	100
	(9)	(5)	(4)	(7)	(25)
Top 100	43.3	15.1	16.3	25.3	100
	(16)	(22)	(26)	(36)	(100)
1977 All sectors					
Top 25	63.6	12.1	8.8	15.5	100
	(10)	(5)	(4)	(6)	(25)
Top 100	44.3	15.9	13.3	26.5	100
	(15)	(25)	(21)	(39)	(100)
1978 All sectors					
Top 25	55.8	11.8	8.6	23.8	100
	(8)	(4)	(4)	(9)	(25)

Table 23—Continued

Year		State Enterprises (no.)		MNCs (no.)	Private National Enterprises (no.)	Total (no.)
			Majority Foreign[a]	"Mexicanized"[b]		
	Top 100	43.8 (23)	15.1 (21)	10.4 (16)	30.7 (40)	100 (100)
1979	All sectors					
	Top 25	57.9 (8)	10.3 (4)	7.4 (4)	24.4 (9)	100 (25)
	Top 100	43.7 (19)	12.5 (17)	11.4 (19)	32.4 (45)	100 (100)
1980	All sectors					
	Top 25	63.6 (9)	7.5 (3)	6.3 (4)	22.6 (9)	100 (25)
	Top 100	47.7 (18)	10.8 (16)	9.9 (18)	31.6 (48)	100 (100)
1981	All sectors					
	Top 25	64.2 (9)	9.5 (4)	3.6 (2)	22.7 (10)	100 (25)
	Top 100	47.5 (18)	11.5 (16)	9.0 (18)	32.0 (48)	100 (100)
1982	All sectors					
	Top 25	69.0 (7)	10.2 (7)	2.2 (2)	18.6 (9)	100 (25)
	Top 100	54.8 (14)	12.0 (23)	6.2 (15)	27.0 (48)	100 (100)
1983	All sectors					
	Top 25	74.1 (8)	6.2 (5)	3.0 (2)	16.7 (10)	100 (25)
	Top 100	61.0 (17)	10.5 (25)	6.3 (15)	22.2 (43)	100 (100)
	Top 200	57.3 (25)	11.9 (57)	6.8 (26)	24.0 (92)	100 (200)

Table 23—Continued

Year	State Enterprises (no.)	MNCs (no.)		Private National Enterprises (no.)	Total (no.)
		Majority Foreign[a]	"Mexicanized"[b]		
1983 All sectors					
Top 300	55.7	12.3	7.3	24.7	100
	(29)	(82)	(53)	(136)	(300)
Top 400	55.1	12.4	7.4	25.1	100
	(36)	(104)	(61)	(199)	(400)
Top 500	54.9	12.5	7.3	25.3	100
	(38)	(121)	(67)	(274)	(500)

Sources: Expansión (various issues, 1975–84); Baird and McCaughan (1979:190–203); Industridata 1980–81; Secretaría de Comercio, Empresas con inversión extranjera mayor de 24.99%; Secretaría de Industria y Comercio (1975); Secretaría del Patrimonio y Fomento Industrial, Dirección General de Informática, unpublished data; Dirección General de Inversiones Extranjeras y Transferencia de Tecnología, Anuario estadístico, and unpublished data; Centro de Información y Estudios Nacionales (1981a), (1981b), (1982a); and Jacobs (1982).

Notes: [a]Foreign participation of 50 percent or greater.
[b]Foreign participation between 25 and 50 percent.

The most difficult task in compiling these data was determining the existence of foreign participation in individual firms. Most of these sources have been utilized for this purpose. The degree of foreign participation in the large conglomerates or "groups" (often including dozens of individual firms) is especially difficult to measure. Though all have some foreign participation, most of the conglomerates were determined to include less than 25 percent foreign investment and thus have been classified as private national enterprises. These include Industrial Alfa, Valores Industriales (VISA), DESC, Empresas ICA, Vitro, Industrias Peñoles, Industrial Bimbo, Sociedad Industrial Hermes, CYDSA, Cementos Mexicanos, Industrias Unidas, Chihuahua, IMSA, Empresas Industrias del Hierro, Industrial Saltillo, and others. Among the largest groups with substantial foreign investment (with the percentage of foreign participation in parentheses) are Empresas La Moderna (45), Celanese Mexicana (40), Empresas Tolteca de México (49), CONDUMEX (48), Industrias Minera México (34), Industrias NACOBRE (40), Industrias Purina (49), and Xerox de México (75).

and no. 500, and the eight government firms within the top twenty-five account for almost all of the state's productive capacity.[35]

Since foreign enterprises have been defined in different ways, table 23 presents information on two different categories: the majority foreign firms (50 percent or more foreign participation), and the Mexicanized foreign firms (foreign participation between 25 and 50 percent). In 1974, the combination of these firms provided more total sales than either the private national or state firms within the top one hundred industrial firms. However, their strength has been weaker within the economy overall and has diminished in recent years. Even in 1974 the public companies were more important within the whole economy, and by 1978 private national corporations were surpassing the combined sales of the two categories of foreign firms.

If one prefers to define foreign enterprises as only those with majority foreign control, the private national firms (those with foreign participation from 0 to 25 percent) have been more significant in all years and in all categories included in table 23. As the MNCs have decreased their contributions among the very largest firms, the representation of private Mexican establishments has grown from 36 of the top 100 in 1974 (with 23.4 percent of sales) to 48 of the top 100 in 1981 (32 percent of sales). The declining percentage of private company sales among the largest 100 in 1982 and 1983 was due to growth in the public sector, paticularly PEMEX, and not to expansion of MNCs. But in contrast to the public enterprises, the private national companies are not as concentrated at the top. The 1983 data show the relative proportions of sales and the absolute numbers of the private nationals steadily increasing in the progression from the largest 25 to the largest 100. Thus, though they are still surpassed by the public sector firms, since at least 1974 the private Mexican companies and conglomerates have been expanding their share of total sales compared to the MNCs. By 1983 private domestic companies were the majority of the top 500 firms (288 were private nationals), were second to the public sector enterprises in total sales, and greatly outnumbered even the combined totals of majority foreign and Mexicanized foreign firms.

Besides assessing their relative proportions of total investment, production, and sales, the roles of national private, public, and foreign capital can be evaluated by analyzing their effects on industrial growth. One of the initial questions posed in this chapter concerned the degree to which the relatively successful pattern of industrialization in Mexico could be attributed to private domestic capital, as opposed to the other sources of capital. This question is addressed here through statistical analysis utilizing industrialization data from chapter 2 along with measures of national private investment, public investment, and foreign investment.

I have employed time-series regression analysis, with industrial value-added as the dependent variable and five independent variables covering the years from 1950 through 1981. The independent variables most relevant to this research are the measures of domestic (private and public) and foreign capital. However, traditional cross-sectional analysis by economists has always identified per capita income and population as the most important predictors of industrial growth.[36] Thus, I have added these two variables to the measures of domestic and foreign investment as the independent variables, and the regression equation is

$$Y = \text{constant} + \sum_{i=1}^{5} B_i X_i$$

where

Y = log of industrial value-added in millions of 1953 U.S. $,
X_1 = log of per capita income in 1953 U.S. $,
X_2 = log of population in millions of inhabitants,
X_3 = log of U.S. investment in manufacturing in millions of 1953 U.S. $,
X_4 = log of public investment in billions of 1955 pesos, and
X_5 = log of Mexican private investment in billions of 1955 pesos.[37]

As is usually the case with time-series data, autocorrelation (correlated error terms) is detected and the ordinary least squares (OLS) procedure of estimating the coefficients would yield inefficient results (Johnston 1972: 8–13, 121–123, 246). Thus, an alternative method of estimating, generalized least squares (GLS), is used.[38]

The results are quite interesting and tend to confirm the relative importance of the private sector to Mexican industrial development (table 24). The traditional socioeconomic variables used as predictors of industrial growth yield opposite results. Population is the most significant independent variable, whereas per capita income is the least significant. It appears that population, as an indicator of market size, is more important in longitudinal analysis than is per capita income in determining industrial growth in Mexico. In comparing the investment variables, all three (national private, public, and foreign) prove to have positive and significant effects on industrialization. This analysis, which covers 1950 through 1981, shows that foreign capital actually has the most significant impact on industrial development. However, the contributions of foreign investment have occurred primarily within the last decade. Excluding the years after 1970 from the analysis, national private capital becomes the most important investment variable in regard to industrial growth, public capital is a close second, and foreign investment is a much weaker predictor of industrialization before 1970. These comparisons before and after 1970 suggest, therefore, that the Mexicanization policies of the 1970s have produced mixed results. Whereas the relative proportions of foreign investment and foreign firms within the economy have been noticeably reduced, external private capital has become a more important contributor to industrial growth. Though Mexicanization efforts in recent years have focused on reducing the dominance of MNCs within certain sectors, they remain concentrated in the most dynamic industrial branches.

Table 24
Regression Analysis

Variable	Unstandardized Coefficient	Standard Error	F
Per capita income	− 0.149	0.120	1.549
Population	1.166	0.154	57.290[a]
Investment			
National private	0.153	0.044	12.375[a]
Public	0.089	0.033	7.185[a]
Foreign	0.295	0.041	52.678[a]
Constant term	0.574		

Note: [a]Significant at the .05 level.

The findings of this chapter provide several interesting and important conclusions and are relevant to a number of the theoretical perspectives outlined earlier. First, the relative importance of private capital and its significant impact on industrial growth affirm the efficacy of the economic role of national industrial entrepreneurs in Mexico, contrary to many conclusions of a weak national industrial sector. Second, the public sector has not become a threat or a rival to the private sector in Mexico and has also contributed positively to the process of industrial development. Public expenditure policies then appear to be one of the political determinants of industrial growth. Finally, several tenets of the dependency literature are found to be valid in Mexico. Postrevolutionary policies have diminished the overall role of foreign investment, but foreign capital has acquired a prominent place in the Mexican economy by concentrating in key sectors. Yet, the quantitative analysis shows that this foreign investment has had a great effect on industrial outcomes only recently. Domestic sources of investment have been more important historically for advancing industrialization. And the recent positive consequences of foreign investment (in terms of industrial growth) are counterbalanced by the negative consequences of concentration and growing balance-of-payments deficits.

Part 2. The Political Role of Industrial Entrepreneurs in Mexico

4. State-Industry Relations: Disaggregating the Authoritarian State

Despite some qualifications, private entrepreneurs have made significant contributions to a relatively successful industrialization process. But economic power and success for private industrialists do not automatically translate into political power. Indeed, the prevailing thesis is that, although Mexican industry may benefit from an "alliance for profits" with the state, entrepreneurs have little influence over public policies affecting them.[1] State-industry relations are said generally to fit the picture of Mexico as an authoritarian state. With the exception of a few, somewhat dated, interpretations focusing on the pluralist aspects of the Mexican system, the trend among social scientists in recent years has been to conclude that Mexico is a predominantly authoritarian system in which a centralized executive in conjunction with the "official" political party controls and manipulates the interest groups, the party system, and the electoral machinery.[2]

However, particularly in the aftermath of the Echeverría *sexenio*, some of the more recent research on the Mexican state has emphasized a critical reevaluation of interpretations of Mexico as an authoritarian system. These analysts posit the existence of considerable autonomy from the state among certain political groups and a political process characterized by bargaining among elite groups with different interests.[3] This chapter contributes to the reevaluation of authoritarianism in Mexico by examining the position of Mexican industrialists vis-à-vis the state and is the first analysis to refine the Mexican authoritarian model in light of state-industry relations.

Particularly in the case of the industrial sector, the contrasts between the Echeverría and López Portillo *sexenios* underline the political significance of relatively independent elite groups.[4] When López Portillo was inaugurated in December 1976, his most immediate task was to restore the confidence of the private sector. Echeverría, his predecessor, had alienated business groups with his populist rhetoric and policies, including fiscal reform, price controls, the expansion of public spending, and agrarian reform. In fact, one of the most striking aspects of the Echeverría presidential term was the vocal and widespread opposition of the private sector.[5] López Portillo sought to reverse this trend and to return the private sector to the dominant political coalition. Within days, the new president reassured entrepreneurial groups by signing an agreement with 140 large companies to coordinate investment projects and by indicating that the landowners affected by Echeverría's expropriations would be justly compensated.

The same pattern seemed to repeat itself in the transition from López Portillo to Miguel de la Madrid. López Portillo, who, like Echeverría and his 1976 expropriations, attempted to leave office under a populist banner, nationalized the banks and established exchange controls only months before his term ended. These policies, along with the devaluations of 1982 and the general overexpansion of the economy in previous years, had greatly disillusioned the private sector. Once again, but with a new president, de la Madrid faced the task of restoring business confidence. Though his austerity package was difficult to accept, entrepreneurial leaders praised his policies as realistic, proclaimed that confidence had been restored, and predicted that economic recovery was imminent.[6]

The private sector and its interest groups have played an important political role in postrevolutionary Mexico. Even in more capitalist societies such as the United States and Western Europe, entrepreneurial groups assume important political functions; in a mixed economy like Mexico's, the relations between the private sector and the government can be critical to the development process.[7] The question of whether Mexican industrial groups act relatively independently of the state or whether they are dependent on and dominated by the state is obviously a significant one with implications not only for the conceptualization of the state but also for explaining policy outcomes and economic progress.

This examination of the relations between industry and the state in Mexico raises fundamental questions about the widespread applicability of the authoritarian label to Mexico. It does not prove that Mexico is a democracy and that Mexican business groups act as freely as their counterparts in the United States. Clearly, in certain periods a strong sense of partnership or shared interests binds the Mexican private sector to the state. However, my conclusion is that the Mexican private sector is considerably more independent of the state than authoritarian interpretations would lead one to expect. In conjunction with the findings of Daniel Levy (1979) that higher education in Mexico enjoys substantial self-rule, my research further substantiates his thesis that at least privileged or elitist sectors of Mexican society have considerable autonomy in the political arena. Thus, the authoritarian model relevant to the Southern Cone should not be uncritically applied to Mexico, which appears to represent a very distinctive variant or subtype of authoritarianism. Specifically, this analysis confirms the relevance of a disaggregated interpretation of authoritarianism or "corporatism" (emphasizing state-groups relations) in which, at least for the case of the private sector in Mexico, state inducements for interest groups are stronger than state constraints over interest groups (Collier and Collier 1979).

The Authoritarian Framework

The authoritarian framework to be addressed here was initially established by Juan J. Linz (1970) and applied to Mexico by Susan Kaufman Purcell (1973). Authoritarianism was stressed in the 1970s as an important alternative to the traditional dichotomy in regime classification between democracy and totalitarianism. The concept of authoritarian political regimes has been particularly relevant to Latin America since the mid-1960s. Authoritarianism has usually been defined as incorporating three characteristics distinct from democratic or totalitarian systems: limited political pluralism, low subject-mobilization, and hierarchical ordering of relationships.[8] Limited pluralism denotes that interest groups are dependent on and controlled by the regime and that the ideology and actions of the groups are more relevant to the regime than to their membership. In instances of low subject-mobilization, citizens are mobilized only to support the state and only in temporary situations. Political participation is at very low levels. Hierarchical ordering of relationships infers centralized and patronal leadership in the political arena. The governing elites (*patrones*) grant benefits to select groups or leaders who then defer to the regime and offer support. This patronal subordination continues down the political hierarchy.

The relationship between the Mexican state and the private sector is examined here principally in light of these three characteristics. The focus within the private sector is on the industrial organizations, though informal groups, other business organizations, and individual industrialists possibly acting alone are not excluded. The principal industrial organizations are the Confederation of Industrial Chambers (Confederación de Cámaras Industriales, CONCAMIN) and the National Chamber of Manufacturing Industries (Cámara Nacional de la Industria de Transformación,

CANACINTRA). Other important national bodies encompassing other economic sectors include the Confederation of National Chambers of Commerce (Confederación de Cámaras Nacionales de Comercio, CONCANACO), the Mexican Council of Businessmen (Consejo Mexicano de Hombres de Negocios, CMHN), the Entrepreneurial Coordinating Council (Consejo Coordinador Empresarial, CCE), the Mexican Bankers' Association (Asociación de Banqueros de México, ABM),[9] the Mexican Association of Insurance Institutions (Asociación Mexicana de Instituciones de Seguros, AMIS), the National Association of Importers and Exporters of the Republic of Mexico (Asociación Nacional de Importadores y Exportadores de la República Mexicana, ANIERM), and the Mexican Employers' Confederation (Confederación Patronal de la República Mexicana, COPARMEX). Finally, the American Chamber of Commerce of Mexico (Cámara Americana de Comercio, CAMCO) primarily is an organization of U.S. multinational corporations operating in Mexico.

Limited Pluralism

The first characteristic of authoritarianism, limited political pluralism, concerns the state's capacity to control and manipulate interest groups. At least the potential for strong state control over business groups in Mexico is provided by the legislation governing chambers and confederations of industry and commerce (Ley de Cámaras, or Chambers Law). This legislation, which was initiated in 1908 and substantially modified in 1936 and 1941, grants semiofficial status to the chambers, imposes obligatory membership, and allows the state to intervene in various facets of the chambers' operations.[10] However, as will be shown below, the actual degree of state interference in the affairs of the business organizations does not approach the potential levels granted by the Chambers Law, and the semiofficial status is seen as more of a help than a hindrance to the chambers and confederations.

The first Chambers Law (1908) recognized chambers of commerce and industry as "legal personalities" and enumerated their functions. However, this law did not compel membership on the part of all businesses, and the chambers remained largely private and voluntary organizations with significant legal autonomy until the 1936 Chambers Law was passed. As other social and economic sectors were being incorporated into the official political party in the 1930s, a new role was also being outlined for the industrial and commercial chambers. For the first time, the 1936 law introduced the requirement of obligatory membership for all private firms except those capitalized at less than twenty-five hundred pesos. The chambers were no longer voluntary organizations, and the legislation even empowered the state to determine which chamber a firm would join. The private sector did not oppose the compulsory aspect of the new legislation, but industrialists did protest their inclusion in a national confederation with the commercial sector. Their opposition led to the passage of the 1941 Chambers Law, which differed from the 1936 Law primarily by providing for separate national industrial and commercial confederations. The 1941 law, with minor modifications in 1960, 1963, 1974, and 1975, has remained in effect.[11]

In addition to the clauses that establish mandatory membership and even allow the state to select the chamber a firm must join, other sections of the 1936 and 1941 laws relevant to government control of business groups include the following:

1. Chambers are recognized by the state as "public institutions with juridical personality," but they are declared to be autonomous.

2. The chambers are designated as the representatives of the private sector before the state, and one of their functions is to consult with the state on policy initiatives and changes relevant to the private sector.

3. The secretary of commerce and industrial promotion decides when a chamber may be created (by withholding recognition) and where a chamber must locate its headquarters.

4. The organization, structure, constitution, and statutes of a chamber must be approved by the secretary of commerce and industrial promotion.

5. Chambers may be dissolved by the state if their membership falls below a specified level, if the chamber cannot sustain itself, or if the chamber does not comply with this legislation.

6. A representative of the secretary of commerce and industrial promotion may attend all meetings of the governing boards of any chambers.

These legal provisions would appear to give the state considerable leverage in controlling all private-sector organized groups. The state can selectively grant recognition to chambers that are supportive of state policies, and it can force firms to join these semiofficial organizations. The state also seems to have considerable influence over the functions and actions of the chambers through its power to approve many organizational aspects of the chambers.

The direct entrepreneurial role that the state has assumed further enhances the relations between it and business groups. Public investment has become approximately one-half of all investment, and close to four hundred public enterprises exist in the manufacturing sector alone.[12] Though the private sector is often critical of these state-owned firms for displacing private capital and for requiring substantial public subsidies, they continue to play an important role in the economy as well as in the organized groups of the business sector.[13] In fact, several chambers, including the National Chamber of the Iron and Steel Industry and the National Chamber of the Filmmaking Industry, include a preponderance of state-owned enterprises. Other chambers, such as the National Chamber of the Construction Industry, include many firms whose principal client is the state. Obviously, in these cases the relations between the state and the industrial chamber are particularly close.

In sum, legal and certain extralegal aspects of relations between the state and the private sector in Mexico appear to be very indicative of limited pluralism under an authoritarian regime. However, the actual degree of government control over entrepreneurial groups has not been as great as these legal provisions suggest. One of the critical characteristics of Mexican business associations is that they are independent of the official party. Mexican politics are dominated by the one official party, the Institutional Revolutionary party (Partido Revolucionario Institucional, PRI), which incorporates three major segments of the population: labor, the peasantry, and the middle class (especially government employees).[14] Thus, whereas labor, *campesino*, and middle-class groups have been tightly controlled by the state through the PRI, entrepreneurial groups have remained outside the party's confines. The private sector appears quite content with its position, since business groups can realize their objectives through other channels and can escape the rigors of party discipline.[15]

In addition to their independence from the PRI, private sector organizations in their actual operations are not restrictively tied to the state by the legislation governing chambers of industry and commerce. In interviews I conducted with officials from various business chambers and confederations, all stated that their semiofficial status under the Chambers Law was not a hindrance or a constraint.[16] They did not feel that the government controlled their activities, limited their influence, or interfered in their functions. They did state that their guaranteed representation in many state agencies, commissions, and boards, along with the requirement that the state must consult with them, were definite benefits of their legal status. Many also said that obligatory membership was a positive factor in that it contributed to the unity of the private sector and guaranteed the representation of smaller firms that otherwise might be apathetic.

CANACINTRA: A "Captive Group"? Most arguments of private sector organization domination by the state focus on CANACINTRA, the National Chamber of Manufacturing Industries. CONCAMIN and CONCANACO, the national confederations of industry and commerce, have been described as relatively independent of the state and even as countervailing forces to encroaching government intervention in the economy.[17] But CANACINTRA has been charged as being created by the government in 1941 and a "captive group" of the state since then.[18] In addition to focusing on the government's role in establishing CANACINTRA, these arguments also point to its ideological affinity with the state and its alleged propensity to alienate much of its membership.

Though CANACINTRA is formally just one of sixty-two industrial chambers, its size and importance rank it with the national confederations. It includes some sixty thousand member firms, with most of its members coming from the chemical, automotive, metallurgical, and foodstuffs industries. Though it is legally a member of CONCAMIN, it has chosen to operate separately from the industrial confederation (interview, 23 July 1979).

CANACINTRA was formed in November 1941, less than three months after the new Chambers Law had been promulgated. The timing has led some authors to imply that the government of Avila Camacho conspired with a select and controllable group of industrialists to pass a new Chambers Law as well as other legislation encouraging industrial growth (the 1941 Law of Manufacturing Industries) and to create an industrial chamber (CANACINTRA) that the state could manipulate.[19] The role of the government in the formative years of CANACINTRA is exaggerated in these accounts, but the chamber's original ninety-three member firms (for the most part recently established industries) did support and benefit from the state's new commitment to promote import-substituting industrialization (Mosk 1950).

Much of the controversy involving the creation of CANACINTRA was due to opposition from the commercial chambers, which had been dominant in the private sector until that time, and to the 1941 Chambers Law and the 1941 Law of Manufacturing Industries. The Chambers Law separated CONCANACO and CONCAMIN and led to the creation of CANACINTRA. The Law of Manufacturing Industries provided fiscal incentives for "new and necessary industries" devoted to import substitution, that is, just the type of industry aligned with CANACINTRA.[20] Commerce and its national confederation, CONCANACO, resented the new emphasis on industrialization and thus worked against not only the 1941 industrial legislation but also against the establishment of CANACINTRA, which became a symbol of the industrial revolution in Mexico and of the substantial state role in promoting that revolution.

In reality, CANACINTRA was simply the representative of those new industries that were at the forefront of the state-supported plan of industrialization. Though CANACINTRA opposed the 1942 Trade Agreement with the United States, it favored most of the state policies of the 1940s and benefited from them. This mutually accommodating relation between the state and CANACINTRA in its early years was the extent to which the chamber was government-created and a "captive group" of the state. CONCAMIN also benefited from the new policies, and its behavior was not terribly different from that of CANACINTRA. Indeed, the first president of CANACINTRA (José Cruz y Celis, 1941 to 1943) was also president of CONCAMIN from 1941 to 1946. In the 1950s even the interests of CONCANACO began to converge more with those of the industrial groups (Vernon 1963:169–174; Shafer 1973:120).

A good illustration of the historical linkages between CANACINTRA and the state as well as of the potency of CANACINTRA is Jesús Reyes Heroles, a technical adviser to CANACINTRA in the late 1940s, who, among other duties, attended the postwar Havana meeting on international trade for the industrial chamber (*Proceso*, 26 November 1979). In addition to his CANACINTRA background, Reyes Heroles has been called "perhaps the most brilliant politician of his generation" (*Latin America Political Report*, 25 May 1979). Since entering politics in 1939, he has served in many capacities, including general director of PEMEX, president of the PRI under Echeverría, minister of the interior (*Gobernación*) from 1976 to 1979, and minister of public education under Miguel de la Madrid. Within the PRI and other official circles, he has often promoted the position of small and medium industrialists (Arriola 1976:480). Reyes Heroles and other state officials sympathetic to CANACINTRA have provided the chamber with crucial links to the decision-making process.

The ideology of CANACINTRA has suggested to some that it is unrepresentative of the industrial sector and obviously a pawn of the state.[21] Specifically, CANACINTRA until recently professed a very nationalistic doctrine, support for a strong state role in the economy, and a cooperative attitude toward labor. Its positive orientation toward organized labor has been particularly vexing to some economic analysts and older entrepreneurial groups in Mexico. In the 1940s, it endorsed labor-intensive industries, income redistribution, higher salaries, and increased standards of living for workers. In 1945 it even signed a pact with the Mexican Labor Confederation (Confederación de Trabajadores Mexicanos, CTM) to support nationalistic policies.

But these actions and ideas were not the result of the government forcing a controlled group of industrial leaders to abandon their constituency. Rather, these opinions represented the self-interests of CANACINTRA's members, which were wholly nationally owned firms and were smaller and newer than the commercial firms or the traditional industrial establishments. As such, they welcomed government protection, the cooperation of organized labor, and policies promoting a larger domestic market and greater economic independence for Mexico. Though the interests of CANACINTRA often paralleled those of the state, the state was not manipulating the ideology of CANACINTRA. In fact, in the past few years the outlook of the membership of the chamber has become more critical of the state's economic role, and its ideology has reflected this change (discussed in more detail in the following chapter).

The government's alleged coercion of unwilling firms to join or stay in CANACINTRA is cited as additional evidence of government control. The example most often given is that of the chemical industry, which is one of CANACINTRA's larger sections. Beginning in the late 1950s, certain chemical firms began to petition to leave CANACINTRA to form a separate chamber.[22] The government never permitted the creation of a separate chemical chamber, but in 1960 a number of chemical industrialists founded the National Association of the Chemical Industry (Asociación Nacional de la Industria Química, ANIQ), a private, voluntary organization not bound by the Chambers Law. Since then, ANIQ has performed all the functions of a separate chamber and has affiliated with CONCAMIN. Other large firms have also successfully broken from CANACINTRA to form their own chambers, for example, the National Chamber of the Beer and Malt Industries and the National Chamber of the Perfume and Cosmetic Industry. In addition, regional manufacturing-industry chambers have come into existence. For example, the Chamber of Manufacturing Industries of Nuevo León was established in 1944 as an alternative to CANACINTRA in that northern state. Thus, though the state can disallow the formation of new chambers, these cases do not substantiate a conspiracy between the state and CANACINTRA to coerce unwilling industries to remain in a chamber that no longer represents their interests.

As the membership of CANACINTRA has grown and matured, the chamber has adapted its policies to reflect the changes and has become less supportive of government incursions into the economic sphere. Despite the departure of large chemical and perfume industries and breweries, CANACINTRA in recent years has included some of the largest industries in Mexico and even some subsidiaries of U.S. multinational companies (such as Pepsi-Cola and Ford). CANACINTRA's positions have reflected many of the concerns of this changing constituency. Its independence grew particularly during the Echeverría *sexenio*. President Echeverría alienated the private sector with his anticapitalist rhetoric and unpredictable populist policies, and CANACINTRA was no exception to the antagonistic posture the private sector took toward him. One of his leading business critics was the president of CANACINTRA from 1976 to 1978, Joaquín Pría Olavarrieta (interview, 10 August 1979; *Proceso*, 26 March 1979). When Echeverría expropriated vast amounts of rich farmland in northwest Mexico in November 1976, regional leaders of CANACINTRA opposed the move and supported the one-day business strike. CANACINTRA and its leadership also criticized increased government involvement in the distribution of basic commodities, increases in minimum wages, the devaluation of the peso, and price controls.

Thus, as its affiliates became more productive and independent of state aid and as Echeverría's policies and rhetoric began to threaten private enterprise, CANACINTRA and its spokespersons became staunch defenders of the interests of the private sector vis-à-vis the state. Even under López Portillo, it opposed Mexico's accession to the GATT and the bank nationalizations, and in the early stages of the de la Madrid government the industrial chamber voiced concern over a variety of issues, including inefficient state enterprises, price controls, dual exchange rates, and taxes on consumption of electricity. If CANACINTRA can somehow be seen as a "captive group" of the state in the 1940s, this argument is hard to maintain in the 1970s and 1980s.

Private Associations and Informal Groups. Aside from questioning the degree of limited pluralism that is enforced by the legal status of chambers and confederations such as CANACINTRA, many important business groups and organizations are independent of the PRI and also are not governed by the provisions of the Chambers Law. Some groups are well-organized associations with publicized members, goals, and functions, but, in contrast to chambers and confederations, they are private, voluntary entities outside the purview of the state. Other groups are informal and loosely defined conglomerates of business figures with some shared interests but no commitment to a concrete organization. Finally, some business executives in effect opt out of all groups—formal or informal, private or semiofficial—and prefer to pursue political influence through individual contacts and channels.[23]

The bankers (ABM), insurance firms (AMIS), foreign-trade merchants (ANIERM), and certain commercial and industrial enterprises (such as ANIQ) are organized as "associations" rather than as semiofficial chambers or confederations. These private associations are purely voluntary and do not have to answer to the requirements of the Chambers Law. Their image is more low-key and apolitical than that of the chambers and confederations, and they do not enjoy the guaranteed access to the state that their semiofficial counterparts possess.[24] Yet, this somewhat aloof profile particularly fits the needs and preferences of the entrepreneurs in banking, insurance, and foreign trade. These economic sectors are more service- and professional-oriented and have less public exposure than retailers or manufacturers. They favor representation in private bodies not so visible to the public eye and not subject to the scrutiny of the state. The industrial and commercial associations include members who, for various reasons, feel alienated from their respective chambers and choose to concentrate their energies on more specialized, private organizations specifically designed to serve their interests.

Though the private associations are more removed from public attention and do not always have the same advantages of representation in state agencies as chambers and confederations, they still have played important and often powerful political roles for their members. The associations are not subject to the guidelines of the Chambers Law, but they can join either the national confederation of commerce or the national confederation of industry. Twenty-six industrial associations, including ANIQ, have affiliated with CONCAMIN and are able to enjoy the confederation's access to the state yet retain their independence from any state control (Confederación de Cámaras Industriales 1983a). The major national associations in other fields (ABM, AMIS, and ANIERM) have established their own contacts with the government and at times have aligned with the confederations to form a united private-sector front before the government. ABM was established in 1928 and from World War II until the bank nationalizations in 1982 was a powerful peak association with almost all private financial institutions as members. AMIS, created in 1946, rose to national prominence in the 1960s and also has included most insurance firms as affiliates. The political ties of ANIERM, in existence since 1944, were displayed when one of its founding leaders (Ricardo García Sainz) became a cabinet minister in the López Portillo administration in 1977.

COPARMEX, the employers' confederation organized in 1929, is another important and independent entrepreneurial group. Though it is really an employers' syndicate under the provisions of the 1931 Labor Law, it has remained a private, voluntary, and fiercely autonomous body. It was established by the influential business leaders of Monterrey and has traditionally been associated with their zealous commitment to free enterprise and limited state intervention in the economy. It is now less dominated by the Regiomontanos (those from Monterrey) and includes over twenty thousand individual firms from thirty-nine regional "centers" from all of Mexico. Yet it remains firmly dedicated to the defense of the rights of entrepreneurs in their relations with labor and with the state.

The American Chamber of Commerce in Mexico (CAMCO) is yet another independent entrepreneurial group.[25] As stated above, it primarily represents the U.S. multinational firms in Mexico. Also, over 80 percent of the *maquiladoras* (in-bond or twin-plant border industries) are affiliated with CAMCO. Created in 1917, it now includes over three thousand corporate members and employs a staff of ninety professionals. Its member firms have been estimated to provide over one-fourth of Mexico's gross national product. The chamber has cultivated close ties with the U.S. Embassy in Mexico, and the U.S. ambassador and the consul general always serve as its honorary president and vice-president, respectively. It also has contacts with other entrepreneurial groups and maintains a high profile in Mexico City through many press releases and conferences, meetings with various government officials, quarterly reports and monthly magazine, and weekly seminars.

The Mexican Council of Businessmen (CMHN) is a little-known, but potentially powerful, organization. Legally autonomous from the state, the CMHN is composed of thirty of the most influential business executives in the country (Basáñez 1982:81–84, 98–102, 210). Its small membership of influential business elites contrasts with the memberships of other trade associations that represent either economic enterprises or other business groups. Another distinct characteristic is its preference for remaining out of the public eye. For example, it neither holds annual assemblies (which are utilized by other groups to gain media attention) nor issues public statements on government policy. But, much like the Business Roundtable in the United States, the cohesive and very private CMHN works behind the scenes to influence political decisions that affect the interests of its powerful members.

The last significant organization independent of the Chambers Law is the coordinating council for the private sector, the CCE, which was established in 1975 and includes representatives of the six major associations and confederations: CONCANACO, CONCAMIN, COPARMEX, ABM, AMIS, and CMHN. Its formation in the last years of the Echeverría administration was a climactic event for the private sector, signifying the desires of business to remain a free and powerful element in Mexican society and to protect the interests of private capital.[26] Feeling somewhat unable to defend itself as a result of its division into various confederations, chambers, and associations, the private sector came together as a powerful voice in the CCE. Its first president, Jorge Sánchez Mejorada (a former president of CONCAMIN), was one of the hard-line critics of the

Echeverría policies and pushed the CCE into assuming a more direct and autonomous political role than that of any other previous business group.[27] Though the CCE initially adopted a more cooperative attitude under López Portillo, it continues to be a staunch defender of the fundamental liberties of free enterprise, as evidenced in its staunch criticism of the 1982 bank nationalizations.

In addition to these private and autonomous organizations, the development of the so-called Monterrey Group (discussed above as the founding force in COPARMEX) is a prime example of the independent spirit of certain Mexican entrepreneurs.[28] The Monterrey Group of industrialists is some two hundred entrepreneurial families from Monterrey, Nuevo León, in northern Mexico. Their economic power is reflected in estimates that they contribute almost one-fourth of the nation's total industrial production. Their political power was made evident when one of López Portillo's first actions was to meet with the leading Monterrey industrialists in 1977 in order to restore their confidence in the government and to extract their pledge to invest one hundred billion pesos in the economy during his administration.

The independence and self-reliance of the Monterrey Group is due to a combination of factors, particularly Monterrey's role as a frontier city and a trade link with the United States. Monterrey is closer to San Antonio, Texas, than to Mexico City, and Regiomontanos have always prided themselves on their regional independence. The industrial network of modern Monterrey began with a brewery and a steel mill, both established before the turn of the century by the still-dominant Garza and Sada families. These and other Monterrey industries (many of which were founded by immigrants) prospered on their own before the government assumed a role of promoting and protecting manufacturing firms. Thus, the Monterrey Group has never depended on government aid and has always opposed "excessive" government intervention in the economy.

The Monterrey Group has also stressed its independence in the political arena. The individual industrialists, merchants, and financiers in the group have given substantial support to the strongest and most autonomous opposition party, the right-wing National Action party (PAN). Though they participate in the organized groups and often are the dominant voice in CONCANACO and COPARMEX, they assert most of their influence through personal ties with high-level officials.[29] One author reports that almost every Monterrey industrialist makes at least one trip to Mexico City a week to speak with personal contacts in the government and that many keep an office in Mexico City to maintain daily interaction with government officials (Derossi 1971:54). These high-level connections were evident in early 1977, when newly inaugurated President López Portillo sought the support of the Monterrey Group and took pains to be photographed publicly greeting one powerful Regiomontano, Andrés Marcelo Sada, in a warm *abrazo* and to accept an invitation to dinner at the home of another, Bernardo Garza Sada.[30] At least for the first five years of his term, López Portillo clearly did not approach the Monterrey business sector as a captive group of the state but rather as a powerful, autonomous entity whose support and cooperation were sorely needed after the enmity Echeverría aroused.

The independence of the Monterrey industrialists was compromised somewhat by the economic difficulties they encountered in the early 1980s.[31] Their problems were an outgrowth of their overambitious expansion between 1976 and 1980 and were compounded by the exchange crisis in 1982. With enormous losses in 1981 and 1982 and a heavy debt burden, the leading Monterrey industry (and largest private company in Mexico), Grupo Alfa, had to seek government aid in November 1981 in the form of a twelve-billion-peso loan from BANOBRAS (the national public-works bank) and was forced to suspend debt payments in March 1982. Its proposal for restructuring its foreign debt included selling off 40 percent of its assets in subsidiaries and keeping only its profitable steel and petrochemical concerns. Almost all other Monterrey industries faced some form of economic retrenchment in terms of reduced production and investment, lay-offs, and the like.

Though the nationalization of the banks had left them more dependent on the state for credit and foreign currency, most Monterrey industralists remained as combative as ever.[32] Vitro (the large glassmaking company) joined the court battles against the bank nationalizations (though Alfa and VISA—the two other Monterrey conglomerates—did not), and the Chamber of Manufacturing Industries of Nuevo León (CAINTRA, the industrial chamber that represents the Monterrey industrialists) attempted to organize a one-day business strike to protest the nationalization of the banks. At its 1983 annual meeting, CAINTRA leaders blamed the policies of Echeverría and López Portillo for the plight of the Monterrey private sector. But in a significant statement at the same meeting, Bernardo Garza Sada (president of Grupo Alfa) stated that the Monterrey industrialists had a great deal of confidence in President de la Madrid, that the large enterprises of Mexico would revive, and that indeed the economic recovery had already begun as a result of the economic measures of the new government. In 1983 the Monterrey Group was a shaken, but still powerful and autonomous, industrial force in Mexico whose support was still needed by the new administration.

Low Subject-Mobilization

The second characteristic of authoritarian regimes is that citizens and interest groups are mobilized only to a limited degree and only to suit the purposes of the state. Hence, in an authoritarian setting, one would expect the private sector to be generally apolitical, individual industrialists not to participate to any large degree in their organized interest groups, those interest groups to concentrate on technical rather than political functions, and entrepreneurs to act essentially in support of state policies. As I shall show, these expectations do not hold strictly true in the case of Mexico.

One of the primary reasons Mexican entrepreneurs do become involved in politics is the importance that economic policymaking assumes in a mixed economy such as Mexico's. The heavy state role in economic ownership, regulation, and aid mandates that entrepreneurs concern themselves with political matters. Entrepreneurs often become personally involved in the implementation of policy, especially as it affects them. Monterrey industrialists have been the most active in pursuing individual interests with high-level bureaucrats and the most effective in influencing the administration of policy, but almost all entrepreneurs engage in rather frequent interaction with the bureaucracy at some level in order to alleviate a problem or gain a favor.[33] Outside their immediate self-interests, the private sector has even played a major role in affecting certain foreign-policy decisions in Mexico (Domínguez 1982:221–222).

Business executives wanting to affect policy choices before they are implemented also seek to contribute to policy formulation through participation in electoral politics, political party affairs, and, ultimately, decision making in the executive branch. Financial contributions to the parties are one way in which the private sector influences and participates in party politics. Many Mexican entrepreneurs, especially in the North and Northwest, have strongly supported the major opposition party, the PAN. The PRI also has had substantial input from the business sector, and several entrepreneurs have participated as economic advisers to PRI presidential candidates in the past.

Entrepreneurs have also successfully run for public office themselves. In July of 1979, an unusually large number of entrepreneurs were elected to the Fifty-first Legislature, and some commentators even forecasted that the trend would lead to the formation of a political party solely representing the private sector (*Excélsior*, 16 July 1979). In 1981 COPARMEX supported the idea of creating a new party for entrepreneurs and the "middle class" (*Nexos*, April 1983); and again in 1983, after a series of verbal battles with the PRI, some entrepreneurial leaders said that the private sector was ready to form its own political party (*Excélsior*, 29 January 1983). This step is unlikely, but the present party most associated with conservative business interests (PAN) did double its elected deputies from Monterrey in 1979. And in the presidential elections of 1982 the PAN received many more votes than any other opposition party (16.4 percent), with its strongest support coming from the industrialized states of México, Jalisco, and Nuevo León.

Finally, though industrialists themselves rarely are appointed to positions in the executive branch, they or their representatives frequently lobby cabinet secretaries or other policymaking officials in the executive branch. Thus, the most important mechanisms that entrepreneurs use to influence policy decisions, including media campaigns, behind-the-scenes maneuvering through personal contacts, open consultation with government officials, withdrawal of support through reduced investment or capital flight, and direct actions such as those described below, are primarily aimed at the ministries within the executive branch and the office of the president.

Entrepreneurs have also partaken of less-traditional forms of political participation, such as business strikes. The private sector has organized two notable strikes of a regional nature in recent years. First, in response to Echeverría's expropriation of one hundred thousand hectares of land in the fertile Yaqui Valley of northwest Mexico, the entrepreneurial chambers of that region struck to protest this executive action and in solidarity with the affected landowners (*Excélsior*, 22 and 24 November 1976). The strike was short-lived, partly because of the entrepreneurs' desire to avoid a confrontation with incoming President López Portillo; however, it was at least partially successful, since López Portillo did agree to compensate the owners for their seized land (*Latin America Political Report*, 13 May 1977). A second business strike occurred in the city of Puebla in October of 1979.[34] A labor conflict arising when a group of bus drivers seized seventy-four buses escalated into an ideological clash when the buses were taken to the campus of the Autonomous University of Puebla. University officials refused to return the buses to their owners. This action incensed the conservative Puebla business leaders, who already resented the university for its "communist" sympathies. The Puebla Business Coordinating Council called for a one-day strike, which shut down approximately 75 percent of the city's businesses. Apparently under some government pressure, the drivers and the university officials returned the buses the next day.

Two entrepreneurial strikes in 1982 were not so successful, but still showed the inclinations of many private sector groups to resort to such direct actions. First, in August many businesses along the U.S. border closed for one day to protest the exchange controls, which particularly affected border-area enterprises. The strike was not as widely supported as its organizers had hoped, but it still was an important manifestation of opposition from a segment of the private sector. Second, the CCE, CON-CANACO, and CAINTRA called for a business stoppage on September 8 to express their displeasure with the bank nationalizations of September 1. But the ABM, as well as the other industrial groups (CONCAMIN and CANACINTRA), feared this action would be counterproductive, and the strike was canceled (*Expansión*, 15 September 1982; *Wall Street Journal*, 7 October 1982; *Proceso*, 31 January 1983; and *Nexos*, April 1983). This did not end private sector opposition to the nationalizations, however, as business leaders utilized court cases, public statements, and other means of public lobbying in attempts to overturn the decision or dampen its impact. In December, de la Madrid did decide to allow one-third of the banks' stock to be sold to the public, with the other two-thirds still held by the state; and by late 1983 the new administration had begun the process of compensating the former bank owners.

In most of their political activities, entrepreneurs have preferred to work through their organized interest groups. Hence, Mexican business executives have participated in substantial numbers in their chambers and associations. For example, in a 1969 survey of a sample of industrialists, 50 percent chose to act through an organized industrial group when faced with an adverse government policy and 70 percent participated in their chamber in some fashion (Derossi 1971:40, 187). In a 1980 survey I conducted of industrial leaders (described in detail in chapter 5), 80 percent said they first preferred to depend on their chamber or association whenever they wanted to influence a government decision. Over 75 percent also disagreed that the business groups ought to serve only technical functions and should avoid politics.

CONCAMIN and CANACINTRA provide excellent examples of the high levels of political activities industrial organizations pursue. CANACINTRA became especially aggressive in the political arena after 1945.[35] One of its major actions in the late 1940s was the organization of the First National Congress of Manufacturing Industries, which was opened by President Alemán. Also in those years, CANACINTRA was active in international economic conferences, in the opposition to the 1942 Trade Agreement with the United States, and in discussions concerning a new tariff law, the 1948 devaluation of the peso, and several tax revisions. In the 1950s, it was especially concerned with policies regarding government industrial credits, the expansion of the domestic market, protection for domestic industries, various energy problems, and the regulation of foreign investment. Among the major issues on which CANACINTRA concentrated in the 1960s were the nationalization of the foreign-owned electrical energy companies, tariff revisions, and fiscal reforms. In a typical year, the political activities published by CANACINTRA in its annual report would include many meetings with the president of the republic and with ministers and department heads in the executive branch, press releases and conferences on policy issues, various public functions discussing economic policies, and the work of fourteen permanent commissions responding to the political needs of member firms. Most recently, as is described in chapter 6, CANACINTRA was one of the groups responsible for convincing López Portillo in 1980 not to take Mexico into the General Agreement on Tariffs and Trade (GATT). The broad scope of the political activities of CANACINTRA has also been reflected in the growth of its annual expenditures, which reached $2.5 million in 1976.

Though not as overtly active as CANACINTRA, CONCAMIN is a much older organization. It was formed at the First National Congress of Industry, which met in 1917–1918 to consider legislative and other means of promoting industrial development.[36] Though CONCAMIN lacked the resources to undertake major political projects in the 1920s and 1930s, the government consulted it often (sometimes the president of the republic) on industrial legislation (Shafer 1973:30–41, 147–148). One of CONCAMIN's primary concerns in this period was labor policy. The Second National Congress of Industry in 1925 concentrated on the creation of a complete social security system.

CONCAMIN significantly increased its commitment to political activities after World War II.[37] For example, the annual report of 1949 (*Asamblea General Ordinaria, 1949*, pp. 1–71) includes seventy pages describing the political activities in that year, with some of the policy areas being industrial credits, social security, new tax laws, and a proposed new chambers law. Principal issues of concern to the confederation in other years have been government subsidies to industry and tariff revisions. CONCAMIN has often been consulted by the government on economic policy. The government sends all proposed legislation affecting industry to it to elicit its reaction. In addition to direct government consultation, CONCAMIN has conducted public campaigns on various issues through newspaper advertisements, radio, television, and its own pamphlets and magazine. It organized national congresses of industry in 1946, 1958, 1964, 1970, and 1976, with each stressing a broad policy aspect of industrial development.

Contrary to the characteristics of an authoritarian regime, Mexican industrialists often mobilize in opposition to a policy initiative or policy change (Solís 1981:98–100). Though they seldom expect to defeat any legislation outright, they usually plan to alter or delay policy so as to extract certain concessions. Also, many business leaders have much faith in their ability to affect policy in the stage of implementation. Their well-founded belief is that the implementation of a policy in Mexico can be very different from its formal intent.

As the private sector developed in the postwar period in Mexico, its relations with the state assumed an adversary nature and the willingness of business groups to criticize policy increased (Smith 1979:211–216). The critical stance of industrialists is evident in survey data, especially in the attitudes prior to the López Portillo administration. In the previously cited 1969 survey, Mexican entrepreneurs were asked to evaluate eight postwar economic policies. None received a majority of favorable responses, whereas two (concerning raw-material prices and custom duties) received a majority of unfavorable responses (Derossi 1971:61). Also, in the 1980 survey of industrialists (see chapter 5) three of the policy areas (prices, labor, and taxes) received unfavorable responses from a majority of the industrial leaders.

The distance between the private sector and the state was particularly great during the Echeverría administration and the last year of López Portillo's term. The 1980 survey showed that the industrial leaders viewed Echeverría as the president most unfavorable to the private sector in the period from Cárdenas to López Portillo. Specific Echeverría policies business groups opposed included the proposed fiscal reform, price controls, the extension of public ownership and of the state's role in distributing basic goods, and the agrarian reform.[38] In addition to public criticism, the efforts of organizations like the CCE, and the 1976 business strike, an even more important form of business opposition to Echeverría was the withdrawal of business confidence, followed by refusals to invest and a growing problem of capital flight from Mexico. These actions were not just selfish attempts to protect earnings and capital; they showed that the private sector could manipulate its own resources to bring strong pressures to bear on the government. Though Echeverría reacted negatively to these business pressures in his last years in office, López Portillo did foresee a need to regain the confidence of the private sector.

Though cooperation between the private and public sectors was partially restored when López Portillo came into office, the entrepreneurs did not stop pressuring the government when business interests were being threatened, as exemplified in the Puebla business strike, in concerns being voiced by CONCANACO and others over the fiscal reforms proposed in 1979, in CANACINTRA opposition to Mexico's accession to the GATT in 1980, and of course in the outcry against the bank nationalizations.

The decision regarding the banks, which was announced September 1 in López Portillo's last *Informe*, began a period of discord between the state and the private sector that even spilled over into de la Madrid's first few months.[39] Soon after the state takeover of the remaining private national banks, entrepreneurial leaders began to decry what they felt was encroaching "socialism" and "statism." They also manifested their opinion that the current political system, as dominated by the PRI, was bent on depriving individuals of their political and economic rights. Once de la Madrid was inaugurated, the private sector focused its attacks on the previous government and the official party and was careful not to criticize the new president or his economic team.

The split between the private sector and the PRI escalated in January of 1983 when CONCANACO organized a conference in Toluca (with representatives from COPARMEX and the CCE also attending) to criticize the "arbitrary acts" (referring to the bank nationalizations and the exchange controls) of the previous administration. On January 28 the PRI took the unusual step of publishing in the major newspapers an advertisement that was a direct response to the private sector criticisms. The official party stated that private sector chambers "are not political institutions nor adequate channels for the expression of ideological positions" and reminded them, in an indirect threat, that they were subject to the control of the secretary of commerce and industrial promotion. However, indicative of their relative autonomy, the entrepreneurial groups were not intimidated and continued their criticisms of the PRI and the previous government.[40]

Throughout this confict with the government party, private sector leaders clearly differentiated between the PRI and the government of de la Madrid and actually praised the latter. In fact, as early as 1980 the private sector had been intent on ensuring an acceptable successor to López Portillo. Industrial and other business leaders began their offensive for affecting the selection process in October of 1980, with speeches in cities all across Mexico exhorting entrepreneurs to make their voices heard (*Proceso*, 20 October 1980). The announcement of Miguel de la Madrid as the chosen successor to López Portillo was well received in industrial circles. And once in office, entrepreneurial groups complimented the de la Madrid economic team for taking the "only options available to Mexico" in order to surpass the economic crisis that they blamed on previous administrations.[41]

Hierarchical Ordering of Relationships

The third characteristic of authoritarian regimes is that relations with the state are organized in a centralized, personalized, and hierarchical fashion. The ultimate *patrón*, the state, co-opts leaders of interest groups so that they are granted certain privileges in return for their unquestioning support. All power and all rewards emanate from the top and derive from personal relationships. Very little grass-roots involvement in political organizations is encouraged or allowed, and no genuine competition for leadership posts exists.

Once again Mexican industrial organizations generally contradict these descriptions of an authoritarian system. The leaders of the chambers and confederations are not beholden to the dominant political elites, the leadership is not oligarchic, and the structure of the groups is not overly centralized. The only aspect of patronal rule evident in the relation of Mexican industries to the state is personalistic style of influence. The importance of personal contacts and personal relations is still relevant to the political effectiveness of business representatives. Yet, even the nature of these personal contacts sometimes indicates the independence of the private sector. In his analysis of the political and economic elites in Mexico, Peter Smith concludes that considerable "social distance" exists between entrepreneurs and the political elite. He states that "entrepreneurs and politicians interact in an atmosphere of uncertainty, distrust, suspicion, and even disdain" (Smith 1979:145).

CANACINTRA is again the focus of many of the charges that industrial leaders are simply a mouthpiece of the state. A few analysts and even some business leaders who are outside of CANACINTRA and are critical of the chamber for some of its views told me that CANACINTRA is easily manipulated by the state because its presidents always are given important government posts after their term expires. Another author states that CANACINTRA's leadership can be viewed as an "unofficial adjunct" of the PRI (Shafer 1973:56). These views clearly reflect the authoritarian image of the state as co-opting business leaders with lucrative positions in return for their loyalty and support. However, no firm evidence for this link between CANACINTRA and the state has ever been cited. Though some individuals like Reyes Heroles do provide CANACINTRA with sympathetic contacts within the government, there is no indication that CANACINTRA officials or leaders are rewarded with government posts.

To test the hypothesized relationship, I compared a list of the twenty-two different presidents of CANACINTRA since its formation in 1941 to those persons listed in Roderic A. Camp's (1976) compilation of Mexican political biographies from 1935 to 1975. The Camp volume encompasses any individuals who have held major political positions, including those most relevant to possible private sector appointments: members of the president's "Inner Circle"; cabinet members and undersecretaries; managers and assistant directors of major state enterprises and of important boards and agencies; and political party leaders. Of the twenty-two CANACINTRA presidents, only *one* is found in the Camp book and his government posts (director general of CONASUPO and secretary of agriculture) were *before* his term as president of the chamber.

I have made the same comparison for the nineteen presidents of CONCAMIN since 1941. Interestingly enough, of these, who the literature suggests are much more independent of the government than their CANACINTRA counterparts, *three* (one director of CONDUMEX and two secretaries of industry and commerce) are found in Camp's list of political biographies, though in only one of these cases did the government positions follow the term as confederation president.[42] Thus, the hypothesized link between the presidency of CANACINTRA and an illustrious position in the government is disconfirmed.[43]

Intense competition often occurs for leadership positions in the industrial organizations, and no individual entrepreneur or group of entrepreneurs has consistently dominated any major group. As noted above, CANACINTRA and CONCAMIN have had twenty-two and nineteen different presidents, respectively, since 1941. All the other national chambers and confederations also change leadership at least every two years. This situation contrasts sharply with a case such as Argentina's in which one president of the national industrial confederation remained in office for twenty-one years.

The leadership transitions in Mexican business groups usually represent legitimate competition rather than merely changes in names of the individuals in power. The competition has become more open in recent years, and some of the most meaningful transitions have occurred since 1975. In that year CANACINTRA elected its first president ever from the furniture industry, C. P. Amilcar Ranero, who began a trend of increasing independence on the part of CANACINTRA (interview, 17 July 1979). He was followed in 1976 by Joaquín Pría Olavarrieta, one of the most vocal opponents of the Echeverría expansionist policies. Juan Manuel Martínez Gómez was elected president in 1978 as one of the chamber's few presidents from the foodstuffs industry, and he continued to stress an independent line for CANACINTRA. In 1983 Ignacio Barragán de Palacio was re-elected for his second term as president, as most CANACINTRA presidents serve two years almost automatically. But Barragán de Palacio had to defeat two serious challengers, and some of the chamber's council members were openly critical of his leadership—again demonstrating the lack of oligarchical control within the organization.

CONCANACO has experienced some of the most bitter struggles for leadership of all the business groups in recent years. In 1977, Carlos Sparrow Sada, the former president of the Chamber of Commerce of Obregón and leader of the 1976 business strike against Echeverría, unsuccessfully challenged the incumbent president of CONCANACO, Víctor Manuel Gaudiano. Sparrow Sada was seen as the head of a "radical" group supported mostly by small, provincial business leaders, whereas Gaudiano was viewed as the representative of the large entrepreneurs centered in Mexico City (*Análisis Político*, 7 February 1977). The following year the provincials and Sparrow Sada threw their weight behind the successful candidacy of Guillermo Zamacona, from Monterrey. Zamacona was not perceived as a threat by the large entrepreneurs and they along with Gaudiano supported him (*Análisis Político*, 3 April 1978).

Two important elections of business leaders in 1979 resulted in the selection of individuals who favored a more cooperative attitude toward the government, and their ascension to power was a boost to the initial rapprochement policies of López Portillo. First, the election of a new president in CONCAMIN saw Pría Olavarrieta (the former president of CANACINTRA) challenge the favored Ernesto Rubio del Cueto (*Análisis Político*, 2 April 1079). Pría Olavarrieta was the activist and hard-line candidate, and Rubio presented himself as more low-key and conciliatory. The election of Rubio was assured in March when thirty-three industrial chambers agreed to support him at the upcoming annual assembly. Second, the CCE saw one of its strongest presidents, Jorge Sánchez Mejorada, replaced by a sharply contrasting industrialist, Prudencio López (*Proceso*, 30 April 1979). Sánchez Mejorada was an ally of Pría Olavarrieta and had even proposed forming a broad political alliance to defend private enterprise from further encroachments of the public sector. López, however, was less aggressive and preferred a more harmonious relationship with the state.

The CCE changed its tone again in 1982, under its new president, Manuel Clouthier. After the accusations by López Portillo against the so-called *sacadólares* (those he blamed for capital flight, allegedly including Clouthier), the institution of exchange controls, and the expropriation of the banks, the CCE under the leadership of Clouthier became quite critical of López Portillo and his new policies. In September it lamented the "corrupt, inefficient, and almost totalitarian 'statization' of the economy,'' and Clouthier said Mexico was becoming an "infantile" nation due to "state paternalism" (*Nexos*, April 1983, p. 27).

One of the primary reasons that the industrial groups have not been controlled by an oligarchy has been that the systems of choosing the leadership have encouraged broad representation. For example, voting strength in CONCAMIN is allotted according to the size of the financial contribution, so that smaller firms and smaller chambers can increase their voting strength through a larger contribution (Brandenburg 1958:33–35). In addition, at least three seats on the Executive Commission of CONCA-MIN are guaranteed to chambers with less than three votes (Confederación de Cámaras Industriales 1983a). In CANACINTRA, voting for the Directive Council is by sections, which represent types of industry, and by delegations, which represent geographic localities ("Estatutos de la Cámara Nacional de la Industria de Transformación," *Diario Oficial*, 11 June 1976, pp. 14–29). Members of the council are prohibited from being elected for two consecutive two-year terms. Thus the leadership tends to be diverse in background and changes frequently.

Some authors suggest that the divisions among the entrepreneurial groups are produced by a government strategy of "divide-and-rule," which is described as exemplary of patronal rule (Purcell and Purcell 1977:196). Though some differences do exist, the role of the state in fomenting them is overemphasized. The greatest division among business organizations is that between the confederation of commerce (CONCAN-ACO) and the confederation of industry (CONCAMIN), and this differentiation primarily resulted from pressure from the industrialists who wanted a separate confederation for industry established. The distinctions between CANACINTRA and CONCAMIN also are not directly attributable to state manipulation, and in fact the ideological beliefs of the two groups as reflected in the 1980 survey are not very different (see chapter 5). Until the mid-1970s, CANACINTRA did support the state more than any other business group, but it also had represented newer and smaller industries more dependent on state aid. After 1975 the industrial chamber began to place more distance between itself and the state, and under the guidance of Pría Olavarrieta CANACINTRA was even more critical of state policies than was CONCAMIN. Finally, divisions within the organizations have arisen not from state interference promoting one set of business leaders over another but from relatively open competition among entrepreneurs with genuine differences of opinion and approach.

Conclusion

In analyzing the degree of authoritarianism in terms of limited pluralism, low subject-mobilization, and hierarchical ordering found in the relations between the state and the private sector, I have emphasized a number of points suggesting that industrial organizations are rather autonomous of state control and manipulation.

1. Unlike other political actors, the private sector is not incorporated under the dominant political party, the PRI, and is not subject to the constraints of party membership.

2. The state has seldom intervened in the running of the industrial organizations, choosing leaders, or banning any chambers, and the obligatory nature of membership is not a hindrance to their autonomy from the state. Despite periodic threats of the exercise of state control, the industrial groups have retained considerable independence.

3. CANACINTRA is not a "captive group" of the state. It has always acted in the interests of its membership, and since 1975 it has become more independent of the state. Firms are not forced to remain in the chamber, and several groups have broken from it to form their own chambers.

4. Many formal business groups are not covered by the Chambers Law. These are private, voluntary organizations, often with national constituencies, as in the cases of the ABM, AMIS, ANIQ, COPARMEX, and the all-encompassing CCE.

5. Certain informal groups, particularly the Monterrey Group, have gained immense political and economic power based on self-reliance and opposition to increased government intervention in the economy.

6. Mexican entrepreneurs are politically active, do support their various organizations, and often oppose government policies. Business opposition was particularly strident during the Echeverría years, but even under López Portillo, business executives maintained their independence and became openly critical in his last year.

7. The state has not co-opted industrial leaders with favoritism and rewards to selected individuals or groups. For example, this research has disconfirmed the hypothesized link between the presidency of CANACINTRA and a high-level government post.

8. The industrial organizations themselves are run in a relatively democratic fashion. The members are guaranteed rather broad representation, the leadership changes frequently, and many elections are openly contested.

The strongest evidence for authoritarian control of industrial groups in

Mexico is the legislation governing all chambers and confederations, but the provisions are unevenly applied. This legislation provides for (1) compulsory membership, (2) guaranteed representation in and consultation by the state, (3) limits on the formation of chambers and on the freedom of firms to choose among chambers, and (4) state approval of the rules and structure of all chambers and confederations. In discussing specific aspects of authoritarian control over interest groups (often labeled "corporatism"), David Collier and Ruth Collier (1979) have made the distinction between "inducements" and "constraints." The first two provisions of the Mexican chambers legislation are clearly inducements, and the latter two are constraints. In a truly authoritarian setting, one would expect the inducements to build the groups' support for the state (the "carrot") and the constraints to keep the groups in the firm grip of the state (the "stick"). But in the case of Mexican business groups, the inducements have been more salient than the constraints. Mexican industrialists feel that they have reaped the benefits of compulsory membership and guaranteed representation but have not had to pay the price in terms of oppressive restrictions on formation and procedure. Indeed, the state has seldom if ever openly intervened in the operations of Mexican chambers.

There is no doubt that the Mexican state has the legal capacity for direct intervention in the chambers. The critical question is why it has seldom exercised its option. One plausible argument is that the state feels no need to control the business groups, because the state and the private sector have a mutual interest in maintaining a capitalist development strategy in Mexico. Thus, neither threatens the other and they have a common stake in the "alliance for profits."

Certainly, there is some truth to this argument. However, it ignores an important and inherent degree of independence on the part of the Mexican private sector. For example, when Mexican entrepreneurs felt their basic interests threatened at times by Echeverría, they responded not only with political opposition but with autonomous economic decisions that crippled the economy and contributed to a near political crisis in late 1976 (loss of confidence and rumors of a military coup). The private sector withheld investment during the Echeverría *sexenio*, and in 1976 capital flight from Mexico to the United States escalated to a frightening $150 million daily in mid-November. By 1976 inflation had reached almost 25 percent, and the rate of economic growth had declined to a level below the rate of population growth.

The actions of the private sector showed that Mexican entrepreneurs wielded considerable economic power which could be used as a political tool, and that government needed to restore the confidence of Mexican business. López Portillo in his first years did establish a more harmonious relationship with industry and commerce, but entrepreneurial groups did not sacrifice their independence for more beneficial policies and again stridently criticized government economic policies in 1982. This disharmony that frequently arises between Mexican presidents and business groups demonstrates not only that the state does not control the private sector but also that private capital does not dominate the state. The private sector and the state remain mutually exclusive (with some exceptions) and independent powers with shared interests in many policy areas but not all.

Though my findings do emphasize the relative autonomy of the private sector in Mexico, especially in comparison with the authoritarian states of the Southern Cone, they do not prove that Mexico is a pluralist or democratic society or that the balance of power is moving away from the state. Mexico in an aggregate sense is an authoritarian regime with a powerful state. Yet, it is an important variant or subtype of authoritarianism in regard to state-industry relations. Beyond the usual differences of Mexico as a civilian, one-party, authoritarian regime, this chapter emphasizes inducements for industrial groups over constraints and more autonomy for the elitist sectors than for the popular sectors. Thus, one should differentiate among additional dimensions relevant to an authoritarian framework. Little variance is found among the traditional aspects of limited pluralism, low subject-mobilization, and hierarchical ordering. However, the distinction between inducements and constraints is relevant to Mexican industrial organizations, and the need to differentiate among different sectors in society exists.

5. The Political Ideology and Perceptions of Industrial Elites: Mexico and Venezuela Compared

An important and necessary complement to the macrolevel analysis of state-industry relations is an understanding of the belief systems of individual industrialists that undergird the political actions of their respective chambers and confederations. The ideological orientation of industrialists can be just as significant an aspect of their political role as the degree of autonomy of industrial organizations from the state or the level of political participation of industrial groups. Differences in ideological orientation and commitment can lead to different policies being advocated and different levels of effectiveness in promoting those policies. The political beliefs of industrialists are particularly salient to the extent that the actions of trade associations reflect the aggregation of the political preferences of their individual members. To examine the question of a unified industrial ideology and other related issues, this chapter shifts to a microquantitative analysis of the political ideology and perceptions of Mexican industrialists as revealed in survey research. A comparative perspective is added by juxtaposing the findings from the Mexican sample with a similar, though smaller, sample of Venezuelan industrialists.

The focus here is on "industrial elites." Of course, the analysis in chapter 4 emphasized that the industrial sector in general is an elitist sector, at least compared to the mass-based groups such as labor or *campesinos*. But the survey research described in this chapter specifically concentrates on the industrial leaders within the most important industrial organizations. The assumption is that these individual industrialists are the primary sources for both the dominant political beliefs and the political influence of the industrial sector.

Much quantitative research has been done on the socioeconomic behavior of industrialists in Latin America. The first comparative studies were coordinated in Latin America by Fernando H. Cardoso in the early

1960s.[1] These surveys, as well as other studies, have concluded that a number of domestic and international factors have obstructed national private economic initiative and capital in Latin America and that Latin American entrepreneurs generally have maintained traditional values while resisting innovative changes. On the other hand, microlevel, quantitative studies of the political orientations of Latin American industrialists have not been as complete or as conclusive as the socioeconomic literature. Though a few studies have made some valuable contributions to the explanations of the political behavior of Latin American entrepreneurs, the literature on the political belief systems of Latin American industrialists continues to lag behind that concerning socioeconomic values.[2]

Specifically for Mexico, only two studies have utilized survey research on economic elites: a national survey of 143 Mexican entrepreneurs done in 1969 by Flavia Derossi (1971), and interviews in 1968 and 1969 with 54 leaders of the private sector in Guadalajara and Monterrey conducted by John Walton (1977). The Derossi book largely fits into the socioeconomic literature of Latin American entrepreneurship; the Walton study emphasizes the political economy of specific urban centers. The other microlevel analyses have focused on political elites in Mexico. Roderic Camp (1980) has examined the relationship between education and political recruitment for individual political leaders in Mexico, and Peter Smith (1977) has compared his data on Mexican political elites with the Derossi data on economic elites. A number of the conclusions of these studies are used as a point of departure for this chapter, to wit, that the Mexican entrepreneurial class contains some new and dynamic sectors; that industrial elites show some signs of political efficacy; and that the relationship between economic and political power structures in Mexico is generally competitive.[3]

I use Venezuela as a point of comparison primarily because it represents a more open and competitive political system with a strong private sector. Since the restoration of democratic electoral politics in 1958, Venezuela's private sector has assumed an important political role and has remained largely independent of political parties and of the state.[4] The leading trade associations are the Venezuelan Federation of Chambers and Associations of Commerce and Production (Federación Venezolana de Cámaras y Asociaciones de Comercio y Producción, FEDECAMARAS), the Industrial Chamber of Caracas (Cámara de Industriales de Caracas, CIC), and the Venezuelan Council of Industry (Consejo Venezolano de la Industria, CONINDUSTRIA). The CIC, a regional association created in 1939, is the oldest of these associations. Its parallel national organization, CONINDUSTRIA, was created in 1969. FEDECAMARAS, established in 1944, is the Venezuelan federation of all economic sectors.

Though some attempts have been made to set up a corporatist structure, especially through functional participation in economic planning, the independent power of the private sector and its propensity to conflict with the state have prevented the evolution of a corporatist framework under state control. On a number of important economic policy decisons (from regional economic integration in the 1960s to exchange control in the 1980s), the Venezuelan private sector has manifested an independent and often strident voice on behalf of its interests. Though not always successful in influencing state policy, it has maintained its autonomous voice. Hence, one might expect Venezuelan industrialists to demonstrate considerable ideological differentiation from the state and to exhibit a strong commitment to political action. Venezuela, then, is used as a "criterion variable" representing a relatively autonomous private industrial sector whose political orientation can be compared to that of Mexican industrial elites.

The Sample and Questionnaire

The Mexican data analyzed in this chapter are from mail surveys received from 109 leading industrialists in the summer of 1980.[5] Obviously, the definition and composition of "industrial elites" in Mexico can vary greatly. My focus is on the leaders of the political interest groups (chambers and confederations) to which all industrialists, except the very smallest, are required by law to belong. The sample to which the questionnaires were mailed includes industrialists who were elected officers in 1980 of the two most important organized groups of industrial entrepreneurs in Mexico: CONCAMIN and CANACINTRA.

I do not claim that this sample is scientifically representative of either the largest or the most powerful (if that could be defined) industrialists in Mexico. However, it does include those industrialists elected by their peers as the principal decision makers in the two most influential industrial trade associations in Mexico. These individuals were not the full-time employees (*funcionarios*) of the chambers and confederations but were the industrialists who formed the leadership cadre of the groups. CONCAMIN is the only national industrial confederation in Mexico, and CANACINTRA stands above all the other industrial chambers in its political importance and has assumed an identity independent of CONCAMIN. Thus, this is a purposive or judgmental sample of Mexican industrial elites that incorporates the leaders of the major organized groups of industrial entrepreneurs in 1980.

The most significant omission of this sample, in terms of incorporating all the elements of the national industrial elites, is the lack of a specific subsample representing the so-called Monterrey Group. Not only do they represent a large concentration of the nation's industrial might, but they are viewed as being particularly independent of the dominant political forces in Mexico City and of the government's political party, the PRI. But since they are a small, informal group without an organized membership, I made no attempt to include them as a specific subsample in this study. Besides, several chambers that encompass many Monterrey industrialists, such as the National Chamber of Steel and Iron Industries, the Chamber of Manufacturing Industries of Nuevo León, the Textile Chamber of the North, and the National Chamber of the Brewery Industry, are automatically included in the CONCAMIN sample. In addition, numerous articles and books have analyzed the influence and ideology of the Monterrey Group.[6]

The entities in Venezuela comparable to CONCAMIN and CANACINTRA are the CIC and CONINDUSTRIA. Thus, the leading industrialists from these two groups, which have almost identical memberships, compose the Venezuelan sample of "industrial elites." Contrary to the Mexican situation, no identifiable informal groupings of Venezuelan industrialists (comparable to the Monterrey Group) exist. And I did not use FEDECAMARAS because it is a peak association that includes economic sectors in addition to industry.

The questionnaire principally involves fixed-response questions (Likert-scale items) pertaining to industrial political influence, sectoral consciousness, views on foreign investment, opinions on the economic role of the state, attitudes toward labor, evaluation of specific economic policies, and impressions of various presidential administrations (see appendix E). Additional questions (primarily open-ended) solicit demographic or background data on education, father's occupation, nationality, age and size of company, the firm's industrial branch, and its dependence on foreign capital.

The questionnaire was sent to the presidents of all 89 chambers and associations in CONCAMIN, to 236 officers (the president, vice-president, and sometimes other elected posts) of the 77 active sections of CANACINTRA, and to 161 leading industrialists from the 15 sections of both the CIC and CONINDUSTRIA (as listed in their mutual publication, *Producción*). The response rate was 34 percent for CANACINTRA (81 responses), 31 percent for CONCAMIN (28 responses), and 20 percent for the CIC and CONINDUSTRIA (32 responses).

The respondents generally reflect the various divisions in the groups. All seven major "councils" in CANACINTRA are represented properly, and

64 percent of the sections are represented. The only organizational division within CONCAMIN is between chambers and associations, both of which are proportionally represented in this sample. All but the smallest section of the CIC and CONINDUSTRIA are represented in the Venezuelan responses. In terms of the industrial branch of activity of the respondents, the only biases are a slight overrepresentation of foodstuffs and beverages in the CONCAMIN group and a small underrepresentation of textiles, electricity, and the automotive industry in the Venezuelan group. Otherwise the industrial branches have roughly proportionate representation.

Differences between CANACINTRA and CONCAMIN

The survey sample specifically included leaders from both CONCAMIN and CANACINTRA in order to investigate the degree to which these two groups represent different industrial interests. As discussed in chapter 4, much of the literature has maintained that the existence of CANACINTRA apart from CONCAMIN represents a successful state strategy of "divide-and-rule" the private sector. More specifically, CANACINTRA has been charged as being little more than a pawn of the state, whereas CONCA-MIN has been recognized as a more legitimate, countervailing force to government economic intervention.

These arguments focus on three points of difference between the two groups: constituency, ideology, and links to the government. CONCAMIN is said to be particularly representative of the older, larger industrial firms. On the other hand, CANACINTRA is said to represent newer, smaller enterprises (the "infant industries") that benefited from the state's commitment to import-substituting industrialization beginning in the 1940s. According to many authors, these differences in constituency groups have also produced ideological distinctions.[7] CANACINTRA is labeled the more "progressive" or "leftist" of the two in that its members are purportedly more critical of the impact of foreign investment, favor a large degree of government intrusion into the economy, and adopt a much more conciliatory attitude toward labor. Finally, CANACINTRA has been reported as having suspiciously close relations with the state apparatus and with the PRI.

These survey data offer an excellent opportunity to test the theory that the groups exhibit substantial differences and that CANACINTRA is especially left-leaning and supportive of the state. I use two statistical techniques to test the null hypothesis, that these two samples have been drawn from the same population, that is, that in a statistical sense they are random samples from the single population of "industrial elites." The alternative hypothesis is that these two samples are from statistically different populations—which is the argument made in most of the literature. The two techniques I employ here are the Mann-Whitney U Test (M-W) and the Kilmogorov-Smirov Test (K-S).[8]

I have applied these two tests individually to the seventy-four survey items that are at least ordinal measures (the survey contains eighty-four items total, reproduced in appendix E). The results reject the null hypothesis of no difference for only seven of the seventy-four items (summarized in table 25). And of these seven items, only three show the rejection of the

Table 25
Mann-Whitney and Kolmogorov-Smirov Tests

Item No.	Mann-Whitney		Kolmogorov-Smirov	
	Z	**P**	**Z**	**P**
7[a]	− 2.836	0.005	1.569	0.015
10	− 2.582	0.010	1.309	0.065
22	− 2.470	0.013	1.167	0.131
27	− 2.041	0.041	0.988	0.283
59	− 2.845	0.004	1.171	0.129
65[a]	− 2.555	0.011	1.442	0.031
79[a]	− 2.923	0.004	1.433	0.033

Notes: These are tests of the null hypothesis of no difference between the two samples. If P (significance) is less than 0.05, the null hypothesis is rejected. In other words, larger differences between groups are indicated by higher absolute values of Z (test statistic) and lower values of P.

[a]Both tests indicate the rejection of the null hypothesis for these items.

null hypothesis according to both tests (items 7, 65, and 79). The actual differences for these three items are reproduced in table 26, which shows that even in these cases the distinctions between CONCAMIN and CANACINTRA are not great. For items 7 and 79 (gauging participation in one's industrial association and perceptions of policies under López Portillo, respectively) the majority of cases for both samples are clustered in the top half of the scale, though the modal categories are reversed. Hence, no major substantive differences exist for these items. Item 65 asks for the gross value of production of the respondent's firm in 1979. The mean values shown in table 26 provide the only confirmation (CONCAMIN tends to represent larger firms) for any of the claims of vast differences between CANACINTRA and CONCAMIN. Yet, items measuring the age

Table 26
CONCAMIN and CANACINTRA Differences

Item 7: I am an active participant in the affairs of my national industrial association (%).

	SA	A	U	D	SD
CANACINTRA	37.0	55.6	3.7	1.2	2.5
CONCAMIN	71.4	21.4	7.1	0	0

Item 79: Do you think the policies of López Portillo have been favorable or unfavorable to the industrial sector (%)?

	VF	SF	N	SU	VU
CANACINTRA	23.3	58.9	9.6	5.5	2.7
CONCAMIN	55.6	37.0	3.7	3.7	0

Item 65: What was the value of gross production in your company in 1979 (millions of pesos)?

	Mean Value	Minimum	Maximum
CANACINTRA	393	2	5000
CONCAMIN	689	6	3070

Notes: SA = strongly agree; A = agree; U = undecided; D = disagree; SD = strongly disagree; VF = very favorable; SF = somewhat favorable; N = no opinion; SU = somewhat unfavorable; VU = very unfavorable.

of the firm (item 63) and the number of employees (item 66) do not prove a statistical difference. So, at least among its leaders, CONCAMIN does not include older firms or more "conservative" industrialists than those in CANACINTRA.

The overwhelming conclusion, then, is that these samples of CONCAMIN and CANACINTRA can be considered as drawn from the same population of industrial elites. This disconfirms the predominant theme in the literature that the two industrial groups are dissimilar in regard to constituency, ideology, and links to the government. Of course, one plausible explanation is that CANACINTRA changed significantly in the 1970s, especially during the Echeverría administration. The existing literature could correctly reflect pre-1970 distinctions. But the populism or reformism of Echeverría might have instilled more unity and independence in the private sector, especially moving CANACINTRA in the conservative direction.

In any case, as of 1980 the leaders of CANACINTRA and CONCAMIN were essentially of like mind, though certain demographic differences (gross value of production) persisted. This unity lends some support to the notion that the ideology of Mexican industrial elites reflects an independent attitude and sectorial consciousness. At least the similarities between CONCAMIN and CANACINTRA disprove theories that the state or other groups are manipulating differences among Mexican industrialists. The following sections then examine the *total sample* of industrial elites in Mexico as compared to the sample of Venezuelan industrial elites.

Demographic Variables

For both the Mexican and Venezuelan samples, the average industrialist in this sample is well educated, upper class, and native-born. Over 90 percent of the respondents in both cases have a university education, and most are either *licenciados* or *ingenieros* (both equivalent to Master's degrees). Their family background, as indicated by their father's occupation, is predominantly upper class. For Mexico, the modal category of father's occupation is industrialist (30 percent) followed closely by professionals such as doctors and lawyers (20 percent) and large merchants (28 percent). The remainder are scattered among landowners (6 percent), working-class jobs (6 percent), and small business executives (1 percent).

The breakdown in Venezuela is remarkably similar. Some differences between the countries do exist, however, in the place of birth of the industrialists. Though both samples show a majority of native-born industrialists, this tendency is much more pronounced in Mexico. The Mexican industrial elites are overwhelmingly native Mexicans—94 percent. Even 76 percent of their fathers were born in Mexico. By contrast, only 56 percent of the Venezuelan industrialists were born in that nation, and 53 percent of their fathers were born outside Venezuela. Hence, there is less immigrant influence among the Mexican industrialists.

In addition to these personal characteristics, the survey information shows that industrialists' firms are extremely large and were established on the average within the last three decades. The mean values of 1979 gross production per firm are $20.5 million U.S. for Mexico and $18.4 million U.S. for Venezuela, and the average numbers of employees per firm are 592 for Mexico and 888 for Venezuela. Thus, the Mexican firms in this sample are larger than the Venezuelan firms according to gross production, and the Mexican firms have achieved a higher level of labor productivity.[9]

The average age of the industrial firms in both countries is twenty-seven years (or an establishment date of 1954); over 75 percent of the Mexican firms have been established since the end of World War II. Correlations among these variables and the industrial branch of the firm show that for both countries the older firms are the larger establishments and tend to be concentrated more in the consumer-goods industries. Conversely, the younger firms are more focused in capital goods, which substantiates the industrial progression from consumer to intermediate to capital goods.

Economic Dependency

In measures gauging their degree of dependence on foreign economic resources, the majority of firms prove to be reasonably self-sufficient (see table 27). The questionnaire asks whether they depend on foreign companies for (1) raw material and other inputs, (2) technology, or (3) credit or capital. In a procedure similar to Cardoso's (1974:189–190), I produced a summary measure of dependency by adding the three responses, with 0 for a "no" response and a 1 for a "yes" response (producing a scale from 0, or least dependent, to 3, or most dependent). Almost a third of the Mexican sample are totally self-sufficient, and over 50 percent have summary scores of 0 or 1, indicating little international dependency. However, fewer Venezuelan firms are completely self-sufficient (only one-tenth of the total), largely because of a greater dependence on foreign companies for providing the necessary inputs. So, the degree of dependency for the Mexican industrial elites proves to be somewhat less than that for their Venezuelan counterparts.[10]

A number of demographic characteristics have been associated with the

Table 27
Measures of Economic Dependency
(Percentages)

Item 71: Does your firm depend on foreign companies for:

	Venezuela		Mexico	
	Yes = 1	No = 0	Yes = 1	No = 0
A. the purchase of parts, products, or raw materials?	83.3	16.7	47.5	52.5
B. technology?	41.4	58.6	47.5	52.5
C. credit or capital?	24.1	75.9	26.3	73.7

Summary measure (A + B + C):

	Self-Sufficient		"Internationalized"	
	0	1	2	3
Mexico	30.3	28.3	31.3	10.1
Venezuela	10.3	44.8	31.0	13.8

degree of economic dependency of a particular firm. Specifically, the more "internationalized" industrial corporations are often said to be the larger firms in the more advanced industrial sectors. Given the importance sometimes attached to the international economic dependency of a corporation, I correlated the summary measure of dependency from this survey to several other characteristics of each establishment. The findings produce *no* statistically significant associations in either Mexico or Venezuela between economic dependency and a firm's age, its size, or its industrial branch. Thus, these data do not support any proposals relating these variables to the degree of dependency of foreign economic resources. This is not to conclude that economic dependency is not a significant explanatory factor in many outcomes—only that certain demographic qualities do not explain (or co-vary with) the economic dependency of a firm.

Ideological Orientation

Among the crucial political and economic issues that the ideological orientations of industrialists throughout Latin America determine are whether to align themselves closely with other economic sectors, whether to support or oppose new foreign investment, whether to promote cooperation with the state or to favor state economic intervention, and whether to support efforts at class cooperation.[11] Most of the literature stresses the lack of sectorial consciousness on the part of Latin American industrialists, and many analysts conclude that the ideology of Latin American entrepreneurs is loosely defined and easily manipulated by the state.[12] In order to examine the ideological orientation of the Mexican industrial elite, I have created summary scales from individual Likert items measuring the four principal dimensions of industrial ideology: sectorial awareness (industrial differentiation from other economic sectors); perception of foreign investment; attitude toward the economic role of the state; and opinion of labor. I have calculated reliability coefficients to determine which items to use for the scales.[13] The specific items that form the most reliable scale for each dimension (three items for sectorial awareness and four items for the others) are enumerated in table A-4 in appendix E.

The argument that the Mexican industrial class is divided has already been disproved in the comparison of CONCAMIN and CANACINTRA. Related to this question of unity within the industrial sector is the issue of its relations with other economic actors. As stated above, many social scientists conclude that Latin American industrialists do not perceive their distinct sectorial interests and that the industrial sector has not broken from the traditional dominance of the agroexport elites in Latin America.

Yet, in the specific case of Mexico, one could argue that the revolutionary upheavals, particularly the changes in the 1930s, enabled the emerging industrial sector to develop a strong role independent of the traditional elites.[14] The sectorial awareness scale in this survey confirms precisely this conclusion. The scale includes items that show interests separate from and opinions critical of other sectors. Though the summary scale has values ranging from 3 to 15, it is analyzed as a trichotomous distinction among those who do not perceive distinct industrial interests, those who are exactly neutral, and those who do perceive distinct industrial interests. In overwhelming fashion, 78 percent of the Mexican respondents fall into the last classification. For comparison, the Venezuelan industrial elites also demonstrate significant sectorial awareness (72 percent), although to a lesser degree than the Mexican group.

The three remaining scales measure industrial elite opinion toward foreign investment, the state, and labor. These scales are aggregated to a trichotomy among positive, neutral, and negative categories. The results tend to contradict assertions that a substantial segment of industrial opinion—specifically those industrialists most dependent on state aid—is unnaturally "liberal" (for example, favorable to state economic intervention, antagonistic to foreign investment, and conciliatory toward labor). In the first place, no differences exist in these scales between CONCAMIN, which has been said to represent legitimately "conservative" views, and CANACINTRA, which has been said to be uniquely liberal and state-dominated. Second, the combined Mexican sample, as well as the Venezuelan group, decidedly congregate around attitudes showing a positive view of foreign capital, support for less government economic intervention, and a critical evaluation of the role of labor. On the foreign investment scale, 75 percent of the Mexican respondents fall into the positive category with regard to the role of foreign capital. The Venezuelans are even more supportive of foreign investment, with over 95 percent in the positive classification. These industrialists state that foreign investment is necessary, has produced good results in Mexico and Venezuela, and does not have too much control over the respective economies. On the state economic role scale, 82 percent of the Mexican respondents and 78 percent of the Venezuelan respondents are critical of the state's intervention in the economy. In particular, nationalizations of industries are strongly opposed, more private initiative is firmly supported, and government economic intervention is seen as overly excessive in both nations at the present time.[15] Finally, on the labor scale, 67 percent of the Mexican respondents and 56 percent of the Venezuelans feel that labor, especially organized labor, has been a detrimental force in the economic development of their countries. The industrialists demonstrate a distrust of labor leaders and a feeling that strikes have hurt the economic development of their country.[16]

On the important question of government intervention in the economy, the opinions of the industrial leaders in this 1980 sample are quite consistent with the professed viewpoints of other representatives of private enterprise in Mexico. Despite the existence of separate industrial interests in many areas, the critical stance of industrialists in this survey toward the economic role of the state closely parallels the ideology of other private sector organizations and leaders expressed over the last decade or so.[17] The industrialists here as well as the private sector in general do accept and support the mixed economic system in Mexico and the important role that the state must play in this system (item 19 in the questionnaire). In an international conference COPARMEX organized in 1971 on the economic roles of the private and public sectors, many Mexican entrepreneurial leaders alluded to the complementary positions of the state and private initiative.[18] The president of COPARMEX, Roberto Guajardo Suárez, emphasized that the "private sector is only one part of the social organism"; and Alfredo Santos, president of CONCANACO, referred to the balance between the private and public sectors in Mexico's mixed economy. Over a decade later, in its 1983 *Declaración de principios: Nuestra doctrina social* (p. 21), COPARMEX reiterated this theme of cooperation when it stated that one of the most important factors in the dynamism of the economy "is the reciprocal confidence between the private sector and the state."

However, at the same time that entrepreneurial leaders recognize the state's role in a mixed economy, they also stress that the private sector should be supreme. For example, at the 1971 COPARMEX conference, Bernardo Garza Sada (then the head of VISA, and recognized leader of the Monterrey Group) depicted private initiative as the "motor of economic development" and said that "the private sector is the people and the public sector is the group of persons that represents the people." In a more recent declaration of entrepreneurial ideology, the umbrella organization of the private sector, the CCE, stated very clearly that private enterprise is the basis of the economy and that public sector economic intervention should be limited to providing public services and activities where private capital is insufficient.[19] And in its 1983 *Declaración de principios* (p. 4), CONCANACO specifically rejected the "rectoría económica del gobierno" (roughly, the control of the economy by the government) because it restricts the liberty of private initiative.

The respondents in this survey echo the theme of private-enterprise dominance in a mixed economy and generally agree that the Mexican state has exceeded its proper economic role (items 22 and 20). In a particularly timely response, the CONCAMIN and CANACINTRA industrialists state their strong opposition to further nationalizations of private enterprises (item 21). This opinion was reflected in the harsh reactions of other private sector leaders to the 1982 nationalization of the Mexican banking system. In one of the more extreme comments, José María Basagoiti, head of COPARMEX in 1982, argued that the Mexican people had lost their freedom with the September 1982 decree expropriating the banks (*Expansión*, 16 February 1983). Though not always as critical as Basagoiti, all private sector organizations did side with the bankers in opposing the nationalizations. Thus, at least on the issue of state intervention in the economy, the industrial leaders here are in close agreement with the stated opinions of other private sector representatives.

Though a general consensus on ideological questions exists among the industrialists in this survey, certainly individual industrialists vary in the *degree* to which they recognize industrial interests, favor foreign investment, and criticize the roles of the state and labor organizations in economic development. And one might expect certain background characteristics to affect these variations in ideological orientations, in particular, the size and age of the industrial firm as well as the degree of international economic dependency of that firm. The older, larger, and more dependent firms might produce the most conservative orientations. To test this proposition, I examined bivariate measures of association for the relationships between the four ideological scales and four independent demographic variables: gross production, number of employees, age of the firm, and the summary measure of economic dependency. In the Mexican case, the results largely disconfirm any effect of these demographic variables on ideology. Of the sixteen measures of association, only two are statistically significant, and even these two relationships are not very strong. The correlation coefficient between age and the foreign investment scale is 0.18 (significance level of 0.04 and explaining less than 4 percent of the total variance) and that between the value of gross production and the state economic role is 0.15 (significance level of 0.08 and explaining less than 3 percent of the total variance).

Furthermore, the direction of these two relationships is somewhat surprising. Mexican industrialists from older firms tend to have more critical views of foreign investment, and industrialists from larger firms tend to be more supportive of state intervention in the economy. Possibly, older enterprises resent the recent encroachment of multinational corporations, and larger firms have benefited somewhat more from state aid. In any case, these demographic variables for the Mexican industrial elites have an almost negligible effect on these dimensions of industrial ideology.

In contrast to the Mexican data, the expected relationships between the background variables and ideology are partially substantiated by the Venezuelan sample. Five of the sixteen measures of association are statistically significant, and the directions of the relationships follow the predicted pattern. First, industrialists in the more dependent firms and the larger firms (as measured by gross production) tend to maintain lower levels of sectorial awareness. Second, the industrialists with the most positive attitudes toward foreign capital are from the largest firms (as measured by number of employees). Finally, the oldest and largest industrial enterprises (as measured by gross production) tend to produce industrial entrepreneurs who are especially critical of organized labor. Thus, the Venezuelan data (but not the Mexican data) provide some evidence that the industrialists from the more dependent, older, and larger firms are more likely to support foreign capital, to criticize organized labor, and to reject the notion that the industrial sector has distinct interests apart from other economic sectors.

Perceptions of Political Participation and Influence

Much of the literature on Latin American industrial entrepreneurs also concludes that they have not been active participants in the political process. As a consequence, one could conclude that industrialists have had little success in influencing public policies. This phenomenon was addressed at the aggregate level in chapter 4 in terms of low subject-mobilization. But these conceptualizations are examined at the microlevel here in light of survey items relevant to political influence and participation.

These survey results, at least for the industrial elites in this sample, contradict the impression that industrialists are not politically mobilized. More specifically, the respondents exhibit a high level of political participation in their organized interest groups. For example, 80 percent of the Mexican industrialists and 60 percent of the Venezuelans say they turn to their industrial association whenever they want to influence a public-policy decision. At the other extreme, only 3 of the 109 Mexican industrialists and one of the 32 Venezuelans say it is useless even to attempt to influence policy by any means. The Mexican industrial leaders also strongly support the political role of their industrial trade associations. In some Latin American nations, especially the more repressive regimes, trade associations are confined to service functions, such as conducting seminars on technical topics and publishing apolitical pamphlets. However, in this Mexican sample, over 75 percent oppose the notion of limiting organized industrial groups to service functions. They clearly prefer that the industrial groups continue to press the interests of their members in the political sphere. The Venezuelan industrial elites are not quite as committed to a political role for their trade associations, as only 50 percent of that sample opposes limiting industrial groups to service functions.

Of course, a commitment to political participation does not guarantee success in influencing policy. Hence the next question to be examined is the degree of influence the industrial elites have in affecting policy, in terms of initiation, delay, defeat, or alteration. Obviously, the focus here is on the industrialists' self-perceptions of their political influence. Survey instruments cannot be unobtrusive indicators of political influence, but they do serve as measures of what the respondents perceive to be their political impact.

Several of the Likert-scale items address the political influence of industrial entrepreneurs in postwar Mexico and Venezuela, and the responses to these items do not affirm a particularly strong belief in the political power of the industrial sector. Both samples divide evenly over whether the industrial sector has achieved much success in influencing postwar economic policies, and a majority (57 percent in Mexico and 81 percent in Venezuela) actually says that the concerns of industrialists are *not* well represented in government policy. Some of the limitations of industrial influence are indicated by the widespread belief in both nations that the industrial sector does not *act* as a unified political force (though my analysis confirms that the two major groups of industrialists in Mexico are ideologically similar) and that industrial influence depends more on the actions of a few, principal industrialists than on collective actions.

As another indicator of political influence, the survey asks the industrialists to rank ten political actors in terms of their influence on policy and the benefits they derived from public policies (table 28). Their responses support the previous finding that a limited number of major industrialists exert most of the political power within the industrial sector. Other than the somewhat cynical attitude that politicians are most influential, the most powerful actors prove to be bankers, large industrialists, and workers. Within the private sector, bankers and large industrialists are perceived as particularly successful in the political arena, whereas the high rating of workers undoubtedly reflects the privileged position of organized labor within the dominant coalition. Along with the critical evaluation of organized labor discussed above, one could infer that the industrial elites resent the disproportionate power labor unions wield. The only difference in these rankings between the Mexican and Venezuelan samples is the wider disparity of scores in Mexico. This might be explained by the existence of a more moderate political consensus in democratic Venezuela.

Table 28
Political-Actor Rankings

Political Actors	Influence on Policy[a]		Benefit from Policy[a]		Average of Both Rankings	
	Venezuela	Mexico	Venezuela	Mexico	Venezuela	Mexico
Bankers[b]	5.4	4.0	4.5	3.7	4.95	3.85
Merchants	6.1	5.5	4.7	4.5	5.40	5.00
Multinational corporations	6.1	5.3	5.8	4.8	5.95	5.05
Large industrialists[b]	4.7	4.3	5.0	4.3	4.85	4.30
Small industrialists	6.2	6.9	5.8	6.4	6.00	6.65
Landowners	6.6	7.7	5.4	7.7	6.00	7.70
Workers[b]	3.9	4.3	4.1	5.0	4.00	4.65
Peasants	5.6	6.3	5.8	7.4	5.70	6.85
Military	6.1	6.8	6.1	6.6	6.10	6.75
Politicians[b]	2.8	2.8	4.3	3.1	3.55	2.95

Notes: [a]Mean rankings with the lowest values indicating the highest rankings.
[b]Those political actors with the most influence and the greatest benefits.

The general perception from the Likert-scale items of little industrial influence in the political arena is clarified somewhat by examining specific policy issues. The degree of industrial impact on public policy appears to vary substantially according to the issue area. The questionnaire asks the respondents to evaluate six policy areas (credit, prices, protectionism, labor, public spending, and taxes) in terms of whether the policies favor the industrial sector and whether industry exercises any influence over the policies. The results for both countries are essentially the same. A majority see only two policy areas (credit and protectionism) as favoring industry and believe the industrial sector influences strongly only one policy (protectionism). Policies regarding prices, labor, and taxes are viewed as unfavorable to industry, and public-spending decisions receive a mixed response. Besides the perception of strong industrial influence on protectionism, the industrialists see credit and pricing policies as reflecting only moderate industrial influence and feel they exert little or no influence on expenditure, labor, and taxation policies. These findings do show an increased perception of industrial influence in Mexico over the last decade: the Mexican entrepreneurs in the Derossi survey (1971:61) of 1969 were asked to evaluate eight postwar economic policies; none received a majority of favorable responses.

Adversary Relations with the Political Elite

One of the most important aspects of the development of the Mexican industrial sector in the postwar period has been the emergence of an adversary relationship with the state. Though political and economic elites have not become so polarized that their differences have the potential for destabilizing Mexico, the industrial sector has evolved into a crucial countervailing power to the state. The competitive nature of state-industry relations has been posited before and is supported by these survey data. Peter Smith (1977) substantiates what he considers the "social distance" between Mexican entrepreneurs and the political elite. Comparing the backgrounds of economic and political elites, he maintains that they belong to different social strata, frequently disagree over policies, and are really competing elites.

Several results from my survey confirm the notion of a split between the public and private sectors. As discussed above, industrial elites in Mexico are quite critical of many economic policies, and their ideological orientation reflects the gap between the state and industrial entrepreneurs. Most significantly, the industrialists staunchly oppose the state's increasing role in the economy. Also, they generally support foreign investment in Mexico, whereas the state has traditionally adopted a more antagonistic view of foreign capital. Though the symbolic nationalism of the state often is more rhetoric than deed, this still suggests an ideological difference between the political and industrial elites. Finally, the industrialists in the Mexican sample are critical of the role of organized labor, which has always been an important ally of the Mexican state. The industrial leaders appear to disapprove of the self-serving aims of their labor counterparts, who have been more easily co-opted and controlled by the state. In Venezuela, where the private sector has often been in conflict with the state, the survey data depict a similar pattern of the ideological distance between industrialists and the state.

The industrial sector's independence from the state in Mexico was particularly evident during the Echeverría presidency. Echeverría alienated the industrialists as well as other private sector elements with his attempts to initiate populist policies and his rhetorical attacks on private enterprise. He frequently criticized entrepreneurs, especially the Monterrey Group, as being "profoundly reactionary and enemies of the people's progress" and even "bad Christians." As might be expected, the leaders of CONCAMIN and CANACINTRA in this sample have a very negative evaluation of Echeverría. In a nearly unanimous voice (94.5 percent), they state that they were not satisfied with the policies of Echeverría, whereas only 36.1 percent say they were not satisfied with the López Portillo policies (though this was before the bank nationalizations and exchange controls of 1982). In reviewing all presidents since 1934, Echeverría is by far the least popular with the industrial elites. Over 80 percent feel his administration was unfavorable to the industrial sector; no other president, including Cárdenas, has even a majority of the industrialists responding negatively.[20] By comparison, the least-liked Venezuelan president in the period since 1936 (Herrera Campins) receives a negative review from only 56 percent of the Venezuelan industrialists (compared to Echeverría's 80 percent). Though an adversary relationship between industry and the state is not unique to the Echeverría presidency, the greatest cleavages certainly existed during his term.

Summary and Conclusions

This analysis of survey research from leaders of the two principal industrial organizations in Mexico has produced five major findings concerning the ideology and political role of those industrial elites.

1. Contrary to assertions that CANACINTRA is a tool of the government and has a different viewpoint from CONCAMIN, the leaders of the two groups do not contrast in terms of either political opinions or socioeconomic characteristics. Hence, both groups are interpreted as being equivalent samples taken from the same population of industrial elites.

2. The Mexican industrial elites exhibit several consistent demographic characteristics. As individuals they are predominantly upper class and native-born, and their firms tend to be quite large, reasonably new, and generally independent of foreign influence. The youngest firms are also the smallest firms (though still comparatively large) and tend to come from the capital-goods branch.

3. The industrialists exhibit ideological unity in terms of recognizing distinct industrial interests, having a positive view of foreign investment, supporting less government economic intervention, and criticizing the role of labor. Most of their political viewpoints are not those favored by the state. These opinions hold constant, despite variations in the demographic characteristics of the industrialists or their firms.

4. The degree of political mobilization or participation of the Mexican industrial elites appears to be substantial, though their political influence is limited to certain policy areas (especially protectionist policies). However, the industrialists also recognize the inability of their sector to *act* as a unified political force.

5. In agreement with previous findings, the industrialists in the Mexican sample demonstrate an adversary approach to their relations with the state. They are critical of most government policies, their political opinions generally are in opposition to official views, and they emphasize their particular alienation from the Echeverría administration. These results further substantiate the relative autonomy of the industrial sector from the state, but the evidence of industry-state conflict refutes converse theories that powerful economic elites constrain state autonomy.

The survey of the Venezuelan industrial leaders produces almost all of these same results. The differences between the Venezuelan and Mexican industrialists, then, are predominantly a matter of degree. But the contrasts are, nonetheless, significant in that they show a group of Mexican industrial elites that are stronger, more autonomous, and more influential than their Venezuelan colleagues. Specifically, the Mexican industrial leaders have a greater tendency to be native-born and their firms are less dependent on foreign companies. Also, they show a stronger commitment to the distinct interests of the industrial sector (more independent from other economic sectors), they are more critical of the roles of the state and organized labor, and they are less supportive of foreign capital. Finally, the Mexican industrialists perceive themselves to be more politically active and more involved in their trade associations as political interest groups. These comparisons are particularly significant, given the independence and autonomy of the Venezuelan private sector within a more democratic political system.

In a comparative perspective, these findings stress the potential for important variations in the political role and the ideology of industrial entrepreneurs across countries. Several characteristics of the Mexican industrial elites (and of the Venezuelans, as well) do not fit the generalizations too often applied throughout Latin America. These Mexican industrialists exhibit considerable economic and ideological autonomy from the state, from foreign investment (less dependence on foreign resources), and from other economic sectors. And despite the generally authoritarian nature of the political system, the Mexican industrial sector has remained active politically and has espoused a clear ideology that cannot be easily ignored by the decision makers within the government.

Part 3. Industrialists and Policymaking

6. A Typology of the Policy Process and a Case Study of the GATT Decision

The ultimate test of the degree of authoritarian control over interest groups involves the freedom of those groups to oppose or initiate policy changes and their ability to effect those changes. The discussion of industry as a political actor in Mexico is not complete without exploring whether industrialists have any real impact on policy. Hence, this chapter and the following focus on some of the outcomes or outputs, in terms of public-policy decisions, of the political interactions between industry and the state. More specifically, the analysis turns to an examination of the policy process in Mexico, the role (or strategy) of industrialists in that process, and several policy decisions and trends of recent years affecting the industrial sector.

Typology of Policy Process

Research into business influence on policy in the United States led scholars to create different categories of policy decision and to posit that business effectiveness varied according to the nature of the policy decision. A typology of policy process, or policy arenas, as some authors prefer, then evolved from attempts to explain apparently contradictory interpretations of the influence of interest groups. A particularly important divergence of opinions occurred in relation to the impact of business leaders on the tariff issue in the United States. E. E. Schattschneider (1935) found that in the 1930s business lobbies were quite successful in gaining specific protective tariffs. On the other hand, Bauer, Pool, and Dexter (1972) discovered in the 1950s that the business groups were not very influential with regard to tariff legislation. In resolving the differences between these classic case studies, Theodore Lowi (1964) said that the different conclusions were each time-specific and that one needed to develop a distinction in issue areas among distributive, regulative, and redistributive policies. Different processes then could be observed in the various issue areas. According to Lowi, distributive policies require highly disaggregated and individualized decisions involving nonscarce resources. Regulative policies are also individualized in their impact but are made by application of a general or aggregate rule. Finally, redistributive policies are much broader in their effects, which include the transfer of resources from one group to another.

Though these distinctions have been applied in an informative manner to Western Europe (Smith 1969) and to Latin America (Purcell and Purcell 1977), they have been criticized for their lack of depth and conceptual clarity. These critiques have led to substantial revisions of the original Lowi distinctions, with the most complete refinement being that of Michael Hayes (1978). Lowi defined his three issue arenas in terms of six categories or attributes, but he provided no specific dimensions by which to classify his distinctions. Hence, Hayes (ibid.:138) states that "Lowi's issue arenas are not really distinct conceptual types at all" and proceeds to derive a more explicit typology of policy process according to two underlying dimensions, which I have relabeled as relations among interest groups and policy response of the state. Relations among interest groups are either consensual or conflictual. Consensual relations infer that the policy process is a positive-sum game among the active participants. If some groups are being deprived, they are unaware of their losses. On the other hand, conflictual relations imply a zero-sum game among participants who are active on both sides of an issue. The policy response of the state may be either inaction, "privatized" policy, in which the meaningful policy decisions are left to the implementation stage, or policy by decree or law, in which a specific allocation of resources is made by the politically accountable individuals or institutions (the executive or the legislative body).

These two dimensions form six categories in the typology of policy process (see table 29). Consensual processes include noninterference, self-regulation, and distribution:

(1) Noninterference is a case in which a consensus against government intervention exists and none of the interest groups pressure the state for action.

(2) In a self-regulatory process, a coalition of groups acquires government sanction of their autonomy or monopoly; that is, businesses are officially allowed to regulate themselves. One of the most often-cited examples is the case in which an industry is given the power to license its own occupational categories.

Table 29
Policy-Process Typology, Mexico

State's Policy Response	Relations among Interest Groups	
	Consensual	Conflictual
Inaction	Noninterference	Nondecision
"Privatized" policy	Self-regulation	Regulation
Policy by decree or law	Distribution	Redistribution

Source: Hayes (1978).

(3) Distribution involves explicit policymaking by decree or law. A group or coalition of groups utilizes influence to gain particularized benefits, which are granted through official decrees or legislation. In the absence of opposition, which is either nonexistent, inactive, or unaware, political bodies allocate specific rewards to the active group. In studies of U.S. politics, this has been referred to as classic "pork barrel" politics.

The three conflictual policy processes are nondecision, regulation, and redistribution:

(4) In case of nondecision, established groups are able to block fundamental change or reforms. If a policy is enacted, it is only a symbolic response to the demands for change.

(5) Regulatory processes involve significant opposition and may produce change, but the policy is decided as it is implemented. Both sides in an issue lobby the executive or legislature, which enacts vague legislation so as not to alienate either side. Group conflict is resolved and policy decisions are quietly made in the bureaucracy or in the courts—outside the public eye. As Hayes (1978:149) states, "Examples abound here from the area of business regulation, hence the label generally assigned to this category."

(6) Redistribution denotes that an explicit choice between contending groups is made at the stage of formulating policy. Resources are transferred between groups by means of political decisions by the legitimate policymakers rather than by means of administrative fiat. Of course, other policy processes may also result in the transfer of resources, notably distribution and regulation. But the identifying aspect of redistribution is the explicit recognition of winners and losers. Conflict over the policy exists, and the government choice between conflicting interests is not hidden from any of the attentive groups.

The influence of industrial interest groups on a policy may depend in part on the particular process relevant to that policy; that is, influence may vary according to the relations among interest groups and the policy response of the state. One plausible argument is that the industrialists' greatest influence will be in policies of a positive-sum nature (consensual). A united front can be presented on an issue and benefits can be allocated either by allowing self-regulation or by granting specific rewards through legislation. Of course, industrial influence may be exercised in conflictual processes, but it will be less evident. Under either consensual or conflictual relations, the influence of industrial associations may be greatest when the state response is either inaction or "privatized" policy. Business groups have more power when policy is hidden from political view and is either not formulated or decided by bureaucrats. The least industrial influence occurs as policy decisions are shifted to the public arena (policy by decree or law). These factors suggest the reason why Latin American industrialists prefer to exert political influence "behind the scenes" and to establish their more important political ties with the ministries responsible for economic policy.

Regulatory Policy Process in Mexico

The most common policy process in Mexico has been regulation.[1] Conflict often arises among different economic elite sectors or between elites and popular sectors, and the choices of allocating scarce resources among these groups are left to the agencies that must implement policies. Hence, the executive and the rubber-stamp Congress often pass vague legislation giving bureaucrats considerable leeway in administering policy. The interest groups that hope to affect policy are keenly aware of the flexibility of the legislation and focus much of their attention on the institutions that apply policy once it has been enacted by the legislative and executive branches.

Among the most important economic policies in postwar Mexico have been protectionist and promotion policies designed to encourage industrial growth.[2] Though these programs have involved an explicit policy decision to emphasize import-substituting industrialization, their specific impact has been determined in the implementation stage. Until the mid-1970s, the protectionist goals had been reached through a system of import licenses, which were especially susceptible to regulatory politics. Commercial groups generally opposed the vigorous employment of import licenses to restrict foreign trade, and industrial branches conflicted over the particular priorities utilized in granting or denying licenses. The application of these import controls did achieve progressive import substitution (from consumer to intermediate to capital goods), but many individualized decisions on import licenses were made that benefited or harmed particular industries. The other component of industrialization policies, industrial promotion, has focused on tax exemptions and public credit. Here again the legislation has been imprecise and the effective decisions have been made largely by administrators. Most of the public credit allocations have been made by the National Development Bank (NAFINSA), and the tax exemption legislation only stipulates that the qualifying industries are to be "new and necessary."

Mexico has also adopted many important policies to regulate the flow of foreign investment (see chapter 3). During the Echeverría administration alone, three new laws on foreign investment were passed: (1) the Law to Promote Mexican Investment and Regulate Foreign Investment (1973); (2) the Law on the Transfer of Technology (1973); and (3) the Law on Inventions and Trademarks (1976). Ostensibly, this and other legislation tightly control foreign investment in Mexico by forbidding foreign capital in certain economic areas, requiring majority domestic ownership in all enterprises, and setting limits on imported technology and the use of foreign trademarks. But in reality these mandates are loosely applied, and exemptions to the strict requirements are allowed whenever the state is convinced of the need for foreign capital in a particular sector. These exemptions are granted quite frequently, so domestic and foreign entrepreneurs are often clashing over the application of the legislation.

Regulatory policies were especially evident in the López Portillo government. One of his most important economic initiatives was the call for fiscal reform, which met with considerable business opposition (*Latin America Economic Report*, 5 January 1979). Of particular interest to industrialists were a new value-added tax (IVA) and tariff reform. The IVA replaced a 4 percent sales tax with a 10 percent value-added tax and went into effect on 1 January 1980. Entrepreneurs, however, stressed their intention to influence the implementation of the new tax so that it would be less inflationary and less cumbersome (*Proceso*, 16 July 1979). The tariff reform, effective 1 July 1979, was designed to "rationalize" the tariff structure, that is, to lower tariff barriers to imported products gradually. This measure also was resisted by industrialists, who hoped to minimize its impact as it was implemented.

Another significant policy initiative of López Portillo was the formulation of various economic plans, including the National Plan of Industrial Development (discussed in detail in chapter 7). These plans are excellent examples of vague legislation that defers crucial policy decisions to the various government agencies administering the provisions. The Industrial

Plan emphasizes such broad goals and programs as 12 percent annual industrial growth, decentralization of industrial production, investment projects financed by petroleum earnings, diversification of exports, and increased production of foodstuffs. But the crucial decisions concerning the plan involve specific matters such as which industries receive tax exemptions and public credit, where to locate public infrastructural projects, and what types of projects to finance. These decisions are to be determined largely by the regulatory agencies within the executive branch.

The early stages of the de la Madrid administration also saw the predominance of regulatory policies. Though the new direction of the government toward austerity was clear, the specific allocation of scarce resources in many areas was left to the discretion of those implementing the new policies. One of the best examples is foreign-exchange policy, specifically the granting of foreign currency to private companies. Criteria were established for the availability of dollars for certain imports, but these criteria (as well as those regarding the payment of private sector foreign debt) were applied in a very flexible manner. Hence, entrepreneurs were not certain of their access to foreign currency until their specific applications were processed (interview, 24 March 1983). New policies on foreign investment, import duties, reduced subsidies, tax increases, and even price controls were also vague and thus subject to influence at the implementation stage. Regarding price controls, though an explicit decision was made to remove them on all but three hundred basic products, the government announced that "flexible supervision" would be maintained on some twenty-two hundred products to avoid steep price increases. Finally, de la Madrid formulated a new economic plan, the National Development Plan 1983–88, which, like its predecessors, left many of the crucial decisions to the government officials administering the plan.

As in the regulatory policy arena, several Mexican economic policies have been subject to a nondecision policy process, in which private industry has been able to protect its interests by delaying or defeating a policy change. The 1976 Law on Inventions and Trademarks has been seen by most of the private sector as costly and unnecessary. Though unable to prevent its enactment, industrialists have successfully prevented its complete application. Thus, a law formally passed by the legislature has not been fully carried out by the bureaucracy due to business opposition. In many cases, the private sector has even defeated a proposed policy change before it is formulated. Though López Portillo pushed through some of his proposed fiscal reforms, entrepreneurs stymied a fiscal reform program devised by Echeverría in 1970 and 1971 (*Análisis Político*, 20 November 1978; and Solís 1981:67–77, 98–100).

Agrarian reform is another area in which private economic interests have blocked any real movement. Except for Echeverría's widely publicized expropriations of farmland in November 1976, meaningful agrarian reform has been a nonissue in postwar Mexico.

Another area ripe with nondecision has been devaluation. Despite increasing overvaluation of domestic currency, Mexican politicians have traditionally preferred a controlled and stable exchange rate. Though the issue is a complex one, the private sector also has appreciated the security of a set rate of foreign exchange. The result of this delay and nondecision has been to send shock waves through the economy whenever devaluation becomes unavoidable, as in 1976 and 1982.

Finally, in a decision to be examined as a case study in the next section, after two years of negotiations and debate over Mexico's entry to the General Agreement on Tariffs and Trade (GATT), López Portillo announced in March of 1980 that he would "postpone" Mexico's accession. Small and medium industrialists had been the most vocal opponents of the push for Mexico to join GATT.

The policy processes of self-regulation and redistribution have been much less relevant to state-business relations in Mexico than have regulation and nondecision. One of the few instances approximating self-regulation in economic policies was pricing policy under López Portillo. In 1977 and 1979 the business sector announced widely publicized programs of voluntary price stability. These measures can be seen as a form of self-regulation on the part of the private sector, but they also resulted at least in part from government pressure. López Portillo made it clear to business groups that he could no longer hold down wage demands without more cooperation from entrepreneurs. Thus, the announced programs were not as voluntary or spontaneous as the business associations claimed.[3]

Explicit redistributive policies have been evident only in a few instances, primarily in the 1930s, with substantial agrarian reform and the nationalization of railroads and petroleum companies. These redistributive policies have essentially disappeared in the postwar era (Kelley 1981:5). Agrarian reform has been insignificant and the nationalizations since the 1930s generally have not matched the redistributive effects of the earlier events. The profit-sharing decision of 1961–1963 has been referred to as redistributive in intent, but its actual impact has been only mildly so. In the implementation of the policy, many influential firms have been able to bargain with the government to reduce its effect (Purcell and Purcell 1977:213). The only clear example of a significant redistributive policy since the 1930s is the bank nationalization of 1982 (the lack of private sector influence in this decision is discussed later in this chapter).

GATT and the "Song of the Sirens"

A particularly relevant and important case study of the role of industrialists in the policy process in Mexico is provided by the 1980 decision not to join the General Agreement on Tariffs and Trade.[4] Though this is an instance of a nondecision policy process, and not the regulatory process most common in Mexico, it does underline the influence of industrialists on economic policy and substantiates many of the conclusions from Part 2. The Mexican government under López Portillo had initiated negotiations for entry in January 1979, and a Protocol of Accession was completed in October and published throughout Mexico in November. Four months of intense debate over the terms of Mexican entry ensued. Despite widespread expectations of a pro-GATT decision, President López Portillo brought the national debate to a stunning climax on 18 March 1980 when he declared that Mexico would not accede as a contracting party to the GATT. This decision, though it actually represented the rejection of a policy proposal, was undoubtedly the most difficult choice López Portillo faced and was clearly among the most significant policy determinations of his *sexenio*.

The Negotiations

Several objective conditions made Mexico's entry to the GATT a relevant issue in the late 1970s. In the first place, the General Agreement had become more sympathetic to the demands of developing nations. The original GATT (created in 1948) included few Third World and only three Latin American nations (Brazil, Cuba, and Chile). By 1979 the eighty-three contracting parties to the international body contained fifty-two developing nations (eleven from Latin America). The major change benefiting the less-developed countries (LDCs) occurred in the mid-1960s, as Part IV, "Trade and Development," was added to the original General Agreement. This section allowed for nonreciprocity on the part of LDCs and for the reduction of trade barriers in developed countries to the export products of the Third World. In the 1970s a number of provisions of the Tokyo Round of multilateral trade negotiations were formulated specifically for the LDCs. The developed nations agreed to extend "special and differential" treatment to the developing countries in regard to the various nontariff codes, and the principle of non-reciprocity envisioned in Part IV was given a firmer legal standing.

Though Mexico did not sign the final document, it did actively participate in the Tokyo Round and did reach bilateral trade agreements, under the auspices of the Tokyo Round, with the United States and eight other developed countries or groups of countries. These bilateral agreements appeared to be quite favorable to Mexico, and may in fact have been signed by the developed nations as an enticement to Mexico to enter the GATT. In the bilateral negotiations, Mexico offered concessions on 328 products totaling $503 million in 1976 and representing 4.4 percent of the total import items in that year and 8.5 percent of the total import value. The concessions involved setting tariff limits in some cases and eliminating import permits in other cases. Yet these concessions were no threat to domestic industries fearful of foreign competition. Only 21 items were going to have actual tariff reductions over the transition period, and only 34 items would have their import licenses removed (Glade 1980:19–20). So Mexico's concessions were not a very significant move in the direction of freer trade. On the other hand, the developed nations offered Mexico substantial tariff concessions on 248 products totaling $612 million in 1976.

In addition to the overtures of the GATT toward the LDCs, Mexico's level of development was making GATT membership more appropriate. Table 30, which includes the six most advanced Latin American nations, shows that by a number of macroeconomic measures Mexico has achieved the second-highest levels of economic development in the region. In terms of GDP, domestic investment, total trade, and value-added in manufacturing, Mexico is second only to Brazil (and total trade in Mexico is even greater than that in Brazil); the next most advanced nation, Argentina, lags significantly behind Mexico. Yet, of the six nations, only Mexico and

Table 30
Comparative Levels of Economic Development, 1983
(Billions of 1982 U.S. $)

	Argentina	Brazil	Chile	Colombia	Mexico	Venezuela
Gross domestic product	57.1	220.3	18.7	28.8	156.3	41.0
Gross domestic investment	9.3	45.0	2.1	6.3	27.2	17.1
Total trade in goods and services	12.6	25.0	9.7	9.3	29.2	15.4
Value-added in manufacturing	13.6	53.1	3.7	5.9	36.6	7.4

Source: Inter-American Development Bank, *Economic and Social Progress in Latin America.*

Venezuela are not members of the GATT. Thus, many Mexican officials felt that as Mexico achieved an advanced status among Third World nations it was incumbent upon it to participate in the multilateral trade discussions of the GATT.

Changes within the GATT itself as well as the economic development of Mexico, then, provided the context in which Mexico began to negotiate entry in January 1979. The GATT Working Group on Mexican Accession met five times in 1979. In October the group produced the Protocol of Accession along with a Report of the Working Group.[5] Mexico then had until 31 May 1980 to decide whether to accept the negotiated protocol. The chief terms of the protocol were the following:

(1) A time period of twelve years in which to eliminate the remaining import permits;

(2) Incorporation of the bilateral tariff concessions negotiated in the Tokyo Round;

(3) Acceptance of the new Mexican system of tariff valuation;

(4) Allowance for the continued use of export subsidies and controls in Mexico;

(5) The right to implement the National Industrial Development Plan of March 1979 and to continue granting certain tax incentives to industry;

(6) Full rights to manage internal development policies and to protect industry and agriculture;

(7) Recognition of Mexican protectionist policy toward rural products and of the priority given to the agricultural sector, especially the basic foodstuffs; and

(8) The rights to ignore any provisions of Part II of the GATT (which covers nontariff trade barriers) that are incompatible with existing Mexican legislation.

Many observers within and outside Mexico stated that these terms were unusually flexible. For example, the *Wall Street Journal* (19 November 1979, p. 32) quoted certain Mexican analysts as considering the terms "extremely liberal," and U.S. economist William Glade (1980:3) said in a February 1980 seminar held in Mexico that the protocol "appears to be virtually unprecedented in the freedom explicitly reserved for an entering country to continue to design policies to conform to its own preferred strategies for development."

The Debate

After the Protocol of Accession was completed in October of 1979, López Portillo called for a national consultation and debate over whether

Mexico should accept the terms. Some observers have suggested that López Portillo was stalling for time in order to convince the Mexican public of the wisdom of GATT participation (*Economist*, 10 November 1979, pp. 86–87). If this was his strategy, the plan backfired. In the final analysis, López Portillo was the one who apparently became convinced that adherence to the GATT was too costly in political terms.

The national debate was a significant event in the domestic political environment for a number of reasons. First, the president's call for diverse opinions on a controversial issue was a positive signal of further movement toward political reform. López Portillo was not about to transform the state in a radical fashion, but the call for debate was another aspect of political liberalization. Second, the debate produced genuine dissension and criticism, aired in public forums. The discussion was not strictly controlled by the government, and the differences of opinion both within and outside the government became well known. Finally, the debate actually affected the outcome of the policy decision. The March conclusion to the national consultation was quite unpredicted, and the domestic pressure released by the debate in part caused the president to reverse himself on the GATT question. In his speech declaring the postponement, López Portillo referred to the significance of the diverse opinions on GATT that had been expressed during the previous five months and announced his decision by saying that "*after receiving various contradictory opinions* I have resolved that this is not the opportune moment for Mexico to enter this commercial system" (my emphasis).

Whereas the openness of the national consideration of the GATT question was remarkable for Mexico, it is also true that the discussion took place primarily at the elite levels of the political and economic systems. This case thus reaffirms the existence of relative political autonomy for the elite groups only. Neither the opposition nor the proponents represented any mass-based political movements. All were either economic, intellectual, or governing elites. The national press did follow the GATT story closely, and many editorials, columns, and articles were written on both sides. However, the national dailies are not widely read by Mexicans and they are not noted for significantly touching the lives of the masses. The most important and influential events were the many luncheons, seminars, meetings, and so forth, that were sponsored by the interested parties. These were the principal means through which groups attempted to influence the decision. But with few exceptions these were sponsored by elite groups, such as an industrial chamber or a professional association of economists. The ostensibly mass-based groups, the labor unions, for example, were not heavily involved in the debate and, in any case, are infamous for being centrally controlled by the governing political party. Still, even at the elite level, the degree of discussion and disagreement that was allowed represented a significant amount of political freedom for Mexico.

Most of the arguments posited in favor of GATT accession related to either the economic benefits or the advantages of multilateral participation. The economic benefits most often mentioned included greater access to foreign markets and improved efficiency, productivity, and quality through competitive incentives. A study by the Brookings Institution (Cline et al. 1978:207–227) projected that Mexican exports would be among the Third World's leading benefactors from the tariff reductions of the Tokyo Round. Addressing the concerns over the increasing emphasis being placed on petroleum exports, the GATT was also argued to be a means for product diversification in the export sector. The positive repercussions stemming from increased competition and efficiency were said to include a reduction in the inflation rate, the attraction of new private investment, and even the redistribution of income.

Arguments citing the advantages of multilateral participation usually began with the facts that a majority of nations (111), including many LDCs, are members of the GATT and that these nations represent from 80 percent to 90 percent of international trade. Hence, Mexico ought not isolate itself from this forum and should join the most important and representative organization setting policy for international trade. Furthermore, it was argued that the GATT provides many legal rights to member states. For instance, outside of the GATT Mexico would have no legal defense against compensatory import levies, which are specifically incorporated in the 1979 U.S. Trade Law. However, within the GATT the Mexican protocol allows for nonreciprocity and special preferences granted to LDCs, as affirmed in the Tokyo Round. In response to the mounting criticism against the protocol and Mexican entry, GATT supporters claimed that the protocol granted considerable flexibility and autonomy to Mexico, along with the legal rights of GATT membership. Even in his speech announcing the rejection of the GATT, President López Portillo praised the Mexican delegation to the GATT and said that they had "negotiated the best of the protocols that might have been obtained."

The opposition arguments concentrated on two broad issues: the loss of sovereignty, and the economic disadvantages of accession. Many critics claimed that joining the GATT would be bending to U.S. pressure, and would increase Mexico's economid dependency. The GATT, critics argued, would benefit only the developed nations by increasing their foreign trade to the detriment of the LDCs, as evidenced by data showing that the share of worldwide exports centered in the United States, West Germany, Japan,

France, and Great Britain grew from 39 percent in 1950 (roughly when the GATT was formed) to 65 percent in 1978 (Bonilla 1980:45). Many also feared that Mexico would not be able to enjoy the GATT privileges accorded LDC members, since Mexico, as one of the advanced developing countries, was targeted for "graduation" from preferential treatment. Besides, they pointed out that Mexico could participate in multilateral trade negotiations (like the Tokyo Round) and could enjoy bilateral generalized systems of preferences without being a member of the GATT.

One of the major economic disadvantages cited was that the sudden exposure to foreign competition would lead to massive bankruptcies among the small and medium industrialists. The case of Argentina in 1979 under the liberalization policies of José Martínez de Hoz was often used as an example of foreign competition producing widespread business failures. In addition, opponents theorized that GATT participation would increase economic and social inequalities and worsen unemployment and other problems of poverty while benefiting only the modern and efficient large capitalists. They also maintained that any increase in supply for consumers would heavily favor the middle and upper classes. In sum, critics argued that Mexican accession would harm the majority of Mexicans, especially the lower classes and the smaller entrepreneurs, while working to the advantage of the upper classes and the large industrial firms.

The Decision and Industrial Influence

This "nondecision" for postponement is best seen as an example of the domestic political constraints operating on the president. In this case, those domestic constraints were posed primarily by an important group of industrialists aligned with the intellectual elite and certain government officials. The assertion that López Portillo actually reversed his stand on the GATT (or decided contrary to his personal beliefs) is crucial in claiming that domestic constraints had a significant impact on the decision. Though López Portillo was careful to maintain a degree of aloofness from the national debate, no one doubts that, even after making the decision, he favored GATT membership. As finance minister under Echeverría, López Portillo had led the Mexican delegation to the Tokyo Round and had demonstrated his support for these multilateral talks and for trade liberalization in general. As president, he initiated programs to reduce the level of protectionism in Mexico independent of the GATT question. After Mexico began negotiating GATT accession, he hinted at his support several times.[6]

Some evidence points to movement within the executive branch on the GATT issue before the decision was announced. On various occasions government officials had maintained that GATT entry would not require modifications of the 1979 Industrial Plan. But in February 1980, Alberto Pérez Aceves (subdirector of studies and projects in the Ministry of Resources and Industrial Promotion) admitted that GATT entry might necessitate some revisions of the Industrial Plan (*Proceso*, 18 February 1980). This position had been a major argument of the GATT opponents, and Pérez Aceves's statement was early indication (though largely ignored at the time) that the defenders of the GATT were beginning to retreat. Still the president gave no hint of having changed his mind, and immediately before the announcement all predictions in Mexico and in the United States were that Mexico would accede to GATT membership.

Thus, López Portillo did change his position, and my thesis is that the domestic detractors of the GATT were the principal constraining forces that prevented him from taking Mexico into that international body. As contrasted with the supporters of the GATT, who were relatively timid in their efforts, the opponents were quite forceful. Their effective mobilization of political forces blocked the policy initiative and produced the "nondecision." Gradually the critics of Mexican entry came to dominate the debate and no doubt convinced the president that he had much to lose and little to gain by a positive decision. The opposition, though not necessarily more powerful than the groups supporting entry, at least on this issue was much more vocal, more organized, and more vehement.[7]

The protectionist elements within the private sector led the opposition forces, with help from the nationalists in the intellectual community and government planners. The protectionists were concentrated in CANACINTRA, and the nationalists were focused in the National College of Economists (CNE). CANACINTRA and the CNE were undoubtedly the two most powerful and determined opponents of GATT accession. The government planners were primarily from the Ministries of Resources and Industrial Promotion (Industry), Labor, Agriculture, Finance, and Foreign Relations.

Though the membership of CANACINTRA has become more diversified in recent years (to include some of the largest industrial firms in Mexico), the chamber has retained its historical commitment to protectionist policies. It has always been influential on trade issues and was the major force behind Mexico's opposition to the Havana Charter in 1948 as well as the Mexican abrogation in 1950 of the 1942 Trade Agreement with the United States. Hence, its opposition to the GATT was the logical extension of its previous activities to defend protectionist trade policies.

CANACINTRA did not officially oppose Mexico's entry until February 1980, but it had exhibited substantial skepticism throughout the national debate. Because of its past involvement in trade issues, one of the critical questions in the national debate was whether CANACINTRA would oppose the Protocol of Accession or remain neutral. In December 1979 meetings with several cabinet ministries, CANACINTRA communicated the serious reservations it had about Mexico's entry, especially the fear that foreign competition would result in the failure of hundreds of medium and small industrial firms (interview, 15 June 1980). Apparently these reservations were never resolved, and at the thirty-ninth Annual Meeting of CANACINTRA the outgoing president, Juan Manuel Martínez Gómez, announced that the chamber favored postponing GATT entry for twenty years. In covering the meeting, the Mexican press gave particular attention to the fact that President López Portillo and industry secretary José Andrés de Oteyza, who were both in attendance, smiled knowingly at the applause greeting Martínez Gómez's statement against the GATT. Perhaps they realized the impact his pronouncement would have on the final decision. During the following month, the new president of CANACINTRA, José Porrero Lichtle, actively promoted the chamber's anti-GATT opinions, especially at one of the CNE forums and at a conference in Saltillo sponsored by the Mexican Institute of Financial Executives.

As the largest Mexican industrial chamber whose voice is especially strong on trade policy, the strident opposition of CANACINTRA was crucial in defeating GATT entry. CANACINTRA devoted most of its resources in the three months preceding the decision to expressing first its reservations and then its outright opposition to GATT membership (interview, 21 June 1980). All of the group's public relations work (including its publications, its annual assembly, press statements, and speeches) was dominated by the GATT discussion, and its leadership was particularly active in utilizing political contacts (such as Reyes Heroles) and in communicating with key ministry officials.

CANACINTRA's position was especially influential, since it was the only group within the private sector to manifest a strong position. Most of the other elements of the private sector remained neutral, although some groups assumed a moderately favorable stand on the GATT. But those promoting Mexico's entry were decidedly low-key. The Monterrey Group apparently favored accession, though it did not forcefully press its case either in the media or before the government. The strongest manifestations of the group's position were some statements by Bernardo Garza Sada, the head of the Alfa economic conglomerate and recognized leader of the Monterrey Group, who welcomed GATT entry and said his colleagues did not fear foreign competition (*Análisis Político*, 19 November 1979). COPARMEX and ANIERM also came out in favor of the GATT; however, CONCANACO and CONCAMIN—both of which tend to be representative of the larger enterprises—did not take a stand on the GATT question. Because of the lack of unity in the private sector, the CCE, which normally serves to solidify the private sector around an issue, also stayed neutral in the debate (interview, 28 May 1980). Thus, CANACIN-TRA's strong opposition dominated the stage in terms of the views of the private sector and played a major role in influencing López Portillo.

The second major opposition voice came from the intellectual community, especially the CNE, which is the largest professional association of economists in Mexico. Its members, most of whom were trained at the prestigious National Autonomous University of Mexico (UNAM) (interview, 1 July 1980), are well connected with the political elite.[8] Furthermore, CNE membership includes many important *técnicos* (professionals with expertise in demand by the state) who are increasingly moving into cabinet-level posts.[9] Mexico is no exception to the Latin American trend of recent years to bestow increasing political power and national respect on qualified professionals whose specialties include economic policy.

Not only was the CNE one of the most important forces working against GATT entry, but it was also the first group to declare its opposition. In fact, its campaign against the GATT lasted over one year. Shortly after negotiations were initiated in January of 1979, the CNE leadership made known its opposition. The CNE president at the time, Armando Labra Manjarrez, exemplifies the political contacts of the group. He is a former deputy in the national legislature and was the general director of planning in the Ministry of Commerce at the time of the GATT debate. His opinions and those of the CNE became especially well publicized during the organization's Third National Meeting held on 6 April 1979, with López Portillo in attendance.

In October of 1979 López Portillo attended another CNE meeting, at which he was exposed to the most severe attacks on the GATT to that point. The CNE installed a new president, Manuel Aguilera Gómez, who was even more active in the discussion against Mexican adherence than was Labra Manjarrez. Aguilera Gómez, too, was well placed in government circles as the general director of INMECAFE, a government-owned marketing institute. CNE activities escalated during the national debate, beginning with a series of forums in November 1979 entitled "Mexico before the GATT" and culminating in a similar program in February 1980. Many of the essays presented at these forums were published in the widely distributed CNE journal, *El Economista Mexicano*. Between these forums Aguilera Gómez was busy promoting the CNE viewpoint in interviews with the press, at other public meetings, and in discussions with government officials.

Opposition views took effect within the government through the afore-mentioned ministries committed to a strong state role in planning economic progress.[10] These government officials stressed that the Protocol of Accession and the principles of the GATT negated many aspects of the economic plans developed under the López Portillo administration. In fact, one report suggests that the 1979 Industrial Plan implicitly assumed Mexico would not enter the GATT (*Latin America Weekly Report*, 21 March 1980).

In addition to voicing their own concerns, government critics of the GATT were reflecting the opinions of the various interest groups opposed to Mexico's accession. The two ministries leading the "in-house" attack on the GATT, Industry and Foreign Relations, were also the two cabinet agencies most closely identified with the opposition outside the state. CANACINTRA had good relations with Secretary of Industry Oteyza, and the CNE had excellent contacts in the Foreign Relations Ministry, especially through the undersecretary for economic affairs, Jorge Eduardo Navarrete, who received his degree in economics from UNAM.

The president reached his final decision only after a cabinet meeting on March 10 in which the "planning" ministries formed a majority of five votes cast against GATT entry as opposed to three votes in favor.[11] It is plausible to conclude that this cabinet vote finally convinced López Portillo that a decision in favor of GATT entry would alienate too many political elements, both within and outside the state. Shortly after López Portillo's speech announcing the decision, Oteyza, speaking at the National Assembly of CONCAMIN, summarized the opinions of the anti-GATT ministries when he said that Mexico had rejected the "song of the sirens" and had chosen to protect its independence and self-determination by remaining outside the GATT framework. Navarrete also emphasized Mexico's future pursuit of trade negotiations through organizations more relevant to Third World concerns than the GATT.

The Impact

Mexico's decision to forego GATT membership will have important repercussions. At least in the short term, the domestic impact is likely to be negative in terms of reduced nonpetroleum exports, a larger trade deficit, and more politicized trade relations with the United States. Of course, greater autonomy in trade and economic policymaking and the preservation of many of the smaller, wholly Mexican enterprises may balance these outcomes.

Specifically, the decision was expected to have an immediate negative effect on nonpetroleum exports due to the application of the 1979 U.S.

Trade Law invoking unilateral measures for limiting imports. Also, the cancellation of the U.S.-Mexico bilateral trade agreement negotiated in the Tokyo Round, abrogated by Mexico's refusal to join the GATT, will deprive Mexico of many trade concessions. Operating exclusively in a bilateral framework, trade issues between the United States and Mexico will take on more political overtones, and both countries will have more difficulties coping with domestic protectionist pressures.

In the period since the March 1980 announcement, the trade picture for Mexico has not brightened, with the exception of petroleum. The 1980 and 1981 trade deficits reached record levels of $4.2 billion and $4.8 billion, respectively; and the trade balance in 1982 became a surplus of $5.5 billion only because of the economic crisis that caused imports to plummet over 35 percent from the previous year.[12] Petroleum exports were steadily increasing their share of the total (77.1 percent in 1982), and manufactured exports were diminishing in real terms (only 14.1 percent of total exports in 1982).

Mexico's trade position vis-à-vis the United States has been particularly bad. The Mexican trade deficit with the United States rose to $2.7 billion in 1980 and to $4.7 billion in 1981. Again because of the severe recession beginning in Mexico in 1982, the trade balance with the United States showed a surplus for Mexico (over $4 billion) for the first time in decades. Although the United States exported some $17 billion in goods and services to Mexico in 1981, these exports dropped to about $11 billion in 1982.

Although Mexican exports to the United States in 1982 did increase by $1.8 billion over 1981, a number of specific actions detrimental to Mexican exports threatened any future gains. Beginning in 1980, Mexican products were being removed from the U.S. generalized system of preferences; and by 1983, fifty-six Mexican products had been excluded from preferential treatment. The Mexican Foreign Trade Institute (IMCE) claimed that these actions could reduce Mexican sales to the United States by 30 percent in 1983, though these reports were somewhat exaggerated for political purposes.[13] In addition, with Mexico not a member of the GATT and not a signatory to the Tokyo Round, the U.S. government is obligated to impose a countervailing duty on any Mexican exports benefiting from a subsidy, without having to prove damage. The first such case, in January 1981, involved certain leather apparel, and by March 1983, thirteen cases existed in which countervailing duties had been applied or investigations had begun.[14] Thus, at least in the short term, the implications of the GATT decision for Mexico-U.S. trade are predominantly negative.

With new pressures arising from the financial crisis and with the generally more conservative economic cabinet under de le Madrid, some speculation again centered on whether Mexico would renew negotiations to enter the GATT. Particularly revealing was the presence of Héctor Hernández Cervantes, who negotiated the Protocol of Accession for Mexico in 1979 and who, as secretary of commerce and industrial promotion in the de la Madrid administration, was closely associated with forces favorable to the GATT. Some analysts also suggested that, in exchange for U.S. economic assistance granted in 1982, the Reagan government would try to persuade Mexico to join the GATT. The compensatory duties and the removal of some Mexican exports from the generalized system of preferences were cited as examples of renewed U.S. pressures (*El Financiero*, 15 March 1983).

The official policy of the new government, however, was that Mexico would not accede to the GATT. At the annual meeting of ANIERM in 1983, Hernández Cervantes stated unequivocally that Mexico would not join the GATT and even denied that he had ever favored such a decision. Other government officials confirmed this position, and the private sector in 1983 actually seemed more opposed to the GATT than in the 1979–1980 period.[15] Finally, in May 1983, de la Madrid stated unequivocally that Mexico would not enter the GATT (*Excélsior*, 21 May 1983). Instead of GATT membership, most interested parties, both within and outside the government, favored bilateral agreements and strongly expressed the view that the United States should apply the principle of "proof of damage" to the cases of countervailing duties on Mexican exports.[16]

Industrialists and the Policy Process: Regulation and Nondecision

The most prevalent policy processes in Mexico, regulation and nondecision, have been fairly conducive to the exercise of industrial influence. Regulatory policies are predominant in Mexico because (1) interest groups are more differentiated and more prone to conflict, and (2) the state avoids explicit policy choices and defers much policymaking to the implementation stage. The private sector would probably wield even more influence if self-regulation were widespread in Mexico, but regulatory policies still allow considerable leeway for input from affected business interests. Industrialists certainly prefer regulation to either redistribution or distribution types of policymaking because in a regulatory arena the elite interest groups can work behind the scenes to influence policy as it is implemented. Thus, they develop excellent contacts with key ministry officials, who sometimes have prior links to the business groups or individuals. Among the examples of regulatory policies in which the industrial sector has had some success in shaping policy at the implementation stage are import licenses, tariffs, tax exemptions, public credit, and foreign-investment controls.

The Mexican private sector has also been reasonably successful in numerous cases involving the nondecision policy process. Business interests have been able to delay or otherwise defeat legislation mandating broad changes in the use of foreign trademarks, agrarian reform since the 1940s, fiscal reform under Echeverría, and devaluation in the postwar period. And the choice not to associate with the GATT is probably the most significant example of a nondecision in which the private sector played a pivotal role. In this case, CANACINTRA along with the CNE provided most of the pressure against Mexican entry, and their efforts were successful.

The alliance of CANACINTRA with the intellectual community underlines a common strategy of business groups. The private sector has exercised its most effective influence in those instances in which it has united with other political actors. These two well-organized and powerful groups representing different constituencies overwhelmed the GATT supporters, who were much less persistent in pushing their viewpoint.

The policy process in the GATT decision showed that at times elite groups like CANACINTRA and the CNE enjoy a substantial degree of autonomy vis-à-vis the state. Though the national discussion did not include mass-based organizations or movements to any significant degree, it did represent the further liberalization of the political system at the upper levels. The entrenched bureaucrats and political leaders (almost exclusively affiliated with the PRI) have not been losing their grip on power, but relatively independent interest groups have been able to mount effective challenges to government-initiated policies. In this case, the two most important opposition groups, CANACINTRA and the CNE, were successful in influencing the centralized decision-making process and in blocking the proposed accession to the GATT. Hence, the particular decision confirms the notion that, at least in certain areas, groups representing diverse elite interests can exercise considerable autonomy from state domination and can affect the outcome of the policy process.

The 1982 Bank Nationalization as a Redistributive Policy

The best, and one of the few, examples of a redistributive policy in the postwar period is the 1982 expropriation of the private sector banks. Clearly, political conflict existed over this decision (though much of the conflict was *ex post facto*), significant economic resources were transferred between sectors, and an explicit choice was made between winners and losers.[17] As expected, in a case like this, when the policy arena shifts from the implementation stage to a public decision for redistributing resources, the influence of the private sector is at a minimum. Though the nationalization decision most directly affected another economic sector, industrialists certainly had a stake in the banks (through interlocking directorships and investments) and participated in many of the protests.

Actually, the public debate prior to this decision was not as great as during the national consultation over the GATT. But the announcement, at 2:16 in the afternoon of September 1 during López Portillo's sixth and last *Informe* to the nation, became one of the most publicized and discussed government decisions in recent *sexenios*. Supporters rallied behind the nationalization in mass demonstrations and in a variety of public forums, and detractors (primarily from the private sector) strongly criticized the action in their public pronouncements, attempted to organize a business strike, and initiated court proceedings to invalidate the expropriation.

The nationalization of the banks as well as the implementation of exchange controls had long been demands of the Mexican Left, including the official and independent labor unions and the progressive intellectuals.[18] And these demands had been reiterated just prior to the July 1982 elections and again before the September *Informe*. As early as August 1981, the CTM had petitioned the PRI to include nationalization of the banks and exchange controls in its electoral platform for 1982. These calls were renewed after the February devaluation and also after the August devaluation. In fact, on August 29 a petition for the bank nationalization was signed by forty unions and supported by all the opposition parties except the PAN and the PDM (Colmenares et al. 1982:149).

Despite these consistent pressures, no one (including the Left) seriously thought the government would ever take these actions. The PRI had never recognized these policies as valid and did not include them in the 1982 platform. Neither López Portillo nor President-elect de la Madrid was known to favor bank nationalization or exchange controls. And several key economic advisers, particularly Jesús Silva Herzog (secretary of finance) and Miguel Mancera (head of the Banco de México), clearly opposed them.

The expropriation of the banks was first considered within the government less than a month before the actual decision. After the August 5 devaluation, López Portillo authorized the first studies regarding a state takeover of the banks. And on August 8 the president met with national leaders from all political sectors and told them that the speculation with the peso must be halted. Yet no one outside a few advisers to López Portillo knew anything about a possible nationalization of the banks. In particular, the bankers themselves suspected nothing. The participation of government officials in the last ABM convention in June seemed to demonstrate continued harmony between the bankers and the state (*Comercio Exterior*, August 1982). As late as 12 July 1982, when López Portillo met with sixty members of the ABM, the president even thanked the bankers for their "solidarity, patriotism, and nationalism" (Presidencia de la República, Coordinación General de Comunicación Social, mimeo, 12 July 1982). And the bankers had a close ally in Miguel Mancera.

López Portillo apparently made the decision on August 29, without consulting Silva Herzog, Mancera, or several other members of the cabinet.[19] The advisers who most influenced him on this decision were Carlos Tello (formerly secretary of planning and budgeting and later head of the government bank for the sugar industry, Financiera Nacional Azucarera) and José Ramón López Portillo (the president's son and deputy minister at Planning and Budgeting). The president was motivated by some legitimate concerns about peso speculation, capital flight, and financial insolvency, but he undoubtedly also was hoping to improve his battered political image. The economic cabinet was informed of the decision the night before the *Informe*, and the directors of the public enterprises and other high-ranking officials were told the following morning. De la Madrid was informed of the decision, though he was not consulted. The president-elect later issued statements supporting the bank nationalization (but not the exchange controls, which he reversed in December).

So, in spite of the repeated demands of the political Left, the announcement on September 1 of the bank nationalization was a shock and surprise to almost everyone. The public debate began after the *Informe*. On September 3, the political parties (except the PAN and the PDM) brought more than five hundred thousand persons to the National Palace to support the actions and to praise López Portillo as a hero equal to Cárdenas. Yet the most immediate, concrete, and lasting reactions were from the opponents. Mancera resigned the evening of September 1 as director of the Banco de México and was immediately replaced by Tello. The following day, the president of the ABM said the acquisition of the banks would not solve any problems, and other entrepreneurial leaders called for a national plebiscite on the issue.[20] The CCE issued a statement on September 3 defending the bankers and saying that the state had abandoned a market economy with this decision. Several business groups planned a strike for September 8, but canceled it, fearing such an action would be counterproductive and might not receive complete support within the private sector. The *Wall Street Journal* on September 9 even reported that the U.S. ambassador to Mexico, John Gavin, had cabled Washington expressing concern that Mexico was becoming a "siege economy" and that Silva Herzog was not consulted over the bank nationalization.

Later in September, the bankers filed their most important court challenge to the expropriations, and entrepreneurial groups organized the first of many meetings over the following months to center on the theme of the loss of liberty as exemplified in the September 1 decision. These conferences, held in diverse cities, including Puebla, Saltillo, Monterrey, Torreón, León, Mérida, and Culiacán, culminated in the January 1983 meeting of entrepreneurial leaders in Toluca in which they directly criticized the PRI for limiting economic and political freedoms. In these actions, the private sector was trying to rally national sentiment on its behalf and to pressure the new government to reverse the decision.

Though some influential groups and individuals (including de la Madrid) may have doubted the economic rationale for the bank nationalization, the entrepreneurs were publicly isolated in their opposition. Without any allies and facing a popular decision to redistribute substantial economic resources, the private sector's attempts to influence this policy were doomed to fail. By November, López Portillo had modified Articles 28, 73, and 123 to the Constitution, incorporating the bank nationalization and further legitimizing it. In de la Madrid's inaugural address, he said the nationalization of the banking system was irreversible. And by March 1983, the courts had rejected all of the bankers' arguments against the decision. De la Madrid's major concession was to constitute the banks as *sociedades nacionales de crédito* and to allow 34 percent of their shares to be sold publicly to private or public concerns (Quijano 1983:368–372). But any individual was barred from purchasing more than 1 percent of the bank shares, and de la Madrid stressed that the banks would remain under the control and administration of the state. The only other consolation to the former bankers were government decisions in August and September of 1983 to sell the banks' shares in 450 companies and to pay a compensation of over one hundred billion pesos to the previous bank owners (*Latin America Weekly Report*, 2 and 16 September 1983; *Comercio Exterior*, September 1983, pp. 808–810).

Thus, in the case of this important redistributive policy decision, the private sector did not wield significant influence. And, contrary to theories that the entrepreneurial class dominates the state, this decision illustrates the state's continuing considerable power independent of private capital influence. The greatest consolation for the private sector was knowing that such policies have been very few in postwar Mexico: the regulatory and nondecision policy processes remain predominant, and in these arenas the private sector continues to exercise considerable influence.

7. Industrial Development Strategies and Petroleum Policy

The prominence, importance, and influence of the industrial sector were especially heightened during the presidency of José López Portillo. He came to power in 1976 after the tumultuous years of the Echeverría *sexenio*. The latter's term ended in near chaos with the sudden devaluations of the peso, the shocking expropriations of rich farmland in the Northwest, the near total alienation of the private sector, and genuine concern about the stability of the presidential succession. But López Portillo did assume the presidential sash as planned on 1 December 1976 and quickly displayed his determination to restore political calm and to reassure business leaders about their role. In his inaugural address he unveiled his commitment to a new direction through his "Alliance for Production" when he pledged "an unremitting democratic effort to change existing circumstances, even the most difficult of them." He further stated that he would "stimulate the dynamic, effective collaboration of every sector" and would guarantee "the legitimate expectations of businessmen."[1]

Despite some setbacks, the industrial sector generally prospered over the next five years, as López Portillo showed that he was a trusted friend of the private sector. Only in his last year, when the economic crisis hit Mexico and López Portillo reacted with devaluations, bank nationalization, and exchange controls, was this harmonious relationship destroyed. De la Madrid then not only faced the task of restoring private sector confidence after another unstable pre-inauguration year, but also confronted the difficulties of the worst economic crisis in decades.

"Shared Development" versus the "Alliance for Production"

No strong indications before his inauguration pointed to any significant changes that might occur under López Portillo. As is always the case in Mexican politics, Echeverría had personally chosen his successor after weighing the political pros and cons of the leading candidates. In September 1975 Echeverría made the surprising selection of López Portillo, who was generally not considered one of the most likely *tapados* (presidential contenders). A lifelong friend of Echeverría, López Portillo had served admirably as treasury secretary since 1973. But his greatest shortcoming was that as a *técnico* he lacked a strong political base. Of course, some have argued that this lack of political connections was an asset in the eyes of Echeverría, who wanted to continue wielding influence after his term of office (Smith 1979:288–292). At any rate, the two men were close associates and Echeverría did hand-pick his successor. Thus, one could reasonably have expected a continuation of policies after the inauguration. But this was not to be. On assuming office, López Portillo immediately set out to "be his own man," and many of his policies, particularly those in the economic sphere, were quite different from those of his predecessor.

More than any other president, Echeverría tried to emulate the populist style, rhetoric, and policies of Lázaro Cárdenas, the leftist president in the 1930s. As was the case with López Portillo, there were no indications of his plans when he came to office in 1976 to succeed the conservative Díaz Ordaz. Echeverría, as minister of Gobernación, was closely linked to the hard-line policies of Díaz Ordaz, especially the 1968 killings of hundreds of students at Tlatelolco. But in almost all areas, including domestic economic policies, Echeverría as president turned to the left. The principal tenets of his expansionist economic programs were income redistribution, an enlarged economic role for the state, controls on foreign investment, and a sometimes openly hostile relationship with private business. This new development strategy, as solidified in documents drawn up by the Secretaría de la Presidencia in 1973, became known as "*desarrollo compartido*," or shared development. In essence it abandoned economic growth as the *only* goal of development and also stressed economic justice, increased employment, better income distribution, improved standards of living, and reduced external dependence (Bueno 1977a; and Yúnez Naude 1979:222–224).

Echeverría was quite vocal in his support of income redistribution, but his policies often contained more rhetoric than results. He seemed committed to revising Mexico's regressive tax structure, but he achieved only marginal tax reforms in 1971 and 1972 (Hansen 1974:xii–xxix; Purcell and Purcell 1976). Real wages did increase under Echeverría, he made some substantial improvements in public housing, and he strongly supported agricultural development, particularly the subsistence sector (Grindle

1977). Overall, however, Echeverría was not able to fulfill his rhetorical commitment to redistributing income in Mexico.

He produced more concrete results in terms of enlarging the public sector and restricting foreign capital.[2] From 1971 to 1976 government expenditures rose much faster than the inflation rate. Much of the spending increases were in current expenditures, including outlays for housing, education, and agricultural development; but the most spectacular advances were in government-owned enterprises and public works. This enormous growth in the public sector was not adequately financed and thus led to more borrowing abroad, growth in the money supply, and higher budget deficits. Other initiatives that had a major impact during Echeverría's *sexenio* were the 1973 laws requiring Mexicanization for all new firms and the registration and review of all technology transfers. These pieces of legislation served to control and restrict the entry of foreign capital and technology into Mexico and were the heart of Echeverría's unfavorable stance toward the growing role of foreign investment in the Mexican economy.

Echeverría's antagonistic attitude toward private capital was not limited to foreign entrepreneurs but extended to domestic business as well. As public expenditures and inflation accelerated, private investment and business confidence in the government diminished. The private sector became increasingly alienated from the administration, and the various business associations and confederations even formed the Consejo Coordinador Empresarial to present a united front against the excesses of the government. Echeverría's treatment of the conservative Monterrey Group was especially harsh. He continually berated them for not contributing to the overall development of Mexico, so the Monterrey industrialists were among his earliest antagonists. But other industrial groups, including CONCAMIN and CANACINTRA, also came to oppose the Echeverría policies quite forcefully.

His troubles with the private sector, his desire to revive populist and leftist policies, and the deterioration of the economy climaxed in his final turbulent months in office in the fall of 1976. The first of Echeverría's unexpected moves was a devaluation of the peso. The inflationary trend had caused the peso to become critically overvalued. A devaluation in the early years of his *sexenio* was vetoed as being politically unfeasible, but by 1976 a substantial devaluation of the peso, which had been fixed at a constant exchange rate for twenty-two years, was unavoidable. In two sudden devaluations in August and October 1976, the peso fell to almost one-half its previous level vis-à-vis the U.S. dollar. These actions shocked the private sector, which responded by sending enormous sums of money out of the country. Capital flight peaked at about $150 million in mid-November, and altogether $3 billion to $4 billion left Mexico in the last half of 1976.

In the short period from August to November 1976, Echeverría attempted to solidify his identification with the left wing in Mexican politics by coupling the devaluations with the sharp and widely publicized attack on conservative business interests in Monterrey and with the expropriations of 100,000 hectares of fertile farmland in the northwestern states of Sonora and Sinaloa (the Yaqui Valley). The president's actions created opposition throughout Mexico and also contributed to widespread confusion. One manifestation of the opposition was the one-day general strike of entrepreneurial chambers of the Northwest to protest the seizure of the land without compensation. The lack of support and the uncertainty of the political situation became so severe that rumors of a military coup circulated. The inauguration of López Portillo less than two weeks after the expropriations was a welcome relief to many Mexicans.

Economic recovery was López Portillo's top priority on assuming office. He wanted to renew the confidence of the private sector, halt the inflationary spiral, and restore the pattern of economic growth based on a healthy industrial sector. The key to his strategy was restoring the confidence and cooperation of business groups, and he wasted no time in establishing better relations with the private sector. His inaugural speech emphasized the calming of political forces and the need to rely more on private industry. Mexican business leaders were quite pleased with the stance of the new president, and 140 large companies signed an agreement with the government on December 10 to coordinate their investment plans so as to achieve the goal of creating 300,000 jobs (*New York Times*, 26 December 1976). This action marked the end of a five-year slowdown in private investment.

The ties between López Portillo and private business were developing into what he called the "Alliance for Production," which was to stress joint planning between the private and public sectors. Some of the initial policy decisions associated with the Alliance for Production were stricter control of public expenses, tax exemptions for export products of firms owned wholly by Mexicans, reduction of taxes on enterprises, and increased prices for basic goods (*Análisis Político*, 4 July 1977).

As the Alliance for Production became more solidified, Mexican businesses continued to profess their support of López Portillo. In April 1977 the Monterrey Group, which had been so hostile to Echeverría, pledged its cooperation with the new government and announced a program to invest 100 billion pesos in Mexico over the following six years. In turn López

Portillo stressed the contrasts between his *sexenio* and the previous one by describing the Monterrey industrialists as "profoundly nationalist." The national federations of chambers of commerce and industry capped his first year in office by issuing a ten-point program of concessions timed to coincide with the president's first state of the union address. Among the principal concessions to the government were promises to increase wages, hold down prices, and accelerate investment.

Almost all of López Portillo's initial cabinet appointments, especially in the economic ministries, were satisfactory to business interests. These appointments also reflected his desire to establish his independence from Echeverría (Smith 1979:298–313). The four top economic posts were in the hands of individuals who had been his associates and loyal supporters in the past. The treasury secretary, Julio Rodolfo Moctezuma Cid, had worked with the new president for twenty years and had been in charge of his presidential campaign. The secretary of resources and industrial promotion, José Andrés de Oteyza, and the head of Planning and Budgeting, Carlos Tello Macías, had both been with López Portillo in various bureaucratic posts in the past. Finally, Fernando Solana, head of Commerce, knew López Portillo from their teaching and administrative days at UNAM. The private sector had no complaints about these new ministers (though entrepreneurs did strongly criticize Tello later) and were particularly pleased with several other appointments: Carlos Hank González as *regente* of the Federal District, Oscar Flores Sánchez as attorney general, Jorge Díaz Serrano as director of PEMEX, and Romero Kolbeck as president of the Banco de México.

Later changes in the ranks of the economic ministries were even more to the liking of business groups. A clash over the 1978 budget developed between the monetarist Moctezuma and the expansionist Tello. López Portillo had both resign in November 1977, but Moctezuma (who reemerged as head of PEMEX in June 1981) was vindicated by the naming of conservative replacements for both posts and by an austere budget for 1978. David Ibarra Muñoz, a traditional economist and former head of the national development bank (NAFINSA), replaced Moctezuma, and Ricardo García Sainz, an active leader in various private sector associations, replaced Tello. In a further move to the right a month later, Jorge de la Vega Domínguez replaced Solana at Commerce, and Solana took over as education minister in place of the cabinet's last *Echeverrista*, Porfirio Muñoz Ledo. De la Vega Domínguez was a pragmatic economist with close ties to the president.

One of the last changes in the economic ministries occurred in May 1979, as the economy was beginning to expand rapidly, thus fueling inflation.

Again, López Portillo opted for a shift to the right and replaced García Sainz, who was seen as ineffective and subordinate to the only remaining expansionist in the cabinet, Oteyza. García Sainz's replacement, former deputy treasury minister, Miguel de la Madrid Hurtado, was expected to add weight to the arguments for restrictionist budgetary policies. Of course, de la Madrid was named the PRI's candidate for the presidency on 25 September 1981, in a move that pleased most industrialists. He was replaced at Planning and Budgeting by Ramón Aguirre. In March 1982 Jesús Silva Herzog (the undersecretary at Treasury) replaced his boss Ibarra Muñoz, and at the Banco de México Kolbeck was replaced by his deputy, Miguel Mancera. Both Silva Herzog and Mancera were close associates of de la Madrid and were strongly supported by the industrial sector.

The only cabinet change of the López Portillo *sexenio* that clearly displeased the private sector was the resignation of Mancera in September following the bank nationalization and the naming of Carlos Tello Macías to succeed him. By this time, Tello was one of the leading antagonists of the private sector. His views had become particularly well known through his two books, the first defending the Echeverría policies (Tello 1979) and the second (coauthored with the parliamentary leader of the Mexican Unified Socialist party) stressing protectionism, nationalism, government spending, and centralized planning (Tello and Cordera 1981). But Tello was director of the Banco de México only for the remaining three months of the López Portillo administration.

The emphasis on financial conservatism was evident in López Portillo's first three budgets. Though not willing to sacrifice economic growth, which rebounded in 1978 after two years of negative per capita growth, spending policies from 1977 to 1979 were generally deflationary. After having steadily increased throughout Echeverría's *sexenio*, the federal deficit diminished in 1977. The absolute value of the deficit increased again in 1978 and 1979, but, according to Inter-American Development Bank sources, the deficit expressed as a percentage of GDP steadily decreased from 1976 to 1979. The projected budgets for 1978 and 1979 were slightly less restrictive than the 1977 budget, which had no increase in real terms. The 1978 projections were for a 24 percent nominal increase and 10 percent real increase in federal spending, and the 1979 budget planned for a 23 percent nominal increase and 6 percent real increase. Significantly, most of the increases were not for current expenditures but for capital investment, especially in petroleum. PEMEX was to receive 60 percent of total public investment in 1978 and the biggest single chunk (20 percent) of total public expenditures in 1979.

The trend to keep actual expenditures within the planned budgets was also noteworthy in López Portillo's initial budgets. Overspending as a percentage of planned expenditures steadily decreased, from 15.4 percent in 1975 and 32.6 in 1976 to 7.9 percent in 1977 and 2.9 percent in 1978 (*Latin America Economic Report*, 7 September 1979). These budgetary policies obviously benefited private industry, especially since all spending increases concentrated on capital rather than current expenditures. These policies also were within the typically austere guidelines of a "letter of intent" negotiated between Mexico and the International Monetary Fund in return for $1.2 billion in long-term credit.

The 1980 and 1981 budgets were the most expansionist of the López Portillo *sexenio*. Government spending decisions for 1980 in particular signaled a retreat from the earlier objective of combating inflation. The priority now was economic growth, boosted by government expenditures that rose to 37 percent of the GNP in 1980 from 33 percent in 1979. Of course, petroleum revenues were feeding this expansion, and in 1980 government income increased 19 percent in real terms. The 1980 budget still emphasized energy and capital-intensive industries. In 1981 the budget was projected to rise 31 percent over 1980 figures, though growth in public sector investment was expected to moderate slightly. One result of these budget increases was that public foreign debt reached enormous proportions by 1980. The external public debt of Mexico in per capita terms or as a percentage of national output was by far the largest in Latin America.

In reaction to these mounting deficits and the overheating economy, in 1980 private industrialists became openly critical of López Portillo for the first time.[3] Undoubtedly, these criticisms were also motivated by a desire to affect the upcoming selection of the next president. In any case, prominent industrial entrepreneurs and leaders of various industrial interest groups began speaking out openly against numerous economic policies. Among the favorite targets were the subsidies granted to state-owned enterprises that were operating at a loss. In one instance, the director of the Cámara de la Industria de Transformación de Nuevo León, Humberto Lobo, exhorted López Portillo in March 1980 to sell unprofitable public companies to more efficient private capitalists. In addition to budgetary policies, other representatives of the industrial sector were critical of exchange rate and credit policies. The overvalued peso was severely damaging many manufacturers (particularly those with export potential), and the pain of restrictive credit through high interest rates was being felt throughout the industrial sector.

Partially as a result of this industrial input, the 1982 budget was again more conservative. Though it provided a nominal increase of 28 percent over 1981, this represented no rise over the previous year in real terms.

Even before the 1982 budget was announced, government expenditures were cut 4 percent in July 1981 to trim the deficit and to adjust for reduced oil revenues. The minimum wage for 1981 was increased about 33 percent over 1980—a level that did not meet the demands of labor but did please business executives and industrialists. These moves, along with the designation of de la Madrid as the next president, did much to mollify the private sector in 1981. Apparently, the semioffensive of 1980 on the part of entrepreneurial leaders brought some successes in 1981.

López Portillo reversed the Echeverría policies of promoting subsistence agriculture and land reform. Though he refused to overturn the 1976 expropriation decree of the former president and believed it politically impossible to return the land to its former owners, he did respond to private sector concerns by providing just compensation for the land and assuring the large agribusiness sector that any future agrarian reform would concentrate on unproductive land rather than on fertile and profitable farms similar to those seized by Echeverría (*Latin America Political Report*, 13 May 1977 and 1 September 1978). López Portillo's major policy initiative in the agricultural sector was the introduction of the Sistema Alimentario Mexicano (SAM), an agrarian plan to achieve self-sufficiency in basic foodstuffs. Announced in March of 1980 and commenced in May of the same year, the SAM involved fiscal and monetary incentives for the production of such food staples as corn and beans. López Portillo claimed some success for the SAM with 5.3 percent growth in agricultural value-added in 1980 (compared to a 0.7 percent decline in 1979) and some bumper crops in 1981.[4]

López Portillo also drastically altered the Echeverría initiatives on regulating foreign capital. He achieved a more harmonious relationship between foreign investors and the Mexican government, as well. He abandoned Echeverría's nationalist rhetoric and recognized a need for more foreign capital to aid Mexico's economic development. He did not change the legislation but he did implement it in a much more flexible manner. Exemptions to the Mexicanization requirements were granted when the foreign investment was seen as providing technology or capital otherwise unavailable. Hence, U.S. investment in Mexico increased substantially after 1977.

Another policy area in which favoritism toward the private sector was obvious was wages and prices. López Portillo was reluctant to control prices, yet wages were held down. Through parts of 1977 and 1978, the state kept annual wage increases in public enterprises at 10 percent, and overall wages increased slower than price levels. Price controls were removed for automobiles in July 1977, and nearly 150 basic commodities were freed from price ceilings in February 1978. In one of the biggest shocks to the population, petroleum and diesel prices were allowed to more than double in December 1981. In other areas, López Portillo was content to rely on voluntary price control programs supposedly initiated by private sector groups in well-publicized programs in 1977 and again in 1979. Ironically, the president continually praised labor for its sacrifices and criticized the private sector for not fulfilling its promises of higher investment and slower price increases. This theme was part of each of his state of the union addresses from 1977 to 1979. Yet, official policies persisted in favoring entrepreneurs and allowing real wages to decline (*Latin America Weekly Report*, 11 January 1980).

López Portillo introduced a number of fiscal reforms in 1979, even though Echeverría had been unsuccessful in significantly reforming the tax system. These policies were among the few issues on which the private sector generally opposed the president, and his popularity with business regarding other measures probably aided in successfully enacting various fiscal reforms. Changes included a plan to reduce the tax rates for lower income groups, but the most important initiatives were a value-added tax and the restructuring of tariffs.[5] On 1 January 1980 a 10 percent value-added tax (IVA) replaced a 4 percent sales tax, but entrepreneurs who believed the value-added tax to be too complex and inflationary were hopeful of influencing the policy in the implementation stage. Most analysts agreed that the IVA would be inflationary, at least in the short run, but it is a more efficient tax to collect and has reduced tax evasion in Mexico and generated additional revenues. Finally, the IVA is a regressive tax that does not address the problem of the disproportionate tax burden of the lower-income groups.

In a previous reform of protectionist policies, López Portillo had already begun to replace import licensing with tariffs. Out of seventy-six hundred products formerly requiring import licenses, only two thousand needed them by 1980 (Cándano Fierro 1980). Another change, effective 1 July 1979, was designed to "rationalize" tariffs by calculating duties according to the "normal value" of the imported product rather than its "official price." This reform of the tariff structure was designed to produce gradually lower tariffs and to promote greater efficiency in domestic industries. As such, this and earlier trade liberalization measures were a concern to the small and medium industries that might suffer from increased foreign competition, though these industrialists did achieve some success in trade policy when López Portillo announced in March 1980 that Mexico was not joining the GATT.

The 1980 GATT decision was followed in 1981 by measures intended to improve the deteriorating trade balance, since Mexico was facing a record balance-of-payments deficit of $11.5 billion. The twin objectives were to lower superfluous imports and to increase exports of manufactured goods. The former goal actually required some reversals of the previous trade liberalization policies. In the summer and fall of 1981 some tariff barriers were raised and some nonessential imports were banned. Production quotas for 1982 were issued for the automotive industry in an effort to minimize the trade deficit in that sector. Also, beginning in 1981, even prior to the devaluations of 1982, the peso was subjected to a series of minidevaluations (about 1 percent a month).

Responding to declines in manufactured exports in real terms and pressure from CONCAMIN and CANACINTRA for an effective export promotion policy,[6] in 1981 López Portillo instituted a number of measures to foment the export of manufactured goods. Export incentives administered through export promotion committees were created in February to support exporters deemed able to compete internationally. In May export performance criteria were established for foreign-owned automobile companies, which previously had generated substantial trade deficits. And in June, the Banco de México announced that it would support exporters with a fund of fifty billion pesos for 1981.

In summary to this point, then, many contrasts between the Echeverría and López Portillo presidencies are evident in economic policy. Though they were close friends and López Portillo owed his job to Echeverría, the policy differences emerged as soon as the succession was complete. Whereas Echeverría was more of a populist, with his *desarrollo compartido* strategy, López Portillo favored the private sector under his Alianza para la Producción, at least for his first five years in office. Echeverría stressed income redistribution, greatly enlarged the public sector, limited foreign investment, and alienated the domestic private sector. López Portillo, on the other hand, restored the confidence of business and industry, reversed agrarian reform, welcomed foreign capital, held down wages, and initiated some trade liberalization. However, since López Portillo faced some new international and domestic economic events, his presidency was not the classic conservative reversal of the Echeverría years that it is sometimes depicted to be. The most significant new factor was that he had to confront the twin opportunities (and problems) of Mexico's entering the 1980s as both an advanced developing country and an oil-exporting nation. The difficulties arising partially from these new developments manifested themselves in 1982.

Economic Crisis of 1982 and de la Madrid's Recovery Program

The economic statistics for 1982 starkly reveal the depth of the recession into which Mexico had fallen: real GDP growth was a negative 0.2 percent; growth in the manufacturing sector was a negative 2.4 percent; inflation was at 100 percent; unemployment doubled; and total external debt was $80 billion. A number of exogenous and endogenous factors had contributed to the two key problem areas: disequilibrium in the external sector, and deteriorating public finances.[7] The exogenous factors included the 1980–1981 world recession, the rise in international interest rates in late 1979, and the slump in prices and demand for petroleum beginning mid-1981. These events substantially reduced revenues and increased costs for the Mexican public and private sectors.

The endogenous factors, however, were probably more salient. In the first place, the economy had become too dependent on petroleum exports; lost revenues in this sector due to erratic pricing policies in mid-1981 were probably the earliest internal precursors of the 1982 crisis. Rapid growth in manufactured imports (related to trade liberalization policies and accelerated growth in petroleum and other sectors) and growing reliance on imported food were also critical sources of trade deficits. Subsidized prices for public sector goods transferred resources from the public sector to the private sector and increased the federal deficit, as did growing public investments in energy and capital-goods industries. Finally, the state turned to external borrowing to finance the budget deficit, which caused the public foreign debt to expand from $20 billion in 1976 to $60 billion in 1982.

The first signal from the government in 1982 of severe problems was the February peso devaluation. The Banco de México allowed the peso to float, and it fell from about twenty-seven pesos to the dollar to forty-eight pesos per dollar in June, when the Banco de México officially reentered the exchange markets to stabilize the rate. A new economic program was also announced in February that included a 3 percent reduction in public spending, reduced imports, and price controls. Except for the price controls and a wage hike granted in March, the government was essentially following traditional monetarist prescriptions of devaluation, reduced external deficits, and decreased government expenditures. Though the devaluation had severely increased their debt burden in dollars, the industrial sector's only complaint regarded the 30 percent wage increase in March. But another austerity package announced in late April mollified most private sector discontent. Public spending was to be cut an additional 5 percent, and the wage hike was to be offset by higher prices of some public and private sector goods. The private sector was also granted some new subsidies and tax breaks.

The first indications of the debt problem came in April and May when Treasury Secretary Silva Herzog said Mexico might have to renew the maturing foreign debt in 1982.[8] By August Mexico had exhausted its reserves, and López Portillo was forced to announce a number of drastic measures to combat the liquidity crisis. Actually, for several months a battle had been brewing between the president's more conservative economic advisers (Silva Herzog and Mancera) and those favoring nationalist reforms and continued expansionism (Andrés de Oteyza, Tello, and José Ramón López Portillo). Though Silva Herzog did convince López Portillo of the necessity of appealing to the IMF and other foreign sources for assistance, the policy initiatives of August and September predominantly reflected the opinions of the "nationalists" within the economic cabinet and were widely applauded by labor and the political Left. López Portillo was quickly losing the confidence of private business.

The "unprecedented bailout" for Mexico beginning in August was the only victory for Silva Herzog and the private sector during this period. In mid-August the treasury secretary announced a four-part plan: (1) a billion-dollar loan from the United States to be applied against future petroleum sold to the U.S. strategic reserve; (2) $1.68 billion in credits from a number of central banks through the Bank for International Settlements in Switzerland; (3) $1 billion in credits from the U.S. Commodity Credit Corporation for grain bought in the United States; and (4) initiation of negotiations with the IMF for a loan package of about $4 billion. Then, on August 23 the postponement of debt payments began with the first thirty-day rollover of principal payments. The IMF letter of intent with Mexico, containing the typical austerity conditions for the recipient country, was released in November (*Unomásuno*, 11 November 1982). The private sector generally applauded these moves as the only realistic option.

The major policy initiatives of August and September, however, produced widespread entrepreneurial condemnation. The advantages of the February devaluation had been reversed by continuing inflation, and financial speculation was further weakening the peso; therefore, in early August López Portillo instituted the first exchange controls (freezing all dollar accounts) along with two rates of exchange: (1) a "preferential" rate for necessary imports and debt servicing (at 49.5 pesos/dollar); and (2) a devalued "free" rate that fell to 115 pesos/dollar before new measures were taken on September 1. The presidential *Informe* of that date then produced the ultimate shock (described by one business magazine in

Mexico as "un golpe") for the private sector. The remaining private banks were expropriated and the exchange controls were fortified and extended, with the "free" rate becoming a government-set rate of 70 pesos/dollar for "ordinary" transactions and the "preferential" rate remaining at about 50 pesos/dollar.

López Portillo had come full circle. He arrived in office determined to restore business confidence, and most of his *sexenio* was marked by a harmonious "Alliance for Production" between state and industry. But overreliance on petroleum exports and an overheated economy contributed to the economic slump in 1982. Hoping to stem the recessionary tide and also looking for political scapegoats, he adopted policies that damaged the industrial sector in particular and the private sector in general. Accused of having socked the nation's wealth away in foreign bank accounts and real estate, the large entrepreneurs (the *"sacadólares"*) once again were in a position of having lost all confidence in the government's economic policies. In the fall of 1982 they were only hoping for more "pragmatic" solutions from the incoming administration.

De la Madrid did not disappoint them, and the contrasts between the policies of the outgoing and the incoming presidents in 1982 were as great as those in 1976. In his inaugural address on December 1 the new president criticized the "financial populism" of Tello and López Portillo and promised "realism" in economic policy.[9] He introduced his "Immediate Program for Economic Reordering" through ten points: (1) reduced growth in public spending; (2) protection of employment; (3) continued public investment in the most productive projects; (4) honesty and efficiency within the public sector; (5) protection of and stimulation for programs providing basic foodstuffs for the popular sectors; (6) fiscal reforms to increase government revenues; (7) channelization of credit toward national development and efficient management of the nationalized banks; (8) "realistic" exchange policy; (9) restructuring of the federal bureaucracy for more efficiency; and (10) constitutional reforms to reinforce the role of the state ("rectoría del Estado") within the mixed economy.

This recovery program was institutionalized through a host of concrete measures over the next month. An austere 1983 budget was sent to Congress on December 7 with a total spending level projected at $100 billion. This amount represented an increase of 44 percent over 1982, but inflation had been at 100 percent. So, the budget deficit was expected to fall from 16.5 percent of the GNP to 8.5 percent in 1983 (in line with IMF requirements). Substantial tax increases (the most controversial being the rise in the value-added tax, from 10 percent to 15 percent) were coupled with drastic reductions in expenditures.

Reversing part of the September *"golpe,"* the exchange controls were relaxed on December 20. The "free" exchange rate floated from 70 pesos to 150 pesos to the dollar, and the "preferential" rate went from 50 pesos to 95 pesos/dollar (and continued to climb slowly toward the "free" rate). To alter the "overprotection" of previous administrations, tariffs were substantially reduced in January and the granting of import licenses was relaxed. Trends in wage and price policies were also reversed. In late December a moderate increase of 25 percent in the minimum wage was announced effective January 1, with another 12.5 percent boost planned for June. Facing a loss in real income, labor was further shocked by the lifting of most price controls on December 30.

To reform the bureaucracy, the old "superministry" with authority over industry, petroleum, and public enterprises (Secretariat of Resources and Industrial Promotion, SEPAFIN) was abolished. In its place, the Secretariat of Commerce assumed responsibility for industrial development (becoming Commerce and Industrial Promotion, SECOFIN), and a new energy ministry was created (Secretariat of Energy, Mines, and Public Enterprises, SEMIP). This reorganization was designed to promote the goals of efficiency and productivity within the public sector. All the high-level cabinet appointments, especially that of Silva Herzog, who stayed at Treasury, and Mancera, who returned to the Banco de México, reflected de la Madrid's commitment to restoring business confidence. Silva Herzog was particularly busy in the first few months. To combat the debt problem, he proposed a debt-restructuring plan to postpone all principal payments through the end of 1984, announced negotiations with Mexico's creditors for an additional five-billion-dollar loan (completed in March), and formalized the IMF agreement with de la Madrid's full backing.

Because the entrepreneurial sector believed that the austerity package was the only option for Mexico, this plethora of measures received its qualified support. The only major initiatives of the early de la Madrid government that disturbed the private sector were the reforms and additions to Articles 25 through 28 of the Constitution. These constitutional changes (the tenth point in de la Madrid's "Immediate Program") essentially declared that the state was to be the guiding and controlling force in the economy. Business groups resented these changes as unnecessary and viewed them as an unwarranted carry-over from López Portillo's bank nationalization. Yet these reforms did not detract from the environment of trust and hope that de la Madrid had restored within the private sector.

Petroleum Policy: "Instant Industrialization" or "Petrolization"?

As I have stated, Mexico since López Portillo has had a dual status as one of the most industrialized Third World nations and also as an oil-exporting nation (with tendencies toward a monocultural economy). These two roles are not necessarily complementary, so one of the unstated goals of government policy since 1976 has been to harmonize petroleum wealth and industrial development.

Since Mexico has received tremendous publicity concerning its petroleum wealth only in recent years, one often forgets that it has a rich tradition of petroleum exploration and production dating back to the late nineteenth century.[10] A small U.S. entrepreneur drilled the first producing oil well in 1876 at Tuxpan on the Gulf coast northeast of Mexico City. This initial effort proved unprofitable, and the first successful commercial well was drilled by U.S. oilman Edward L. Doheny in 1900 near Tampico. U.S. and British concerns then escalated the exploitation of Mexican petroleum resources over the next two decades.

Oil production reached a peak of 0.5 million barrels a day (bpd) in 1921, and at this time Mexico was actually the world's leading exporter of petroleum. However, the industry entered a period of decline caused in part by mounting disagreements between the Mexican state and the foreign oil companies. These conflicts reached a climax in 1938, when President Cárdenas expropriated all the U.S. and British oil interests and concentrated the petroleum industry in the hands of the state-owned monopoly, PEMEX. Mexico would not be a major international source of petroleum again until the late 1970s.

In the postwar period Mexican petroleum production did increase slightly, and Mexico did maintain its self-sufficiency in oil until 1970. But domestic demand for energy grew so much in the 1960s that by 1970 the country became a net importer of petroleum products. The oil deficit expanded to a peak of over $250 million in 1974, but the situation began to reverse itself in that year, and by 1975 Mexico again was exporting petroleum.

The first significant new oil discoveries were made in 1972 and 1973 in the Reforma fields in the southern states of Chiapas and Tabasco, and in 1975 the first well in the offshore Campeche field (in the Bay of Campeche) was drilled. These Reforma and Campeche fields in the southern zone have provided the bulk of Mexico's oil production, but other oil and gas discoveries have been made along the Gulf coast, particularly near Tampico and in the northeast near the Texas border, and on the Baja California peninsula.

Though the initial discoveries were made during the Echeverría administration, the size of the oil deposits was not well publicized and petroleum exports were not emphasized until López Portillo came to power. A number of reasons can be cited for the delay.[11] One was technical—the Mexican state did not know with certainty the extent of the reserves and did not want to make projections that might prove invalid. The other reasons were largely political and related to the ideology of the Echeverría administration. In the first place, the Echeverristas were extremely apprehensive of U.S. intentions and feared direct pressure from Washington if the optimistic projections of Mexican petroleum were publicized. Also, the Echeverría team preferred a nationalistic and conservationist ethic of keeping the oil and gas in the ground in order to save it for future needs. They viewed increasing exports as a policy that squandered Mexican resources in order to satiate the energy appetite of other nations. Finally, the expansionist-oriented technocrats within PEMEX wanted to hide the true potential of the oil wealth even from Echeverría for fear that he would use it irresponsibly.

As with a number of other issues, the López Portillo administration quickly adopted a new attitude toward petroleum resources. In a press conference twenty-three days after López Portillo's inauguration, his director general of PEMEX, Jorge Díaz Serrano, outlined their plan to discover more petroleum. In his first *Informe*, the president stated that petroleum represented the best opportunity for Mexico's economic independence and the solution to the country's economic problems. He claimed that proven reserves amounted to fourteen billion barrels, compared to estimates of five billion to six billion barrels cited throughout the Echeverría years.

The enormousness of Mexico's petroleum supplies received even more attention with López Portillo's second *Informe* in 1978, when he put proven reserves at twenty billion barrels, probable reserves at thirty-seven billion, and potential reserves at two hundred billion. Furthermore, he claimed that the "economic crisis" inherited from Echeverría was over and that petroleum would play a key role in future economic development. In each successive *Informe*, the figures on petroleum resources increased. By the fifth *Informe*, in 1981, announced proven reserves had risen to seventy-two billion barrels, and Mexico had become the fourth-largest producer of petroleum in the world.

Actual production increased under López Portillo, but at a rate slower than that for the estimates of reserves. Total production rose from 0.8 million bpd in 1976 to about 2.7 million at the end of 1981. Petroleum exports quickly came to dominate the external sector. Mexico was importing petroleum as late as 1974, but by 1978 petroleum was almost one-third of all exports, over 40 percent of total exports in 1979, 66 percent in 1980, 74 percent in 1981, and 77 percent in 1982.

Though the López Portillo administration obviously overturned the cautious conservationism of the Echeverría government, there were some very important debates over petroleum policy and its impact on industrial development during the López Portillo years. The most optimistic scenario, which was linked to arguments for expanding petroleum production and exports, emphasized the potential for "instantaneous industrialization," which occurs when revenues from petroleum exports suddenly overcome previous obstacles to industrial growth involving the scarcity of capital (Yúnez Naude 1979:210–234). The alternative scenario, termed the "petrolization" argument, claimed that the economy was becoming too dependent on petroleum, with substantial negative results: balance-of-payments deficits (rapid import growth coupled with stagnation in nonoil exports), inflation, and an overvalued peso. The former, or expansionist, point of view was best reflected by the oil "establishment" within PEMEX, particularly its director general, Díaz Serrano. The latter, or restrictive, attitude was often professed in the pages of the publications *Proceso, Unomásuno*, and *Excélsior* by writers like the late Manuel Buendía and Heberto Castillo and usually was best represented in government circles by the secretary of resources and industrial promotion. José Andrés de Oteyza.[12]

Both sides cited statistical evidence to substantiate their arguments. The proponents of instant industrialization could point to government revenues that more than doubled between 1976 and 1979, an extremely good credit rating in international banking circles (until 1982), growth in the gross domestic product averaging 7 to 8 percent annually between 1977 and 1981, and growth in industrial value-added averaging 8 to 9 percent annually between 1977 and 1981. On the other hand, those who feared the "petrolization" of the economy could stress that petroleum's share of the gross domestic product more than doubled under López Portillo, that manufactured exports stagnated in real terms and shrank from over 35 percent of total exports in 1978 to less than 15 percent in 1982, that the balance of payments was incurring record deficits, and that inflation continued to run above 20 percent a year and reached 100 percent in 1982.

This debate over petroleum policy was linked to other economic issues that pitted the economic "liberals" like Díaz Serrano, who wanted to see Mexico advance as rapidly as possible to the forefront of world development, versus "nationalists" in the administration like Oteyza, who preferred to concentrate on domestic solutions to problems of inequality and dependency. The nationalists scored important victories in several areas, with the GATT decision as just one example. But decisions over petroleum production produced the most numerous *apparent* victories on the part of those who feared excessive dependence on the advanced capitalist world. Their arguments were bolstered by events in Iran—a country to which Mexico was often compared at that time. It was quite instructive to Mexicans that Iran under the shah, with his policies of rapid modernization, was falling apart at the same time that Mexico was reemerging as a major petroleum-producing nation. The watchword was to avoid the "Iranization" of the economy.

Along these lines, López Portillo always tried to appear to be emphasizing controlled growth of both petroleum production and the economy overall while announcing the newly discovered reserves. He also frequently stressed that the priorities of Mexican petroleum production were to satisfy domestic consumption and needs and to preserve national autonomy. Reflecting these themes in his fourth *Informe*, in 1980, he boasted that in the exploitation of petroleum reserves Mexico was maintaining a "margin of safety" of more than sixty years compared to about thirty years in most other oil-producing states. He downplayed the significance of petroleum by claiming that "petroleum production is not the ultimate objective of the efforts of this administration." Echoing the nationalist refrain he said, "Mexico's oil is ours and is for our own development. This has been true ever since we rescued it [in 1938] from being squandered at the powerful and materialist hands of concessionaires" (*Comercio Exterior de México*, September 1980, p. 336). In his 1981 *Informe*, a major thesis was that Mexico had not become a "petroleum economy." He stressed that oil was only 7 percent of national output, though he also admitted that petroleum products accounted for over two-thirds of total exports.

Probably the best, and most important, statement of these themes of conservation and nationalism in petroleum policy was the 1980 Mexican Energy Program issued by Oteyza in November.[13] This program established specific goals and targets until 1990 and broader objectives lasting up to the year 2000. It emphatically stated that a principal goal was to end "the present situation of dependency on hydrocarbons" (p. 13). Six specific, but nonquantifiable, aims were enumerated: (1) to satisfy the nation's energy needs; (2) to "rationalize" the production and use of energy; (3) to diversify the sources of primary energy; (4) to integrate the energy sector into the rest of the economy; (5) to know more accurately the extent of the nation's energy resources; and (6) to strengthen the scientific and technical infrastructure. The program also reaffirmed the quantitative limits announced by López Portillo in March 1980: the ceiling for total production was 2.75 million bpd and the export limit was 1.5 million bpd.

The export limit was to remain constant for twenty years (with no single nation to receive more than 50 percent of the exports), and total production was to rise to 3.5 million bpd in 1985 and to 4.1 million bpd in 1990. These ceilings were set low, despite the fact that the technological limit to maximum production was claimed to be between 8 million and 10 million bpd. The publication of this program and its intended coordination with the other national development plans was an obvious attempt by Oteyza and his supporters to bring PEMEX under control.

Another apparent defeat for the PEMEX expansionists under Díaz Serrano occurred in the summer of 1981. With market forces (specifically a world oil glut) pushing for moderate pricing policies, Díaz Serrano engineered a price reduction of four dollars per barrel in early June. Most analysts felt this was a rational move if Mexico was to retain its customers. But the decision was politically unpopular in Mexico, since many interpreted it as "selling-out" to the industrial nations that import Mexico's oil (particularly the United States). Faced with mounting criticism, Díaz Serrano took complete responsibility (or blame) for the price reduction and resigned, saying that he did not want to be an "element of discord." He was replaced by Moctezuma Cid, the former treasury minister, but the real victor seemed to be Oteyza.

As secretary of resources and industrial promotion, Oteyza was nominally the immediate superior of the PEMEX chief. But Díaz Serrano had molded PEMEX into the largest single employer in Mexico and, some say, the most important enterprise in Latin America. Hence, he operated with near complete autonomy from Oteyza. After his resignation, however, Oteyza began to make the major decisions for PEMEX.

The secretary of resources and industrial promotion was determined that Mexico would not bend to the international market forces operating in the summer of 1981, and he began to seek ways to nullify the Díaz Serrano price rollback. This stance was another manifestation of the nationalist perspective that desired to preserve Mexican sovereignty over its petroleum. By raising prices two dollars per barrel effective July 1 (half of the June reduction), Oteyza hoped to recoup some of the lost income. But the results were just the opposite, as customers began canceling orders. Petroleum exports went from 1.43 million bpd in May to just 0.7 million bpd in July. Government revenues lost in that month exceeded $700 million, and the federal budget was cut 4 percent across the board. In effect, Oteyza was forced to retreat from his original pricing policy of July, and on August 5 he reduced prices almost back to the lower level set by Díaz Serrano in June. Though the former PEMEX chief was not resurrected politically, he was at least vindicated. As one oil analyst in Mexico City was quoted after prices were lowered in August, "Today is one of the smoggiest days I've seen here, but I imagine the view from Díaz Serrano's office is crystal clear" (*Dallas Times Herald*, 5 August 1981). By November oil exports were back up to 1.4 million bpd due to a combination of more price decreases and an improvement in the mixture of crude being sold.

Though Díaz Serrano did lose his job, this price fiasco is just one example of the transparency of the perceived triumphs of the nationalists who posited the "petrolization" argument and hoped to reverse that trend. Despite the government's rhetoric to the effect that Mexico was conserving its petroleum, that it was avoiding the pitfalls of an Iran, and that the economy was not dependent on petroleum, despite the publicized ceilings spelled out by the Energy Program, and despite the sacking of Díaz Serrano, petroleum policy during the López Portillo administration was biased heavily in the direction of the growth strategy. From 1975 to 1981 total petroleum production tripled, and even in 1982, when the economic crisis hit Mexico, total production increased 19 percent over 1981 (table 31). Exploration activities increased even more than production, with proven reserves going from 11 billion barrels in 1976 to 72.5 billion in 1983. Common practice was to set a ceiling, reach that ceiling earlier than expected, and then adjust it upwards. In October of 1977 total production was 1 million bpd and the ceiling set for 1982 was 2.25 million bpd. But this level was reached in 1980, whereupon it was increased to 2.75 million bpd with a 1.5 million bpd limit for exports. In June 1982 both of these ceilings were surpassed, and by December total oil production exceeded the government-established limit by 9 percent.

These increases in production in 1982 occurred despite the oversupply of oil in international markets. While OPEC was attempting to support oil prices by reducing its exports 18 percent in 1982, Mexico was maintaining among the lowest prices in the world and increasing its output (Central Intelligence Agency, *International Energy Statistical Review*; and Petróleos Mexicanos). In fact, between 1979 and 1982 Mexico's oil production increased 70 percent while OPEC's production fell 40 percent. Mexico exports about a 50–50 mixture of its more expensive light crude (Isthmus) and its cheaper heavy crude (Maya). The average price for this mixture has undercut OPEC at least since November 1981, when OPEC unified its prices at the reference price of Arabian light. And from February 1982, when Mexico lowered its oil prices immediately after the devaluation, until March 1983, when all international oil prices dropped, the price of Mexican light crude alone was $1.50 per barrel lower than the Arabian light (table 32).

Table 31
Mexico's Crude Oil Production
(Million Barrels per Day)

				Yearly Averages				
1975	1976	1977	1978	1979	1980	1981	1982	1983
0.81	0.90	1.09	1.33	1.62	1.94	2.31	2.75	2.67

Source: Petróleos Mexicanos, Anuario estadístico, and unpublished data.

By the end of the López Portillo sexenio oil had clearly become the engine of growth for the rest of the economy (Corredor Esnaola 1981). Petroleum's share of the gross domestic product had doubled; it accounted for over three-quarters of total exports (compared to only one-third in 1978); and it provided about 30 percent of all federal revenues (compared to only 11 percent as late as 1979). Furthermore, strictures placed on the geographic concentration of customers were not closely followed. Though PEMEX maintained that U.S. exports continued to be only 50 percent of the total in 1982 (Petróleos Mexicanos, Memoria de Labores 1982, p. 16), other reports suggested the U.S. share was closer to 60 percent (Proceso, 31 January 1983). In August 1981 Mexico did become the first country (and so far the only country) to sign a long-term contract to sell oil to the U.S. Strategic Petroleum Reserve, and in 1982 Mexico replaced Saudi Arabia as the principal source of U.S. oil imports. In sum, "petrolization" was occurring and there were few signs of any reversals of direction.

Though the de la Madrid administration made notable changes in other policy areas (exchange rates, tariffs, price controls, for example), the growth strategy for petroleum was not substantially altered with the succession. After peaking in January 1983 at 1.6 million bpd, oil exports did begin a slight decline in February. But this was due more to market conditions (especially buyers anticipating a price decrease) than to any real policy choice. In fact, in January PEMEX announced that the level of petroleum exports would respond to foreign exchange needs, which were substantial (Proceso, 31 January 1983). Government figures in early 1983 forecasted that petroleum was to provide 80 percent of all foreign exchange from exports in 1983 (Wall Street Journal, 24 February 1983). And in February Silva Herzog and at least one government study suggested that petroleum exports could be increased to offset any losses from the inevitable price decrease.[14] The only perceivable difference in the new government's petroleum policy was a more cooperative attitude toward

Table 32

Crude Oil Prices since November 1981, Mexico and OPEC

(Dollars per Barrel)

Type of Crude	API Gravity	Nov. 1981	Jan. 1982	Feb. 1982	March 1983	Oct. 1983	April 1984
Arabian light (OPEC reference)	34°	34.00	34.00	34.00	29.00	29.00	29.00
Mexican light (Isthmus)	32°	35.00	35.00	32.50	29.00	29.00	29.00
Mexican heavy (Maya)	22°	28.50	26.50	25.00	23.00	25.00	25.50
Mexican average[a]		31.75	30.75	28.75	26.00	27.00	27.25

Sources: U.S. Energy Information Administration, *Weekly Petroleum Status Report*; and Petróleos Mexicanos.

Note: [a] Assuming a 50-50 mixture of Isthmus and Maya.

OPEC. Prior to the March price adjustments, PEMEX and other Mexican government officials worked closely with OPEC in deciding on a new price level. Then on March 14, the prices for Mexican light and Arabian light were unified at $29 per barrel, and Mexico pledged not to engage in a price war with other oil exporters.

National Development Plans

Though the Energy Program alluded to the relevance of petroleum policy to the industrial sector, the strategy of industrial promotion made possible by enhanced state revenues was more specifically addressed in two development plans issued in 1979 and 1980: the National Plan of Industrial Development (Plan Nacional de Desarrollo Industrial, or the Industrial Plan), and the Overall Development Plan (Plan Global de Desarrollo, PGD). Actually these were two of the more than ten plans devised by the López Portillo team, which seemed to be adopting a new commitment to economic planning at the national level.[15] But the Industrial Plan in particular was the most important policy initiative among the sectorial programs, and the PGD was significant in that it was an attempt to bring together all the sectorial plans.

Economic development planning actually dates back to the 1930s in Mexico.[16] The government party issued the first two plans: the Primer Plan Sexenal del Gobierno Mexicano, 1934–40, and the Segundo Plan Sexenal 1941–46. But these served primarily political functions, since they addressed social problems and were couched in revolutionary doctrine. However, the next planning experience was relevant to economic policy and projections. In the 1950s the Investment Commission, which functioned directly under the president at that time, prepared the Programa Nacional de Inversiones 1953–58. This document for the first time presented a national plan of investment and included projections for growth in national income and investments.

Two efforts in the 1960s were more ambitious endeavors, but their impact on economic policy or economic growth was still minimal. Partially in response to the requirements of agreements signed under the rubric of the Alliance for Progress, the Secretariat of the Treasury in coordination with the Secretariat of the Presidency drafted the Plan de Acción Inmediata 1962–64, which predicted overall and sectorial growth rates congruent with projected levels of investment. It was more detailed than earlier plans, but it was not widely disseminated even within government circles. The most recent plan prior to López Portillo was the Plan Nacional de Desarrollo Económico y Social 1966–70, written by the Comisión Intersecretarial para la Formulación de Planes de Desarrollo Económico y Social with input from both the Treasury and Presidency secretariats. This plan introduced incentives to private investment and had a proper macroeconomic framework. Echeverría chose not to engage in planning per se (though he clearly enlarged the economic role of the government), but López Portillo greatly refined the art of planning and engaged in a wholesale effort to develop coordinated plans for all sectors. In fact, one of the major accomplishments of his administrative reform in 1977 was to create an upgraded Secretariat of Planning and Budgeting whose primary functions included overseeing the formulation of national sectorial plans and the PGD.

National Plan of Industrial Development.

In February of 1977 Oteyza, as secretary of resources and industrial promotion, submitted to López Portillo an initial industrial programming scheme that made projections for different industrial sectors. These projections suggested that both shortfalls and excesses in investment existed in different industrial groups. The president then instructed the Industry Secretariat to devise a National Industrial Development Plan. In November 1978 Oteyza submitted a plan to López Portillo for the next four years with projections until 1990. After some amendments and changes, the plan was finalized, and its principal arguments were outlined by the president in February 1979. The full plan was made public by Oteyza on March 12, published in the *Diario Oficial* on May 17, and later published in two volumes by the Secretariat of Resources and Industrial Promotion.[17] It contained an analysis of the historical characteristics and failures of the Mexican industrial sector, a description of broad objectives and aims, a macroeconomic framework, and detailed economic projections up to 1990. But the factors that made this industrial plan so unique and important were the specific and concrete designations of the sectorial and regional priorities, the policy instruments to accomplish its goals, the nineteen decrees and laws to accompany it, and the proposed plant and machinery purchases of four state enterprises. For the first time in Mexico, a plan was more than just rhetoric.

It began by outlining the four basic failures of the industrialization process in Mexico: (1) industry relied too much on the domestic market, creating small, inefficient firms unable to compete externally; (2) industry was too heavily concentrated in three metropolitan centers; (3) production was oriented too much toward import substitution in consumer goods; and (4) a few extremely large firms in dynamic branches coexisted with a multitude of smaller firms. The fairly exhaustive list of objectives and aims attempted to address these failures and included the promotion of the production of both basic consumer goods and capital goods, the development of high-productivity industries capable of competing in international markets, taking advantage of natural resources and domestic processing (adding value in Mexico), the integration of the industrial sector through productive branches of capital goods, the achievement of a greater equilibrium between large and small industries, the decentralization of industrial production geographically, increased employment, the stimulation of investment, and a diminished deficit in the balance of payments through industrial development.

The economic projections were quite extensive, estimating gross domestic production, employment, investment (public and private), trade, and value-added, and the data were disaggregated into as many as forty-six different economic sectors. An important characteristic of the plan's projections was that they were divided into two types: (1) "base" projections, which would be achieved under the existing policy framework (without the plan); and (2) "plan" projections, which would be achieved under the new

Table 33
Selected Economic Projections, National Plan of Industrial Development
(Percentages)

Projection	Average Annual Growth Rate				
	1979–80	1980–81	1981–82	1982–85	1985–90
GDP, total					
Plan	8.2	9.5	10.6	10.2	10.5
Base	6.8	6.4	6.9	6.4	6.4
Economically active population					
Plan	3.4	4.1	5.1	5.4	6.7
Base	3.0	3.2	3.8	3.7	4.2
GDP, in manufacturing					
Plan	8.2	9.7	12.4	12.1	10.8
Base	6.4	5.6	7.4	7.0	6.5
Private capital formation					
Plan	9.0	10.4	14.0	12.8	8.9
Base	7.7	6.6	9.6	10.1	7.4
Government capital formation					
Plan	10.0	15.0	20.0	22.3	25.6
Base	9.5	14.0	17.0	19.3	15.5

Source: Plan nacional de desarrollo industrial 1979–82, Vol 1:73–144.

policy framework (with the plan). Of course, in all cases the "plan" projections estimated higher growth rates than the "base" projections (table 33).

A major achievement of the plan was the enumeration of sectorial and regional priorities for industrial development. Seventy priority branches representing 60 percent of industrial value-added were divided into two basic categories. The first category (no. 1 in the plan), with maximum priority, included the agroindustrial sector (particularly food processing and fertilizers), capital goods (machinery and equipment for use in other industries), and other key industrial inputs (especially steel and cement). The second category (no. 2 in the plan), with lower priority, contained nondurable consumer goods (textiles, shoes, soap, paper), durable consumer goods (appliances, furniture, and parts and equipment for transportation vehicles, the health industry, and electronic communication), and intermediate goods (petrochemicals, metallurgical products, and construction materials).

In establishing regional priorities, three geographic zones were created with some intrazone divisions, as well. The goal was to reduce the share of the Valley of Mexico (Mexico City and its environs) in industrial production from 50 percent (the 1979 level) to 40 percent. This goal anticipated that two-thirds of the increase in industrial production would occur outside the Mexico City area.

The first priorities were the frontier and coastal regions, which would promote the exportation of manufactured goods. Thus Zone I was to receive the most preferential stimuli. Zone IA included four industrial seaports (Coatzacoalcos, Tampico, Salina Cruz, and Lázaro Cárdenas in the states of Veracruz, Tamaulipas, Oaxaca, and Michoacán, respectively) and their twenty-four surrounding municipalities. Zone 1B was devoted primarily to urban industrial development and included ninety-nine municipalities from other coastal areas, border regions with potential for expansion, and interior cities previously considered as priorities in the urban development plan. Many of the areas in Zone I were chosen because of their location along the national network of natural gas distribution or because they possessed raw materials that must be processed near their source.

Zone II was labeled the "state priorities" and included those cities that state governors designated as priorities in their state plans for urban development. Obviously, this zone provided considerable flexibility. In cooperation with state entities, the public works and industry ministries at the federal level were charged with integrating state priorities into the decentralization scheme.

Finally, Zone III was concentrated around Mexico City and was assigned the lowest priority. Zone IIIA was the area of "controlled growth" and encompassed Mexico City (that is, the Federal District) and 53 surrounding municipalities (almost all in the State of Mexico). Essentially this area was to receive no incentives. Zone IIIB was the area of "consolidation," which was to receive limited incentives in order to preserve the dynamism already developed but to avoid the negative consequences of more concentration. This zone incorporated 144 municipalities from the states of Hidalgo, Mexico, Morelos, Puebla, and Tlaxcala, all of which surround Mexico City. Hence, Zone IIIB included the outskirts of the industrial belt in the Valley of Mexico.

Apart from sectorial and regional priorities, a special category in the plan was reserved for small industries. An industry was defined as "small" if its investment in fixed assets was less than two hundred times the annual minimum wage in Mexico City. In 1979 this figure was approximately 10 million pesos (or about $440 thousand at the 1979 exchange rate). The plan claimed to be recognizing the important role that small enterprises play in employment and in certain branches (particularly foodstuffs, metallurgy, and basic consumer goods). The desire was that smaller firms would become more integrated with the activities of larger industries (through subcontracting and the like) and that larger firms would become more diversified (fewer oligopolies and more exports of manufactured goods).

All of these priorities became meaningful in the plan as they were matched with specific incentives. The key instrument was a fiscal stimulus through a federal tax credit. The credit would be issued to a firm as a Certificate of Fiscal Promotion (Certificado de Promoción Fiscal, CEPROFI), which would be valid for five years, could be applied against any federal tax not already dedicated by law to a specific purpose, and would replace any current tax exemptions. The tax credit could be given for both increased investment and additional employment generated.

The size of the investment tax credit would be determined by sectorial and regional priorities (table 34). The only credit available to industries in Zone IIIA (Mexico City) would be for the purchase of new machinery and equipment made in Mexico. This credit would be equal to 5 percent of the purchase price. Outside Zone IIIA all small enterprises could receive a tax credit of 25 percent of investment. Regional priorities were considered here in that small firms in Zones I and II could take the credit for investment in both expansion *and* diversification, but small industries elsewhere (except Zone IIIA, with no investment tax credit) could receive the credit for expansion only. For industries other than the small firms, the investment tax credit was either 10, 15, or 20 percent, depending on the sectorial and regional priorities. Industries in sectorial Category 1 and located any-

Table 34
Levels of Tax Credits, National Plan of Industrial Development

Region	Small Firms	Sectorial Priorities			All Industrial Activities	
		Categories		All Others	Purchase of Machinery and Equipment Made in Mexico	Employment Created by Additional Work Shifts
		1	2			
Zone I	25% of Investment	20% of Investment & 20% of Employment	15% of Investment & 20% of Employment	None	5%	20% of Employment
Zone II	25% of Investment	20% of Investment & 20% of Employment	10% of Investment & 20% of Employment	None	5%	20% of Employment
Rest of country	25% of Investment[a]	20% of Investment & 20% of Employment	10% of Investment[a] & 20% of Employment[a]	None	5%	20% of Employment
Zone IIIA	None	None	None	None	5%	None
Zone IIIB	25% of Investment[a]	20% of Investment[a] & 20% of Employment[a]	10% of Investment[a] & 20% of Employment[a]	None	5%	20% of Employment

Source: Plan nacional de desarrollo industrial 1979–82, Vol 1: 181.

Notes: [a]Could be applied only for expansion of productivity capacity within the same industrial activity.
Zone I = frontier and coastal regions
Zone II = state priorities
Zone III = Mexico City and environs
Zone IIIA = controlled growth areas
Zone IIIB = consolidation area

where outside Zone III were offered a credit of 20 percent of investment for expansion and diversification. The lowest rate, 10 percent (for expansion only), was offered to Category 2 industries not in Zones I and II.

To counter any tendency that the investment tax credit would have to substitute capital for labor, an employment tax credit was also made available. This credit was a uniform 20 percent of the annual payroll cost of the additional employment (calculated according to the annual minimum wage in that zone). The regional priorities were significant, since Zones I and II received the employment credit for expansion and diversification of output, whereas Zone III received it only for expansion. Both the employment and investment tax credits were offered to all industries except the small enterprises. But these firms could choose either the "small enterprise" priority (with 25 percent investment credit) or the appropriate sectorial category (with 10 to 20 percent investment and 20 percent employment credit). Finally, in an effort to promote more intensive use of existing facilities, a 20 percent employment tax credit was given for additional work shifts in every region except Zone IIIA.

Another significant tool of industrial promotion in the plan was a scheme of differential (or subsidized) prices for energy and petrochemical products of state-owned companies. In the seaports of Zone IA, new installations or existing plants expanding by at least 40 percent would receive a 30 percent discount on the cost of energy consumption. Petrochemical enterprises would also get a 30 percent reduction on the price of petrochemical inputs, if they exported at least 25 percent of the plant capacity for a minimum of three years. Zone IB was treated in a more complex fashion, with the main criterion being the supplies available in that region. Zone IB industries in the states of Tabasco and Chiapas were to receive a 30 percent reduction on the prices of any two of these inputs: electricity, natural gas, fuel oil, or petrochemicals. A 15 percent discount in the price of natural gas was available to Zone 1B municipalities located along the pipeline networks. And a 10 percent cost reduction on fuel oil was given to Zone IB cities not on the natural gas distribution network. These subsidized prices were not granted to firms outside of Zone I.

The last means of industrial promotion contained in the plan was a vague promise of increased financial support. Increased revenues from hydrocarbon exports were said to provide the opportunity for strengthening state financial assistance (through existing trust funds) for industry, particularly small and medium firms, as well as capital-goods firms. The plan pledged facilitated access to resources and technical services for small and medium industries and widened volume of credit and better terms of credit for capital-goods industries.

Two final aspects of the Industrial Plan further enhanced its utility and preciseness. First, lists were published of the probable purchases of equipment and machinery from 1979 to 1986 by four major state-owned enterprises: PEMEX, the CFE (electricity), SIDERMEX (steel firms of Altos Hornos, SICARTSA, and Fundidora de Monterrey), and Fertilizantes Mexicanos. These projections of future demand were expected to be useful to private companies in a position to supply any of these materials. Second, the plan officially coordinated nineteen laws, decrees, and agreements regarding industrial development that had been promulgated by the state since 20 June 1977. These documents (all of which were previously issued in the *Diario Oficial*) were published in Volume 2 of the plan and fortified its juridical nature.

Overall Development Plan

Whereas the Industrial Plan was a fairly concrete document with clear-cut objectives and specific instruments for achieving them, the Overall Development Plan (PGD) was a more ambiguous attempt to coordinate all the sectorial plans. The original strategy was to begin with an overall blueprint and develop the sectorial plans from that.[18] The more detailed sectorial plans emerged first, however, and the PGD became only an *ex post facto* statement that primarily tried to stress social rather than economic goals.

As stated above, one of the principal functions of López Portillo's new Secretariat of Planning and Budgeting was to devise a comprehensive economic plan. The first plan was drawn up in 1977 as "Programa de Acción del Sector Público 1978–1982" by this ministry. But later the planning secretary, García Sainz, decided to include the private sector and create a true overall development plan. This expanded plan was presented to López Portillo in general outline in March 1979—just as the Industrial Plan was being made public. In May, de la Madrid replaced García Sainz and then set out to put his personal stamp on the overall plan. In its third version, the PGD was released to the public by de la Madrid on 15 April 1980.[19]

In its final form, the PGD was more of a political document than an economic blueprint. It was essentially an attempt to defend the continuation of state participation in the economy and, in a vague fashion, to stress social aims of equality and justice over economic accomplishments. In contrast to the specific objectives, priorities, and instruments of the Industrial Plan, the PGD comprised mostly rhetorical promises for higher standards of living and sustained economic growth. It was an extremely optimistic document, apparently based on a positive-sum approach. It set no additional priorities and seemed to assume that all groups and sectors would benefit from the policies of the López Portillo government. This optimism and ambiguity were evident throughout.

The four objectives of the PGD provided the first indication of its vague yet all-encompassing nature. It pledged to (1) strengthen the independence of Mexico as a democratic nation; (2) generate employment opportunities and maintain a minimum standard of living for all; (3) promote rapid, sustained, and efficient economic growth; and (4) improve the distribution of income among people, sectors, and regions. In the following section, the PGD focused directly on the concerns of labor. It declared that the development strategy was fundamentally geared toward generating sufficient employment opportunities, that petroleum was intimately tied to this strategy, and that the strategy was to be accomplished through twenty-two basic policy actions. However, these basic actions were not noticeably more concrete than the four objectives. Some of the highlights included the strengthening of the state in order to satisfy the demands of society; the reorientation of productive structure toward basic goods and capital goods; the "rationalization" of consumption and stimulation of investment; the use of petroleum as a lever of development; the use of more resources for basic well-being; increased and improved basic education; and controlled inflation. The most specific statements here were pledges to create 2.2 million jobs between 1980 and 1982 and to achieve at least 8 percent annual growth in GDP betwen 1980 and 1982. However, as was the case with all twenty-two "actions," there was no realistic discussion of how they were to be accomplished.

In the last section before the requisite econometric model and economic projections, the PGD differentiated its policy guidelines among seven areas: public spending, "general" economic policy, energy policy, sectorial policy, regional policy, social policy, and policy affecting salaries, prices, profits, and taxes. It emphasized the role of the public sector by anticipating that total public expenditures would rise 12 percent annually from 1980 to 1982 (compared to its projected 8 percent for GDP) and by anticipating that public investment would increase 14 percent annually. Yet, the "general" economic policies were to be oriented toward avoiding inflationary financing and decreasing foreign debt. A forecast of petroleum revenues was made as well as a plan for their distribution. The largest share (almost one-third) was reserved for reinvestment in PEMEX. The PGD basically reiterated the sectorial and regional policies of the Industrial Plan while stating a special attempt to link industry with agriculture and commerce. Finally, it promised to increase the relative proportion of salaries in national income and to establish a generous wage policy.

The PGD did include the normal economic projections, though not as detailed as those found in the Industrial Plan. All of its projections were for the three-year period from 1980 to 1982.[20] It forecasted average annual growth in the GDP at 8.0 percent, with all sectors showing improved growth rates compared to those of the two preceding decades. The most rapid expansion was to be in industry (10.8 percent annually) and the lowest rate was predicted for agriculture (4.0 percent annually). In achieving the employment objectives of the PGD, job opportunities were to increase at a 4.2 percent average annual rate. Total investment was expected to grow at a 13.5 percent annual pace, with public sector investment (at 14 percent) slightly surpassing private sector investment (at 13 percent). The enhanced role of the state in the economy was also evident in the projection that public expenditures as a share of GDP were to average 40.0 percent between 1980 and 1982 (compared to 37.4 percent for the 1977–1979 period and 26.2 percent from 1965 to 1976). Despite this growth, the public sector deficit was to shrink from 6.4 percent of GDP in the 1977–1979 period to 4.2 percent in 1980–1982. Further optimism was found in the balance-of-payments predictions, which called for the current accounts deficit to fall from 2.85 percent of GDP in 1977–1979 to only 0.65 percent in 1980–1982. The PGD revealed the principal source for this balance-of-payments improvement by estimating that petroleum income as a percentage of total current accounts income would average 46.51 percent in 1980–1982 (compared to 18.24 percent in 1977–1979).

Reactions of Industrialists

During the López Portillo *sexenio* the private sector was reported as responding in a fairly positive way to the planning process and to the plans themselves. In particular, the private sector reacted favorably to two aspects of the plans: (1) the forecasts of future economic trends and policies, which gave business leaders a rational basis for decision making; and (2) the lists of upcoming equipment requirements for the public enterprises (FitzGerald 1980:135). More generally, López Portillo's approach was called "participative planning," in which all sectors were consulted and urged to participate in the process (Blair 1980:4–5). Procedures under López Portillo did not in any sense produce a centrally planned economy that simply dictated policy to the various sectors. Rather, as I indicated in chapter 6, these plans are best seen as examples of the regulatory policy process. They presented broad goals and even concrete policy instruments (in the case of the Industrial Plan), but the state retained considerable flexibility in terms of implementing the various plans. And the private sector remained optimistic that its voice would be heard at the ongoing implementation stage.

However, this "participative" and regulatory policy process did not produce unquestioning support from private industrialists for the national development plans. They expressed a number of criticisms with regard to the objectives and impact of the plans and were especially concerned over further state encroachment in the economy and the possible obligatory nature of the plans.

Many industrialists told me that the government moved too fast in formulating the Industrial Plan and devised its various parts in an unorganized and irrational manner. Indeed, the nineteen laws and decrees "coordinated" by the plan often seemed quite independent of one another; hence the Industrial Plan was partly an *ex post facto* attempt to bring together these disjointed promulgations. Industrialists in the urban centers (particularly the Association of Industries of the State of Mexico) also opposed the plan's emphasis on industrial decentralization. Their concern was that regional industries would benefit to the detriment of the dynamic leading industries in the large urban areas. There are indications that such resistance to decentralization efforts will prove quite powerful. For example, an industrial park was begun by the government at Lázaro Cárdenas in 1976, but by 1981 not a single national private sector firm had located there (*Latin America Regional Report*, 13 February 1981). And the data on the tax credits (CEPROFIs) granted under the Industrial Plan show little success in the decentralization efforts of the government (table 35). Despite their preferential status, the ports of Zone I had attracted very few tax credits; whereas the "controlled growth" region of Zone IIIA (principally Mexico City) received considerable tax credits in spite of its very limited incentives.

Though the economic estimates contained in the plans generally were welcomed by the private sector as indicators of future directions, some problems were noted regarding weaknesses of certain projections and contradictions between predictions for different plans. A flaw often cited in the Industrial Plan was its low estimate of inflation. This plan optimistically ignored the negative effects of high inflation, and many correctly felt the assumption of lower inflation would not prove valid and would bias other projections—many of which were already viewed as too high. Possibly in anticipation of not meeting all the goals, Andrés de Oteyza wisely presented both base and plan projections. The base projections were sufficiently conservative so that they would be easy to surpass.

Many industrialists criticized some discrepancy between the respective forecasts of the Industrial Plan and the PGD. In most cases, the Industrial Plan was the more expansionist document. In the 1980 to 1982 period, it

Table 35
Tax Credits (CEPROFIs) Granted under National Plan of Industrial
Development, September 1979–March 1983

Region	Sectorial Priorities (value in millions of pesos)			All Industrial Activities (value in million of pesos)		
	Small Firms	Categories 1	2	Purchase of Mexican-Made Machinery and Equipment	Employment[a]	Total
Zone I						
ports	65	71	80	126	11	353
	(20)	(2,322)	(836)	(16)	(25)	(3,219)
Urban						
industry	1,922	1,286	951	1,701	242	6,102
	(535)	(5,849)	(2,372)	(331)	(245)	(9,332)
Zone II	783	1,067	688	1,122	181	3,841
	(220)	(3,051)	(1,138)	(151)	(179)	(4,739)
Zone IIIA	0	0	0	2,208	0	2,208
				(1,423)		(1,423)
Zone IIIB	284	108	413	381	31	1,217
	(144)	(261)	(701)	(101)	(36)	(1,243)
Rest of						
country	351	674	522	1,131	123	2,801
	(100)	(3,027)	(720)	(170)	(113)	(4,130)
Total	3,405	3,206	2,654	6,669	588	16,522
	(1,019)	(14,510)	(5,767)	(2,192)	(598)	(24,086)

Source: Secretaría de Hacienda y Crédito Público, unpublished data.

Note: [a]New jobs and additional work shifts.

expected 10.0 percent annual growth in the GDP (8.0 percent for the PGD) and 11.0 percent annual growth in industry (10.8 percent for the PGD). It also anticipated greater imports and exports, more public sector consumption and investment, and faster growth in oil. On the other hand, the PGD predicted a higher rate of job creation, higher inflation, and higher growth rates in agriculture. To some extent these differences in the plans reflected the particular orientations of their principal architects (Oteyza for the Industrial Plan and de la Madrid for the PGD). Oteyza was less cautious in pushing for economic growth and was more supportive of the government's economic role, whereas de la Madrid generally favored more moderate growth and greater reliance on the private sector. In any case, the contradictions between the plans were often confusing to Mexican entrepreneurs.

Of course, by 1982 the forecasts of both plans were meaningless, though their projections in terms of economic growth proved reasonably accurate through 1981 (see table 36). Actual annual growth in GDP, manufacturing, jobs, and investment in 1981 were very close to the figures forecasted in the PGD and the Industrial Plan. But the discrepancies in terms of deficits and inflation between plan projections and actuality were substantial and foretold the economic collapse in 1982. Expressed as percentages of GDP, the current accounts deficit was over seven times larger than projected and the budget deficit was triple the expected level in 1981. Inflation in the same year was also almost three times as large as that envisioned. In 1982 most of the growth statistics were negative, the public sector deficit was still expanding, and inflation had ballooned to near 100 percent. The López Portillo administration clearly had not foreseen the enormous disequilibriums resulting from its growth strategy, and the government's 1982 projections were far from the reality.

The Industrial Plan itself contained several apparent contradictions that further confused industrialists. In the first place, it included objectives aimed at promoting basic consumer goods to achieve self-sufficiency in staples as well as developing high-productivity industries to achieve industrial integration and to stress manufactured exports. These goals addressed industrial branches with widely disparate characteristics and needs, and planning decisions could possibly require choices between promoting one branch or another. Also, the seventy priority sectors ranged from foodstuffs to capital goods (altogether totaling 60 percent of value-added in industry), which further suggested that some tradeoffs would have to be recognized. Finally, the plan did not seem to comprehend the problems of wanting to encourage efficient, capital-intensive industries while also generating more jobs. As revealed by the data on tax credits granted under the plan (table 35), investment in capital-goods industries (included in sectorial priority no. 1) proved very popular, with the greatest value of tax credits, whereas the creation of employment attracted little interest, and very few tax credits were granted for the generation of jobs or additional work shifts. Of course, all of these contradictions were indicative of the regulatory policy process in Mexico and were left to be resolved

Table 36

Planning Goals Compared with Actual Achievements, 1980–1982, Mexico

(Percentages)

Plan	GDP	Manufacturing	Employment	Public Investment	Private Investment	Current Accts. Deficit[a]	Public Accts. Deficit[a]	Inflation
PGD, 1980–82	8.0	10.8	4.2	14.0	13.0	0.7	4.2	10.0
Industrial Plan 1980–82	10.0	11.0	4.6	17.5	12.1	0.1	n.a.	8.0–10.0
Actual 1980	8.3	8.8	4.1	18.5	12.8	5.8	2.9	26.3
Actual 1981	8.1	8.0	5.4	17.0	13.6	4.9	14.0	28.7
Actual 1982	–0.2	–2.4	0.8	–12.7	–20.0	2.5	16.5	100.0

Sources: Table A–3; *Plan nacional de desarrollo industrial, 1979–82; Plan global de desarrollo, 1980–82;* Centro de Investigación y Docencia Económicas (1982:10); Banco de México, *Informe anual;* Inter-American Development Bank, *Economic and Social Progress in Latin America;* and Nacional Financiera, *La economía mexicana en cifras* (1981).

Note: [a] As % of GDP.

by the officials administering the plan. Hence, many of the most difficult decisions were postponed until the implementation stage, when individual industrialists would try to influence ministry officials as they made specific choices.

Although the implementation stage of the Industrial Plan provided many industrialists with hopes of affecting its form and impact, questions about how it was to be enforced also created some real concern among them. Not only were they worried about increased public investments, but many expressed fears that in administering the plan the state would force production, investment, and employment goals on unwilling private sector firms. The important question became the plan's obligatory nature, an issue that reflects the theme of the relative autonomy of the industrial sector as discussed in Part 2 here.

The López Portillo administration took several steps to implement the Industrial Plan between 1979 and 1981. First, an interministerial Industrial Development Commission (Comisión de Fomento Industrial) was established to coordinate all decisions under the plan.[21] The Industrial Development Commission was empowered to issue development programs (*programas de fomento*) for each priority sector. According to the plan (pp. 32–33) these programs were the mechanisms for "harmonizing actions with the entrepreneurial sector in order to fulfill and evaluate its course . . . within the framework of the Alliance for Production."

The development programs, which applied to whole industrial branches, superseded the previous manufacturing programs (*programas de fabricación*), which had applied to individual firms. Each development program was to detail specific incentives and measures of protection for the industries in that branch. In turn, the assisted firm would commit itself to achieving predetermined goals for investment, production, prices, exports, and for complete integration with national suppliers. Foreign enterprises would also agree to terms for their Mexicanization within a certain period. Each development program, then, included three aspects: "objectives and targets established under the terms of the plan for each activity; incentives and assistance available for new investment; and agreements that should be entered into by firms undertaking said programs."[22]

Individual firms interested in the incentives were required to register with the Industrial Development Commission for the appropriate development program. Once they agreed to the terms of the program, the proper government departments would award the incentives. The commission was granted the power to verify at any time the information submitted by firms adhering to a certain program. It was also instructed to certify that all commitments were being fulfilled, and the registered firms were required to grant the necessary facilities for inspection. According to the Industrial Plan, "Incentives must be granted in line with commitments, and once agreed upon, *they can become mandatory*" (my emphasis).[23] Any firms found in noncompliance with any of the agreements were subject to the suspension of all incentives and, "where necessary, to the application of predetermined [but unspecified] sanctions."[24]

It was precisely these mandatory aspects of the plan that most troubled the private sector. Carlos Salinas de Gortari, the general director of social and economic policy at the Secretariat of Planning and Budgeting, explained the state's view: "We are telling them [private firms]: If you don't invest enough or if you charge too much for your products we will remove the protection you enjoy from foreign competition. Our private sector is rational; when you have clear objectives and rules of the game then you can work with people. Those who don't come aboard are going to lose out badly."[25] Industrialists retorted that the plan should not be made obligatory for the private sector. At the annual meeting of COPARMEX in March 1979, its president, Manuel J. Clouthier, in the presence of López Portillo, criticized trends (implying the Industrial Plan) toward "a paternalistic state adopting the attitude of supreme benefactor." He said the state should put into effect a sensible and realistic policy "without discouraging the initiative and programs deriving from private investment" (*Unomásuno*, 17 March 1979). Later that month, a former president of CONCAMIN, Luis Guzmán de Alba, also speaking before López Portillo, was quoted as saying that the Industrial Plan should not be "a path of state interventionist policy." On the same occasion, Andrés de Oteyza tried to be conciliatory. He stressed that "the climate is now propitious for constructive attitudes, for a joining of efforts, for persuasion" (*Excélsior*, 30 March 1979).

In a November 1979 meeting labeled "Primera Reunión Nacional de Industrialización," CONCAMIN continued to stress that the private sector would not be coerced. At this meeting Prudencio López, head of the CCE, outlined the three characteristics that entrepreneurial groups wanted to see in the national development plans: (1) obligatory *only* for the public sector and oriented toward private initiative; (2) congruent with economic reality; and (3) accessible for the participation of entrepreneurial, labor, professional, and technical groups (*Análisis Político*, 26 November 1979). At the annual convention of the Instituto Mexicano de Ejecutivos de Finanzas the following year, Ernesto Rubio de Cueto, head of CONCAMIN, emphasized that the state could not impose its objectives on private capital and that individual entrepreneurs should determine their role within the Industrial Plan (*Proceso*, 20 October 1980).

López Portillo began to feel this continual pressure from business groups and in October 1980 he went out of his way to emphasize that central planning was only binding on the public sector (*Latin America Weekly Report*, 31 October 1980). Indeed, the Industrial Plan itself (pp. 33–34) had allowed for the industrial chambers and associations to serve an important role in gaining the cooperation of individual firms in the development programs. This government pledge not to obligate private firms to meet specific goals of national plans, together with the inclusion of the private sector groups in the implementation process, helped to mollify many of the critics from the industrial sector. By mid-1981 several development programs had been signed and there was no evidence available of state coercion, sanctions, or the like applied against private industrialists.[26]

Planning under de la Madrid

Though the de la Madrid team emphasized a strong commitment to national planning, its only concrete accomplishment in the initial stages was to extend the policies of the 1979 Industrial Plan. Only days after de la Madrid was "tapped" by López Portillo (September 1981), Carlos Salinas de Gortari became head of the Institute for Political, Economic, and Social Studies of the PRI and in this capacity quickly presented a *plan básico* to the National Assembly of the PRI on October 5 (Instituto de Estudios Políticos Económicos y Sociales, Partido Revolucionario Institucional 1981; also see *Proceso*, 7 March 1983). This marked the beginning of "democratic planning" under the president-to-be, but it really was the continuation of a planning team that was first formed when de la Madrid became secretary of planning and budgeting in May 1979, and Salinas de Gortari directed the studies for the PGD within the same ministry.

The path to the formulation of the Plan Nacional de Desarrollo, 1983–1988 (PND) was long and complex, but the slow process seemed to serve more of a political than any economic purpose. In October 1981 de la Madrid announced that the *plan básico*, which reflected many of the vague principles of the PGD, would be analyzed by the PRI in consultation with the Mexican people. During the next eight months of the election campaign, over one hundred public meetings were held under this "popular consultation" with all social, political, and economic sectors. On 2 June 1982 Salinas de Gortari summarized the results of these and first presented the seven basic themes later to be emphasized in de la Madrid's inaugural address: revolutionary nationalism; integral democratization; egalitarian society; moral renovation; decentralization of national life; development, jobs, and the fight against inflation; and democratic planning. The planning hierarchy was expanded on July 20 when the PIR formed twenty-seven working groups to analyze the information collected over the previous eight months of "popular consultation."

When de la Madrid was inaugurated on December 1, he was only prepared to announce that the Plan Nacional would be made public in May of 1983. Despite months of studies and meetings and contrary to his prompt actions in other areas, the new government was not prepared to present a national economic plan. On 5 January 1983 a new Planning Law was promulgated that did little more than institutionalize the "popular consultation" and establish a National System of Democratic Planning (*Diario Oficial*, 5 January 1983). Under this National System, the president installed eighteen forums in early February (covering different economic and social sectors) that would hold more public meetings regarding the formulation of the National Plan. These forums and the creation of the new plan were coordinated by the secretary of planning and budgeting, Carlos Salinas de Gortari. As with the multitude of previous meetings, these forums were designed more for public consumption than for legitimate public input. Almost all of them were announced only a day or two before they took place, and participants were required to submit their statements in advance.

The first concrete results of planning under President de la Madrid were announced in late February, when the secretary of commerce and industrial promotion, Hernández Cervantes, presented to the annual meeting of CANACINTRA a Program for the Defense of the Productive Plant and of Employment. This program provided for public sector purchases to promote industrial recovery, new credits for industry, help in restructuring private sector debt, special support for small and medium-size industries, and, most important, the maintenance of the fiscal stimulants of the Industrial Plan of 1979. In May 1983 the Secretariat of Commerce and Industrial Promotion created a Program of Immediate Actions to Support Exports, which essentially simplified the paperwork required for exporters, eliminated almost all export tariffs, and promised a unified exchange rate and increased export credits. But, in advance of the May announcement of the Plan Nacional, the main achievement of the new government in the planning arena was the extension of previous policies. The role of the industrial sector in the planning strategy had not been substantially altered. In terms of the planning process under de la Madrid, entrepreneurs had not increased their input. Though private sector leaders stated in public their belief that the evolving plan would be "realistic and participative" rather than "utopian, centralized, and coercive" (*Proceso*, 7 February 1983), an air of apathy was also evident in private sector reactions to the "popular consultation" (interviews, February and March 1983).

The Plan Nacional de Desarrollo, 1983–1988 was finally announced by de la Madrid on 30 May 1983 (and published in the *Diario Oficial* on 31 May 1983 and in book form by the Secretaría de Programación y Presupuesto in June 1983). Though it was publicized as the blueprint for the de la Madrid *sexenio*, it contained no surprises and essentially elaborated the policies and objectives already put forth by the new administration. The new plan emphasized four broad objectives: to strengthen democratic institutions, to overcome the economic crisis, to recover the capacity for economic growth, and to initiate the required qualitative changes in the nation's economic, political, and social structures (pp. 12, 108–109). The economic and social strategy of the PND was then summarized in six areas, which were remarkably similar to the seven themes presented by Salinas de Grotari in June of 1982 and to the ten points of the recovery program announced by de la Madrid in his inaugural address (pp. 117–149). The plan specifically rejected more concrete declarations of policy or economic forecasts. It also did not include the detailed macroeconomic models of previous plans. Its only quantitative forecasts concerned GDP growth, which was projected to fall two to four percentage points in 1983, recover only slightly in 1984 to an annual growth rate between 0.0 and 2.5 percent, and finally rebound in the period from 1985 to 1988 to average yearly growth rates between 5 and 6 percent.

In terms of industrial policy, the PND did more closely link the industrial sector and the external sector (specifically, manufactured exports) and stated that the fundamental problem within Mexican industry had been overconcentration on the import substitution of consumer goods (pp. 314–337). The key elements of industrial strategy were said to be developing the supply of basic goods, selectively promoting the capital-goods industries to increase industrial integration, encouraging those industrial branches with the potential to export and to acquire foreign exchange, creating a *national* technological base, and fomenting efficient and competitive public enterprises. The leaders of both CONCAMIN and CANACINTRA praised the plan as a positive response to the economic crisis (*Unomásuno*, 31 May, 1 June 1983); however, in concrete terms the 1979 Industrial Plan (as modified slightly by the February Program for the Defense of the Productive Plant and of Employment and by the May Program of Immediate Actions to Support Exports) still remained the policy instrument most relevant to the industrial sector.

Development Strategies in Mexico and the "Cruel Dilemma"

This chapter has described a number of policy shifts vis-à-vis the industrial sector over the last few *sexenios*. López Portillo's Alliance for Production restored the confidence of industrialists after the disastrous (from the point of view of private capitalists) "shared development" policies of Echeverría. The differences between the two *sexenios* were at least partly the result of political pressures common to presidential transitions in Mexico. Substantial demands for change are made on the new leader on assuming office. The outgoing president retains no real influence in the political process, and the incoming president has the opportunity to build a new political coalition (Martínez de la Vega 1976).

The need to achieve political stability and a balance of political forces may also necessitate a policy shift from one president to another. This strategy has enabled the Mexican political system to incorporate most of the significant political groupings, from large capitalists to rural peasants. All of the groups, albeit at different times, must be courted by the political leadership. As one president is perceived to favor, even slightly, a particular group or ideology, the next president must balance the scales by leaning in the other direction. Changes in direction in order to balance the system may even occur within administrations: possibly feeling he had done too much for the private sector and wanting to leave office on a populist note, López Portillo turned toward the Left in his final year.

The transition from Echeverría to López Portillo demonstrated the leverage that the private sector has in this process. López Portillo was under considerable pressure from business groups to show that he was not simply an extension of Echeverría. He immediately set out to form his own political team (*camarilla* or *equipo*) and to establish his own goals. Private industrialists welcomed all of these changes. Thus, he built a political coalition based on the support of the private sector and more conservative forces and stressed a return to confidence in the government. Many of these moves were necessary to restore political calm after the upheavals of Echeverría's final months. To put the economy back in order and even to ensure the continued stability of the one-party system, López Portillo had to shift to the right and appease the groups (such as industrial chambers and associations) that Echeverría had alienated. (After the 1982 bank nationalization and exchange controls, de la Madrid was again under pressure to restore business confidence with a stabilization policy that put most of the burden on the lower classes.)

In facing Mexico's new status as both an ADC and an oil-exporting nation, López Portillo clearly pursued a growth-oriented development strategy. In doing so, he was abandoning most hopes for economic justice and more equitable income distribution. Many authors argue that all developing nations must confront the inevitable tradeoffs between growth and equity; that is, they must decide between emphasizing a quantitative goal like absolute economic growth or more qualitative objectives like human rights and economic equality.[27] Though some policymakers in Third World nations claim that they can stress economic expansion while avoiding the "cruel dilemma" posed by growth versus equality, much empirical evidence suggests that the benefits of "economic miracles" in developing countries are extremely slow in "trickling down" to the masses.[28]

This would appear to be the case in Mexico. Mexico's economic miracle in the postwar era has achieved over 6 percent average annual growth, but little of this growth has benefited the lower classes. According to one well-known study, "The degree of inequality in the distribution of Mexican income, no matter how it is measured, exceeds that of most of the world's developing countries" (Hansen 1974:83). Whereas Echeverría, at least rhetorically, tried to stress economic justice along with growth, López Portillo returned to the strategy of giving top priority to absolute growth. Only in 1982 did he emphasize equity as a public priority.

This growth strategy was particularly evident in two major policy concerns of the López Portillo *sexenio*: petroleum production and the Industrial Plan. As described above, López Portillo often publicly referred to the need to moderate petroleum production so as to conserve this important natural resource. But in reality his petroleum policy was heavily biased in the direction of growth. As a result, the economy was becoming steadily more dependent on petroleum, and petroleum provided almost all the good economic news (increased revenues, GNP growth, and industrial growth), but was also the cause of all the bad economic news (balance-of-payments deficits, inflation, and stagnation in nonoil exports). Petroleum dependence even had political implications, as the perceived economic luxuries of greater revenues caused the initial political reforms of the López Portillo administration (more rights to opposition parties and anticorruption campaigns, for example) to lose their impetus (Cleaves 1981).

The Industrial Plan also reflected the growth strategy that favored the business elites. Its main purpose was to utilize petroleum revenues to stimulate industrial development. Thus, growth in the industrial sector was expected to continue at high rates. On the other hand, it did not recognize problems of maldistributed income, and in fact many of its aspects were predicted to increase inequalities in income distribution (Blair 1980:10–11). The PGD did refer constantly to social goals like improved standards of living, but it was largely a vague political document whose function was to pacify the labor sector. In actuality, it contained no concrete rewards for the lower classes. The only potential difficulties the Industrial Plan presented to private industrialists were the possibilities of decreased private sector autonomy and enhanced government economic intervention. But the private sector, especially through the industrial chambers and associations, did play a role in "participative planning," and the industrialists' stern defense of their independence seemed to have counteracted any mandatory or obligatory factors in it.

8. Conclusion

This book has attempted to bridge the gap between research that classifies Mexico according to "system" variables such as economic dependency and regime type and research that describes Mexico as a unique country with economic and political systems that cannot be described or understood by broad categorizations.[1] Cross-national analyses, and even many case studies, cite Mexico as an example of an authoritarian nation that is economicaly dependent on the advanced industrial world (especially the United States). The one-party state, the penetration of foreign investment, and the geographic concentration of trade serve to substantiate these conclusions. On the other hand, many other authors (usually working from a more descriptive and historical viewpoint) stress that Mexico has many traits that are peculiarly its own. For example, the Mexican Revolution is said to have been the result of a unique blend of political, economic, social, cultural, and religious factors. Even geographically, Mexico exhibits some distinctiveness—Latin America is often divided into the South American nations, the Caribbean nations, the Central American nations, *and* Mexico.

I have undoubtedly emphasized the latter perspective over the former, but only because my objective was to refine overly general classifications of the Mexican state and the Mexican industrial sector. My analysis assumes that Mexico can be usefully compared to dependent, authoritarian states with weak industrial sectors; but I have concluded that in all respects Mexico is an important variant of the general model.

The Mexican Variant

The major findings of this book substantiate how the Mexican case varies from the broad generalizations often applied to development in

Latin America, especially in regard to the industrial sector. I began with a review of the pattern of industrial growth in Mexico and the relative contributions of public, private domestic, and foreign capital. Industrialization in Mexico has progressed more rapidly than in almost all other Latin American countries, and the dynamic industries have been leading this growth in recent decades. In terms of the capital sources for this industrial success, private enterprise, the public sector, and foreign investment have all made important contributions. But in overall comparisons from various perspectives (such as investment, production, sales), the domestic private sector was found to be the dominant factor in almost all instances. And in statistical predictions of industrial growth across time in Mexico, private national investment proved to be a significant contributor to industrialization.

In further understanding this industrial success, I next examined the political role of the private sector. Specifically, I reevaluated the common interpretation of Mexico as an authoritarian regime in which industry, along with other political actors, is dominated by the state. In terms of relations between the state and organized industrial groups, Mexican industrialists have demonstrated considerable autonomy from state control. In particular, the state has employed many more inducements than constraints in trying to enlist the support of the industrial sector. The state has not exercised political control over the industrial groups primarily because the economic power and autonomy of industrialists (as shown in decisions to withhold investment, send money abroad, and the like) can be translated into political independence; that is, the private sector also has some inducements (investment, cooperation, labor peace) it can offer the state in return for relative autonomy. The political ideology of industrial elites was also shown to reflect their sectorial consciousness and their adversary relationship with the political elites. At the same time, industrial entrepreneurs are not shown to be capable of dominating the state. The private sector and the state are essentially separate and independent actors with some shared interests, but with the potential for considerable conflict as well.

Finally, the book has focused on the influence and impact of industrialists in the policy process. Mexican industrialists have had considerable success in affecting policy decisions through two principal strategies: blocking policy initiatives or changes (nondecision), and influencing the implementation of policy (regulatory policy process). The GATT debate is a good example of industrialists preventing a decision, and regulatory policy types have been quite common in Mexico, including protectionist legislation, laws regulating foreign investment, and the fiscal reforms

López Portillo instituted. Many other policies under López Portllo (the Energy Program, the National Industrial Development Plan, and other aspects of the Alliance for Production) signified the influence of private industrialists in the policymaking process. President Echeverría's alienation of the private sector had produced a unified effort to defend the interests of capital and resulted in the much more favorable administration of López Portillo, at least for his first five years.

In sum, Mexico has experienced substantial industrial success, the industrial sector (as well as other elite groups) has enjoyed relative autonomy from the state, and industrialists have wielded considerable influence over industrial policy. These findings suggest refinements in the conceptualizations of Mexico as an authoritarian state under late and dependent development. Mexico acquired certain aspects of modernization quite early relative to other Latin American nations: the industrialization process began before that in any other nation in the region except Argentina; the most rapid expansion of new industrial firms occurred in the 1930s and 1940s; and import substitution in capital goods is evident as early as the late 1930s. Though Mexico's trade relations have always been dependent on the United States, successive Mexican presidents in the postwar period have attempted to control the penetration of foreign capital into Mexican markets. As a result, foreign investment has shrunk from an estimated 50 percent of total investment in 1910 to below 5 percent now. Finally, the Mexican authoritarian state has demonstrated some crucial distinctions, expecially between popular sectors and elite sectors. The incorporation of the popular sector groups (labor and peasants) has closely fit the characteristics of authoritarianism, but relations between the state and elite groups (industrialists in this case) have not necessarily exhibited limited pluralism, low subject-mobilization, or hierarchical orderings. Instead, the elite sectors have operated fairly independently of state controls, and the government has employed incentives or inducements in efforts to win their cooperation.

I do not argue that Mexico is a democratic nation with an independent economy and an omnipotent industrial sector. If one had to dichotomize nations between independent and dependent economies and democratic and authoritarian political systems, Mexico would join most of its Latin American neighbors as a dependent, authoritarian country. Furthermore, its industrial sector has many inherent weaknesses: cyclical growth, concentration, inflationary pressures, and slow expansion into export markets. And the contradictions between Mexico's status as an ADC and as an oil-exporting nation contributed to the economic collapse of 1982. However, my thesis is that these are continuous variables and that Mexico presents substantial variations in all dimensions. Most would interpret these variations as moving in the "positive" direction—toward a stronger industrial sector, toward more independence, and toward more autonomy for certain interest groups.

Linkage among Variables

In focusing on the industrial sector, most social scientists have concentrated on the economic causes and political consequences of industrialization; that is, they emphasize that industrialization primarily has economic determinants and political effects. However, various political phenomena also may have an impact on industrial growth. Therefore, I have adopted a political economy perspective in studying the role of Mexican industrialists in the development process and I have emphasized the relationships among economic and political variables. I have reexamined the arguments concerning the economic causes and the political consequences of industrialization and have considered an additional set of interrelationships: the political causes of industrialization.

Economists have traditionally posited that market-size factors (per capita income and population size) are the primary variables affecting industrial growth. In addition, industrialists and other economic actors can influence industrial progress through their economic function of capital accumulation. Hence, I have combined the traditional market-size indicators with variables measuring the sources of capital investment (public, domestic private, and foreign) in a statistical analysis to predict longitudinal industrial growth in Mexico. The results have confirmed the importance of private national industrialists. Population proved to be the most significant variable (surprisingly, per capita income was the least significant), and domestic private investment ranked second in explanatory power prior to 1970. State investment also had a significant influence on industrial growth, whereas the impact of foreign capital was mostly concentrated in the 1970s. Thus, national industrial investment, especially from the private sector but also from the state, did have a positive and significant impact on industrial growth in Mexico.

Focusing on the political consequences of industrial growth, recent research in Latin America has indicated that advanced stages of industrialization have a tendency to produce authoritarian regime types employing harshly repressive policies (O'Donnell 1973). The Mexican system, however, can be viewed as a more "benevolent authoritarianism," or more accurately, as authoritarianism emphasizing inducements over constraints for elite groups. At least one of the reasons for this political outcome is the autonomy of the industrial sector, which in turn has been a function of that sector's economic power. As stated above, Mexican industrialists can prevent state control or dominance by threatening the withdrawal of economic support or cooperation. Furthermore, at least one author has argued that the stability of an authoritarian regime depends on the degree to which domestic industrialists are incorporated into the dominant coalition and achieve economic success (ibid. 1975:22–41). Another theory states that the early achievement of industrial dominance in a Latin American country aids in the successful inclusion of labor in the coalition and reduces the need to repress labor in later stages (Kaufman 1977). The dominance of industry was established in Mexico by 1940, industry has remained in the governing coalition, and industrial growth has been quite successful. Partly as a consequence of these accomplishments, since 1940 Mexico has had stable, one-party authoritarianism with a heavy industrial orientation and only moderately repressive policies.

The final linkage involves the political determinants of economic growth in general, and industrial growth in particular. This causal direction has long been ignored by most social scientists. One of the few exceptions is a study by Robert Holt and John Turner (1966) that examines the political bases for economic growth in England, France, China, and Japan. They conclude that there are indeed important political prerequisites for economic growth. In the Latin American context, industrialization has also had numerous and important political determinants. In this research I have hypothesized that the political role of industrialists affects industrialization in developing nations, where public policies have been so crucial in shaping economic development. Through their political involvement, industrialists seek to establish the necessary political prerequisites for industrial growth in developing countries: political stability, respect for ownership rights, and policies that aid in capital accumulation, stimulate industry, and provide the necessary infrastructure. In addition, the outcome of the political conflict that often transpires between the emerging industrial sector and the traditional export-oriented oligarchy can be linked to the relative success or failure of the industrialization process. The nature and the success of the industrial challenge to the traditional export sector should have a definite impact on subsequent industrial growth.

The important political role of Mexican industrialists has been confirmed here in terms of its relative independence from the state and its impact on public policies. The political influence of the private industrial sector, then, has been a catalyst in the industrialization process and a stabilizing force in the political process. At relatively early stages, industrialists supported policies that encouraged growth in the dynamic industries. These policies did not lead to industrial dependence on the state or to gross inefficiency in industry. Landowning and foreign elites no longer dominated economic policymaking, and therefore backward-linking or integrated industrial growth was emphasized as early as the 1940s. For example, Mexico established one of the first integrated iron and steel plants in Latin America, and it had the first industrial promotion law that specifically stated import substitution as a goal in 1941.[2] Also, relations between the public sector and private industrialists have been relatively stable. The state has been able to count on the support of the industrial sector (or at least its "responsible" opposition), and industry has been able to rely on fairly impartial treatment from the state and reasonable security in property rights and value.

The mutual respect of industry and the state in Mexico has broken down in only a few instances, and in each case industry's hostility and distrust have been soothed as soon as possible. For example, in the last years of his term, President Echeverría began to alienate the private sector with his spending policies, his anti-imperialist rhetoric, and his attempts at income redistribution. These policies as well as the attitude of the private sector contributed to the substantial outflow of capital to the United States in 1976 and to the first devaluation of the Mexican peso in over two decades. The first goal of incoming President López Portillo in 1977 was to reassure the private sector of Mexico's economic stability. Business confidence was restored and the economy did begin to recover. The same pattern was repeated with the bank nationalization of 1982 and de la Madrid's inauguration.

Another political factor contributing to industrial progress in Mexico was the early industrial challenge to agroexport dominance.[3] This clash between domestic industry and the foreign-dominated export sector was initiated by the Revolution of 1910 during which the private industrial sector supported the struggle against the export elite. Mexican industry consolidated its dominant position in the 1930s and 1940s during the presidencies of Cárdenas, Avila Camacho, and Alemán, and its power was one of the principal catalysts of industrial growth. In the political arena, the industrial groups wielded considerable influence over economic policies after the mid-1930s. Industry also became dominant from an economic standpoint, as it surpassed agriculture in terms of percentage of the national product and became one of the most productive industrial sectors in Latin America.

Partly as a result of industrial dominance and an early state commitment to the dynamic branches of industry, growth in the intermediate- and capital-goods industries in Mexico occurred relatively early. Since industry had already displaced the export elite, the state did not have to assume an active role in favoring it over the other sectors, as it did in Argentina and Chile (Story 1981). Industrialization policies in Mexico were not a part of a state strategy of sectorial discrimination, so they could more rationally focus on industrial promotion as well as on balanced growth. Postwar policies particularly emphasized industrial integration, as protectionist and other policies were designed to stimulate basic industries like the automobile industry and electronics. As a consequence of the various factors, growth in the dynamic industries climbed to over 20 percent annually as early as 1935. Industrial growth rates in these and other industries have remained at relatively high levels throughout the postwar period. Since the issue of industrial dominance was settled before the transition to the crucial phase of import-substituting industrialization, industrialization could progress without the delays and interruptions associated with constant clashes between sectors.

Implications for the Future

The final task here is to determine what this research reveals regarding implications for Mexico's economic and political development. Of course, the immediate question for the political future of Mexico concerns the administration of Miguel de la Madrid. Though the economic crisis of 1982 may not have left him much room to maneuver, his initial policies were generally praised by the industrial sector. This book has documented the political power and autonomy of private industrialists, who have been determined to prevent a repetition of the Echeverría years. Some of López Portillo's last policy initiatives certainly raised the specter of Echeverría's populism in the minds of business leaders. Thus, de la Madrid was under considerable pressure from the private sector to return to the pro-business policies López Portillo espoused prior to 1982.

As early as 1980, the private sector was attempting to influence the choice of a successor to López Portillo. Its political offensive of late 1980 was part of this apparently quite successful strategy. Despite the populist rhetoric of the PGD, de la Madrid was the near unanimous preference of private enterprise. The president is a technocrat with a law degree from UNAM (where he was a student under Professor López Portillo) and a master's degree in public administration from Harvard. He held no elective posts before the presidency, but has extensive experience in various government agencies and ministries. Since 1970 he has served as deputy director of finance at PEMEX, director general of credit at Treasury (when López Portillo was secretary of treasury), assistant secretary of treasury, and as secretary of planning and budgeting. De la Madrid is generally regarded as a fiscal conservative and pro-business. Thus his nomination itself was something of a victory for the private sector, which feared a candidate with closer ties to labor and the Mexican Left. Almost all of his initial policies confirmed his close orientation to the private sector.

The important, long-term implications of any research on Mexico always regard political stability and economic growth. Certainly the political actors who are the focus of this book, domestic industrialists, pose no threat to continued political stability in Mexico. The destabilizing impact of private business elites that may be evident in some Latin American countries (some observers cite El Salvador and Chile as examples) is not a factor in Mexico. As long as their status is secure within a mixed economic setting, Mexican entrepreneurs are committed to maintaining that system and have adopted relatively moderate positions on issues relevant to labor and social peace. In recent decades, few, if any, segments of the entrepreneurial class have demonstrated a tendency to side with right-wing extremists who would seek the overthrow of the existing order in Mexico or even more severe repression of the popular sectors. Of course, completely apart from the role of industrialists, the Mexican political system contains several unique elements (such as revolutionary symbolism and a dominant party) that have co-opted the lower classes while preserving elite privileges. In any case, this research does not lead me to any conclusions that imply a threat to political stability from the private sector.[4]

The final issue involves the prospects for economic growth. Until 1982 many analysts (and international bankers) were very optimistic about the future of the Mexican economy; some stressed that the difficulties beginning in 1982 were simply a short-term "liquidity crisis." Most of my research, in fact, has documented a strong and viable entrepreneurial class operating in a vibrant industrial sector. However, there are a number of problems facing Mexico that pose long-term threats to sustaining economic progress: unchecked inflation, mounting balance-of-payments deficits, an enormous debt, and stagnation of nonpetroleum exports. Undoubtedly, the resolutions to these problems are many and complex, but one factor is common and relevant to them all: an increasing reliance on the petroleum sector.

Numerous and well-publicized advantages for Mexico stemmed from its new oil discoveries: revenues increased; the economy boomed; many jobs were created; some new wealth was generated; a few multiplier effects were evident. But the new income also fueled demand and inflation, increased economic expectations beyond capabilities, boosted imports, contributed to the overvaluation of the peso, produced burdensome international financial obligations (as it attracted foreign loans), and generally overheated the economy. The most direct impact on the industrial sector was the near collapse of the export market for manufactured goods.

These outcomes point to the ultimate irony for Mexico: its two major economic accomplishments (twin status as an oil-exporting nation and as an ADC) may prove to be contradictory. In particular, the concentration on hydrocarbons may be the most serious threat to achievements as an ADC. One of the principal aspects of this elite set of rapidly industrializing Third World countries is their success in exporting industrial products. Yet in Mexico manufactured exports have been declining in real terms in recent years, and among the root causes is overreliance on petroleum exports. The perceived panacea of petroleum revenues has acted as a magnet that draws capital and other resources away from other sectors, thus severely hampering exports of manufactured goods. So, in spite of the general optimism I have expressed about industrial growth and the autonomy of a strong class of national private industrialists in Mexico, the recent economic successes, especially the petroleum boom, contain the seeds for future difficulties and provide challenges for the political and economic elites who desire to continue the pattern of balanced, consistent economic growth.

Appendix A
Sources of and Methods for Collecting Industrialization Data

There is a somewhat misleading tendency to label economic statistics as "hard" data, compared to the "soft" data in most other social sciences. Despite the fact that money or volume of production can be easily quantified into ratio scales, measurement error can be as large in economic variables such as gross domestic product as, for instance, in measures of political democracy. Thus, questions of reliability and validity are just as important in measuring economic variables, and criteria for choosing among indicators of economic variables need to be established. This appendix discusses some of the major problems I confronted in collecting data on industrial production and suggests criteria that should be met whenever possible. The sources of and methods for collecting the industrialization data in Mexico are then described.

The first obstacle to reliability in economic measures is that of changes in relative prices, that is, the situation in which prices of products vary disproportionately. Sometimes a general price index for industrial goods is used to deflate current value figures for each industrial branch. But this procedure can severely bias the results if prices of each branch vary at different rates. Thus, one criterion calls for deflating industrialization data in a more disaggregated manner, using as many different price indices for specific industrial branches as possible.

Even when disaggregated price indices are available, there remains the question of which year to use as the "base year" for price indices, that is, which year's prices are used to value output.[1] Estimates of the growth of the gross domestic product (either for the whole economy or for individual sectors) and its composition can vary depending on which year is chosen as the base year. This can best be shown algebraically in the following example.

Suppose the economy is composed of only two sectors, A and B, and we want to find the growth of the GDP from year 0 to year 1. This will be done using two different years, X and Y, as the base years for valuing output. Table A-1 delineates the prices, quantity, and current value in this hypothetical economy.

Table A–1
Hypothetical Two-Sector Economy

Year	Prices		Quantity		Current Value	
	A	B	A	B	A	B
O	P_{oa}	P_{ob}	Q_{oa}	Q_{ob}	$P_{oa}Q_{oa}$	$P_{ob}Q_{ob}$
X	P_{xa}	P_{xb}	—	—	—	—
Y	P_{ya}	P_{yb}	—	—	—	—
1	P_{la}	P_{lb}	Q_{la}	Q_{lb}	$P_{la}Q_{la}$	$P_{lb}Q_{lb}$

The value of A in year O at year X prices is equal to

$$\frac{P_{oa}Q_{oa}}{P_{oa}/P_{xa}} = Q_{oa}P_{xa}$$

The rest of the data in real values can be calculated in a similar fashion (table A-2).

Table A–2
Real Values Using X and Y as Base Years

Year	Base Year X Values		Base Year Y Values	
	A	B	A	B
O	$Q_{oa}P_{xa}$	$Q_{ob}P_{xb}$	$Q_{oa}P_{ya}$	$Q_{ob}P_{yb}$
1	$Q_{la}P_{xa}$	$Q_{lb}P_{xb}$	$Q_{la}P_{ya}$	$Q_{lb}P_{yb}$

GDP figured at base year X prices would be

$GDP_o = Q_{oa}P_{xa} + Q_{ob}P_{xb}$, and

$GDP_1 = Q_{la}P_{xa} + Q_{lb}P_{xb}$.

The percent of GDP growth would be

$$\triangle GDP \text{ (in \%)} = \frac{GDP_1 - GDP_o}{GDP_o}$$

$$= \frac{Q_{la}P_{xa} + Q_{lb}P_{xb} - (Q_{oa}P_{xa} + Q_{ob}P_{xb})}{Q_{oa}P_{xa} + Q_{ob}P_{xb}}$$

$$= \frac{P_{xa}(Q_{la} - Q_{oa}) + P_{xb}(Q_{lb} - Q_{ob})}{Q_{oa}P_{xa} + Q_{ob}P_{xb}} \tag{1}$$

In a similar manner, percentage of GDP growth using Y as the base year would be

$$\triangle GDP \text{ (in \%)} = \frac{P_{ya}(Q_{la} - Q_{oa}) + P_{yb}(Q_{lb} - Q_{ob})}{Q_{oa}P_{ya} + Q_{ob}P_{yb}} . \qquad (2)$$

By setting equations (1) and (2) equal and reducing, it can be shown that a necessary condition for equality is that relative prices be equal:

$$\frac{P_{xa}}{P_{xb}} = \frac{P_{ya}}{P_{yb}} \text{ or } \frac{P_{xb}}{P_{yb}} = \frac{P_{xa}}{P_{ya}} .$$

It could also be shown that, for the composition of the GDP in similar years to be the same, no matter what base year is chosen, relative prices have to be equal.

In more concrete terms, if industrial prices in 1950 were disproportionately high relative to other sectors, GDP calculated at 1950 prices for any year would overestimate industry's share. Also, if the quantity of industrial output had been growing more than other sectors, the growth rate of GDP could be overestimated.

To counter these problems, the second criterion calls for choosing a base year for valuing output that does not have any disproportionately high prices for any sector. This criterion, however, is probably not as important as the first, that is, disaggregating prices as much as possible. In constructing series of industrial production in Chile from 1914 to 1965, Oscar Muñoz (1971:10–11, 38–40) has compared four different methods: three use disaggregated prices with different base years (1924, 1950, and 1960) and one uses an aggregate price index. The results for the disaggregated series were very similar—average annual growth rates were 4.4 percent (1924 base), 4.2 percent (1950 base), and 4.3 percent (1960 base)—but the aggregate series yielded an average growth rate of 5.1 percent. The difference among disaggregated series with different base years were thus much smaller than the differences between the aggregate series and any of the disaggregated series.

Another problem in compiling industrial production data is that complete information is never available on a year-to-year basis, so indices must be based on periodic censuses and incomplete surveys in intervening years. Also, the industrial censuses are not always comparable, since the definition of industrial activity or the coverage of industrial firms may change.[2] The best one can do in this situation is to use comparable information from as many censuses as possible in deriving production indices. Also, if sample survey data are used to estimate aggregate indices, the relative weights assigned to the sampled industries should be established according to the most accurate and timely information available. Suppose, for example, that an annual survey of the automobile industry were being used to estimate total production in all metal-transforming industries and that automobile production were 10 percent of total production in these industries in a 1960 census and 1 percent in a 1945 census. It certainly would be erroneous to use the 1960 weighting factor of 0.10 as far back as 1945. If no more information on the relative weight of automobile production in intervening years were available, the best method of estimation would be to use some form of interpolation of weights.

Mexican Industrial Production Data: Sources and Methods

Annual value-added data in standardized (1960) prices have been calculated for all two-digit ISIC manufacturing categories, except categories 32 and 39 (which were 0.7 percent and 1.4 percent, respectively, of total manufacturing output, according to the 1970 industrial census), for the years 1929 to 1983 (table A-3). Categories 20, 21, and 22 are combined into one group, as are categories 25 and 26 and categories 35 to 38.

The data for 1929, 1950, 1970, and 1975 come from the industrial censuses for those years.[3] These censuses are relatively comparable in coverage (all establishments) and in the classification of industries. The only problem is that the 1950 figure for category 34 also includes metal mining (ISIC category 12). To make this comparable to the other censuses, it is multiplied by 0.537, since 1960 data from the Banco de México show category 34 to be 53.7 percent of the total when combined with category 12.

Other industrial censuses are not used because the industries covered are not consistent with the 1929, 1950, and 1970 censuses. Censuses of 1935, 1940, and 1945 cover only industrial establishments producing more than ten thousand pesos in total value, and in 1929 these account for around 6 percent of the total output in manufacturing. The results of the 1955, 1960, and 1965 industrial censuses also show that the coverage is not strictly comparable to the censuses used here.

The current value-added figures for 1929, 1950, 1970, and 1975 are deflated by disaggregated price indices from Dirección General de Estadística, *Anuario Estadístico* (various issues), and Banco de México, *Informe Anual* (various issues). The price indices after 1960 from the Banco de México are disaggregated according to each two-digit ISIC category; the indices for 1951 to 1960 from the Banco de México are disaggregated

Table A-3
Value-Added in Mexican Industry
(Millions of 1960 Pesos)

Year	ISIC Category												Total
	20-22	23	24	25-26	27	28	29	30	31	33	34	35-38	
1929	823	1,085	215	166	89	197	49	5	66	97	74	144	3,010
1930	637	903	170	171	90	185	36	7	42	102	79	148	2,570
1931	682	632	160	118	61	117	31	9	38	106	84	153	2,191
1932	671	646	122	136	69	125	25	10	33	111	89	158	2,195
1933	699	802	177	174	86	148	31	16	42	116	95	163	2,549
1934	788	1,168	275	198	96	157	46	35	80	122	101	168	3,234
1935	884	983	224	165	87	139	39	24	58	96	83	146	2,928
1936	753	1,031	298	129	72	113	55	29	70	116	103	192	2,961
1937	901	1,079	310	157	92	143	60	43	108	138	126	247	3,404
1938	1,023	1,066	298	160	98	149	60	48	124	178	167	344	3,715
1939	1,079	1,104	285	194	124	185	60	65	173	92	162	350	3,873
1940	1,112	1,160	283	253	155	214	57	60	171	149	260	502	4,376
1941	1,225	1,236	312	301	176	225	61	62	189	145	251	428	4,611
1942	1,614	1,318	413	366	205	240	78	83	268	181	322	476	5,564
1943	1,879	1,756	501	386	208	220	90	70	239	355	325	409	6,438
1944	2,292	1,914	535	445	229	216	91	84	305	413	422	434	7,380
1945	2,365	2,039	587	501	248	237	103	106	395	515	490	501	8,087
1946	3,120	2,231	712	519	247	239	130	157	607	670	755	768	10,155
1947	3,488	2,076	587	587	269	263	111	166	666	796	892	903	10,804
1948	3,334	2,132	695	744	328	325	137	208	868	844	977	806	11,398
1949	3,790	2,026	668	825	349	351	136	201	869	896	1,332	1,334	12,777
1950	4,473	2,048	643	901	367	373	136	235	1,051	961	1,501	1,495	14,184

Table A-3—Continued

Year	ISIC Category 20-22	23	24	25-26	27	28	29	30	31	33	34	35-38	Total
1951	4,974	1,888	599	940	413	404	125	305	1,209	1,046	1,622	1,695	15,220
1952	5,238	1,950	626	893	423	399	129	301	1,594	981	1,639	1,798	15,971
1953	5,347	1,665	541	823	420	382	110	310	1,715	963	1,559	1,795	15,630
1954	5,604	1,832	601	878	483	424	121	372	1,955	943	1,600	1,932	16,745
1955	6,005	1,858	617	891	528	447	122	422	2,234	1,034	1,730	2,192	18,080
1956	6,399	1,819	611	944	603	492	119	465	2,616	1,098	1,923	2,556	19,645
1957	6,859	1,819	617	990	681	536	119	506	2,798	1,107	2,107	2,940	21,079
1958	7,239	1,815	623	979	727	551	118	630	3,145	1,028	2,175	3,184	22,214
1959	7,470	1,825	634	996	796	582	119	759	3,764	1,031	2,389	3,669	24,034
1960	8,124	1,831	643	1,043	899	634	119	844	4,014	1,066	2,615	4,214	26,046
1961	8,581	1,828	660	874	1,069	684	121	803	4,222	1,042	2,790	4,879	27,553
1962	8,864	1,937	688	987	1,223	721	120	839	4,704	1,180	2,868	4,841	28,972
1963	9,585	1,978	708	1,071	1,329	758	126	914	4,931	1,223	3,410	5,849	31,882
1964	10,436	2,367	884	1,513	1,532	867	148	1,050	5,680	1,420	3,994	7,604	37,495
1965	11,198	2,473	965	1,509	1,653	968	155	1,168	6,737	1,557	4,317	8,894	41,594
1966	11,708	2,737	975	1,532	1,750	1,027	144	1,283	7,633	1,819	4,894	10,249	45,751
1967	12,379	2,870	1,145	1,563	1,892	1,037	174	1,389	8,518	2,039	5,223	10,527	48,756
1968	13,295	3,061	1,240	1,556	2,092	1,143	191	1,505	9,995	2,299	5,790	12,175	54,342
1969	14,131	3,285	1,339	1,689	2,337	1,248	199	1,630	10,995	2,534	6,275	12,983	58,605
1970	15,027	3,619	1,473	1,769	2,557	1,325	212	1,680	12,020	2,672	6,787	14,579	63,720
1971	14,689	3,883	1,535	1,668	2,220	1,247	221	2,073	13,087	2,850	6,634	15,374	65,481
1972	14,986	4,275	1,620	1,780	2,193	1,345	205	2,555	14,744	3,118	7,094	17,301	71,216
1973	15,213	4,702	1,713	1,876	2,278	1,287	223	3,043	16,024	3,560	7,302	20,558	77,779

Table A-3—Continued

Year	20–22	23	24	25–26	27	28	ISIC Category 29	30	31	33	34	35–38	Total
1974	15,217	4,889	1,704	2,050	2,393	1,308	242	3,434	16,457	3,691	7,730	23,581	82,696
1975	15,445	5,063	1,721	2,114	2,113	1,326	235	4,271	16,646	3,916	7,251	25,827	85,928
1976	15,704	5,195	1,799	2,280	2,441	1,418	238	4,791	17,469	4,094	7,572	26,233	89,234
1977	16,503	5,573	1,929	2,425	2,633	1,369	251	4,325	16,982	4,304	8,264	26,729	91,287
1978	17,401	5,660	2,006	2,563	2,912	1,469	273	5,217	17,592	4,716	9,942	31,015	100,766
1979	18,428	6,021	2,151	2,719	3,012	1,620	232	5,127	18,871	5,187	10,490	36,145	110,003
1980	19,775	6,126	2,189	3,015	3,303	1,777	236	5,622	20,692	5,616	10,891	40,410	119,652
1981	21,170	6,482	2,316	3,068	3,432	1,846	250	6,041	22,237	6,116	11,286	44,980	129,224
1982	22,070	5,940	2,181	3,051	3,491	1,859	250	6,342	22,470	5,885	10,296	39,315	123,150
1983	21,801	5,882	2,142	2,610	3,421	1,577	208	5,430	22,849	5,276	9,749	30,415	111,360

into six groups; and the indices before 1951 from the Dirección General de Estadística are only disaggregated into three groups. The 1951–1960 indices correspond to ISIC groups in the following manner: categories 20 to 22 from the index for elaborated foodstuffs (consumer goods); 23, 24, and 29 from the index for nonfoodstuffs (consumer goods); 25 to 29 from the index for paper products (producer goods); 30 and 31 from the index for chemical products (producer goods); 33 from the index for construction materials (producer goods); and 34 to 38 from the index for metal products (producer goods). The indices before 1951 correspond to ISIC groups in this manner: categories 20 to 22 from the index for elaborated foodstuffs (consumer goods); 23 to 29 from the index for nonfoodstuffs (consumer goods), and 30 to 38 from the index for producer goods.

The value-added data for 1960–1969, 1971–1974, and 1976–1983 are from the Banco de México, *Informe Anual* (various issues), and *Actividad Industrial, Cuaderno 1975–1982, Vol. 2, Producto Interno Bruto* data on gross national product in manufacturing, which are broken down according to ISIC categories. The data are deflated by the Banco de México according to disaggregated price indices. Information provided me by the Banco de México shows that these data represent value-added with a base year of 1960. The Banco de México, recognizing that the structure of the manufacturing sector is constantly changing, has used the Laspeyres formula to obtain the indices of volume and the Paasche formula for the indices of value and implicit prices. Manufacturing production indices with 1970 = 100 are made from these data and applied to the 1970 census data to give value-added for 1960–1969 and 1971–1975.

Value-added for 1951–1959 is estimated from manufacturing production indices given in United Nations Economic Commission for Latin America, *Statistical Bulletin for Latin America* (their source is the Banco de México). Not all ISIC categories are covered by these data, so the index for category 23 is also used for categories 24 and 29, the index for 27 is also used for 25/26 and 28, and the index for 34 is also used for 35 to 38. To make the total growth rate for the UNECLA data from 1950 to 1960 equal to that for the data already calculated, the former are "fitted" to the existing 1950 and 1960 data by multiplying the indices by a varying constant computed logarithmically.

Finally, value-added data for 1930–1949 are computed by "fitting" value of manufacturing production indices to the 1929 and 1950 census data. The production indices for 1929–1947 for categories 20 to 24, 27, 30, 33, and 34 are from Secretaría de Economía, Dirección General de Estudios Económicos, "La industrialización de México," *Trimestre de Barómetros Económicos*, no. 8 (March 1948), pp. 50–52. The 1948–1950 indices for these categories are derived from value of production data given in Dirección General de Estadística, *Anuario Estadístico 1951–1952*, which is deflated by the price indices described earlier. For the other categories, value of total production in the industrial censuses of 1929, 1934, 1939, and 1944 are deflated and then expressed as indices. To make the 1929 census data more comparable to the other census data, the 1929 values are subtracted by 6 percent, which is a rough approximation of the share of total production accounted for by establishments with less than ten thousand pesos total output. The years between these census years as well as 1945–1950 are estimated from the indices for the most similar ISIC categories: 27 for 25/26 and 28, 24 for 29, 30 for 31, and 34 for 35 to 38.

Appendix B
Selected "Mexicanized" Firms, 1967–1983

Mexicanized Firm	Foreign Parent[a]	Mexican Partner	Date[b]	Foreign[c]	Activity
Alcan Aluminio	Alcan (Canada)	n.d.	n.d.	48	Metals
Azufrera Pan-americana	Pan. Amer. Sulphur	State	1967–1972	0	Mining
Celulosa de Chihuahua	SNIA Vis-cosa (Italy)	Grupo Chihuahua	1975	14	Paper & chemicals
Cementos Apasco	Hozderbank (W. Germany)	BANAMEX	n.d.	48	Cement
Cementos Tolteca	Portland Cement (U.K.)	Grupo ICA	1971	49	Cement
Cía. Explota-dora del Istmo	Texas Gulf Sulphur	State	1966	34	Mining

Sources: *Industridata 1980–81*; Baird and McCaughan (1979:190–203); Centro de Información y Estudios Nacionales (1981b); Secretaría de Industria y Comercio (1975); Secretaría del Patrimonio y Fomento Industrial, Dirección General de Informática, unpublished data; Dirección General de Inversiones Extranjeras y Transferencia de Tecnología, *Anuario Estadístico* and unpublished data; and *Comercio Exterior*.

Notes: n.d. means no data
[a]U.S. MNCs, unless otherwise specified.
[b]Date of Mexicanization.
[c]Remaining percentage of foreign participation.
[d]On 6 June 1983 SOMEX and DINA announced plans to sell their shares of both Vehículos Automotores Mexicanos and Renault Mexicana to the French firm Regie National des Usines Renault.

Mexicanized Firm	Foreign Parent[a]	Mexican Partner	Date[b]	Foreign[c]	Activity
Cía. Explotadora de Sal	Mitsubishi (Japan)	State	1975	49	Mining
Cía. Industrial de San Cristóbal	Scott Paper	NAFINSA	1978	49	Paper
Cía Minera de Cananea	Anaconda	n.d.	1977	48	Mining
Cía. Minera Río Colorado	Allied Chem.	Industrias Peñoles	1970	40	Mining
Cigarrera La Moderna	Brit. Am. Tobacco (U.K.)	Empresas La Moderna & BANAMEX	1973	45	Tobacco
Cigarros El Aguila	Brit. Am. Tobacco (U.K.)	Empresas La Moderna & BANAMEX	1973	45	Tobacco
Clemente Jacques	United Brands	Grupo VISA	1974	n.d.	Foodstuffs
Cobre de México	Anaconda	State	1973	0	Metals
CONDUMEX (Gpo.)	Anaconda	NAFINSA	1978	48	Electrical
Continental de Alimentos	n.d.	n.d.	n.d.	49	Foodstuffs
Gerber	Gerber	Grupo Coral	1983	49	Foodstuffs
Hoteles Camino Real	Western Intl. Hotels	BANAMEX	n.d.	47	Hotels
Hulera El Centenario	Firestone	n.d.	1978	49	Tires
Industria de Telecomunicación	IT&T	SOMEX & BANAMEX	1968–1974	49	Electrical
Industrias Purina	Ralston Purina	COMERMEX	1978	49	Agriculture & foodstuffs

Mexicanized Firm	Foreign Parent[a]	Mexican Partner	Date[b]	Foreign[c]	Activity
Industrias Resistol	Monsanto	Grupo DESC	1974–1976	39	Chemicals
John Deere	John Deere	BANAMEX	1976	45	Machinery
Kimberly Clark	Kimberly Clark	BANAMEX	1973	43	Paper
La Dominicia	DuPont	n.d.	1978	49	Mining
La Tabacalera	Phillip Morris	NAFINSA	n.d.	11	Tobacco
Magnavox	Magnavox	Grupo Alfa	1979	n.d.	Electrical
Manufacturera 3M	3M	n.d.	1981	n.d.	Machinery & equipment
Massey Ferguson	Massey Ferguson (Canada)	Grupo Alfa & NAFINSA	1979	0	Machinery
Mexicana de Cobre	ASARCO	Grupo Ind. Minera Mex.	1974	0	Mining
Minera Frisco	Union Corp. (South Africa)	BAN-COMER	n.d.	n.d.	Mining
Motores Perkins	Perkins Motors/ Chrysler (Canada)	DINA	1973	33	Auto parts
Motores y Refacciones	n.d.	n.d.	n.d.	43	Auto parts
Negromex	Phillips Petro.	Grupo DESC & Grupo Ballesteros	1967	39	Petro-chemicals
Novaquim	Cyanamid	Grupo CYDSA	1976	0	Chemicals
Organización Roberts	n.d.	n.d.	n.d.	49	Clothes

Mexicanized Firm	Foreign Parent[a]	Mexican Partner	Date[b]	Foreign[c]	Activity
Philco Mexicana	Ford	Grupo Alfa	1975	0	Electrical
Polioles	BASF (West Germany)	Grupo Alfa	1979	40	Petro-chemicals
Polycid	B. F. Goodrich	Grupo CYDSA	1975	0	Petro-chemicals
Química Pennwalt	Delaware Chem.	BANAMEX	n.d.	n.d.	Chemicals
Rassini Rheem	n.d.	n.d.	n.d.	40	Auto parts
Sanborn Hermanos	n.d.	n.d.	n.d.	41	Foodstuffs
Teleindustria Ericsson	L. M. Ericsson (Sweden)	BANAMEX	n.d.	46	Electrical
Texaco Mexicana	Texaco	n.d.	n.d.	40	Petro-chemicals
The Reliance Elec. & Engineering Co. de México	The Reliance Elec. & Engineering Co.	Industrias Reliance	n.d.	49	Electrical
Toledo Scale	Toledo Scale	n.d.	n.d.	49	Instruments
Union Carbide Mexicana	Union Carbide	SERFIN & Grupo Ballesteros	1973–1978	49	Chemicals & electrical
Vehículos Automotores Mexicanos[d]	American Motors	SOMEX	n.d.	4	Autos
Viscosa de Chihuahua	SNIA Viscosa (Italy)	Grupo Chihuahua	1975	0	Chemicals

Appendix C
Selected Newly Established
"Mexicanized" Firms, 1973–1979

Mexicanized Firm	Foreign Parent[a]	Mexican Partner	Date[b]	Foreign[c]	Activity
Aluminio	Alcoa	Grupo Pagliai	1975	35	Metals
Borg & Beck de México	Borg & Beck	SOMEX	n.d.	40	Auto parts
Bujía Mexicana	Champion Sparkplug	SOMEX	n.d.	15	Auto parts
Cía. Minera Lampazos	Union Corp. (South Africa)	BAN-COMER & state	1974	n.d.	Mining
Conelec	Phelps Dodge	n.d.	1973	40	Electrical
Dina Komatsu Nacional	Komatsu (Japan)	DINA	1974	40	Machinery
Dina Rockwell	Rockwell	DINA	1977	40	Automotive
Fibras Químicas	AKU (Netherlands)	Grupo Alfa	1977	40	Chemicals
Hules Mexicanos	Polysar	PEMEX	1975	40	Petro-chemicals

Sources: Same as Appendix B.

Notes: [a]U.S. MNCs, unless otherwise specified.
[b]Date of establishment.
[c]Remaining percentage of foreign participation.
[d]On 6 June 1983 SOMEX and DINA announced plans to sell their shares of both Vehículos Automotores Mexicanos and Renault Mexicana to the French firm Regie National des Usines Renault.

Mexicanized Firm	Foreign Parent[a]	Mexican Partner	Date[b]	Foreign[c]	Activity
Industria de Baleros Continental	SKF (Sweden)	Grupo DESC	1969	35	Metals & auto parts
Industrial Marítima	Barreiro Hmnos. (Spain)	Grupo VISA	1977	40	Foodstuffs
Industrias Cydsa-Bayer	Bayer (West Germany)	Grupo CYDSA	1974	40	Petro-chemicals
Industrias Polifil	Bank of America	Grupo Pagliai & NAFINSA	1974	34	Petro-chemicals
Interruptores de México	Siemens (West Germany)	NAFINSA	1979	33	Electrical
La Encantada	Lacana Mining (Canada)	Industrias Peñoles	n.d.	40	Mining
Met-Mex Peñoles	Bethlehem Steel	Industrias Peñoles	1974	40	Mining
Mexinox	Pechiney (France)	Banco del Atlántico & NAFINSA	1974	40	Steel
Nylon de México	DuPont	Grupo Alfa	1975	40	Petro-chemicals
Petrocel	Amer. Petrofina & Hercules	Grupo Alfa	1973–1978	40	Petro-chemicals
Pigmentos y Productos Químicos	DuPont	BAN-COMER	1973	49	Chemicals
Poliesteres	Bayer (West Germany)	Grupo CYDSA	1974	40	Petro-chemicals
Polycid	B. F. Goodrich	Grupo CYDSA	1975	40	Petro-chemicals

Mexicanized Firm	Foreign Parent[a]	Mexican Partner	Date[b]	Foreign[c]	Activity
Química Fluor	DuPont	BAN-COMER & state	1973	33	Chemicals
Renault Mexicana[d]	Renault (France)	DINA	1978	40	Auto-mobiles
Spicer	Dana	Grupo DESC	1975	40	Auto parts
Tereftalatos Mexicanos	Amoco, St. Oil, & Celanese	NAFINSA & SOMEX	1975–1978	n.d.	Chemicals
TF de México	Taylor Forge	Grupo Pagliai	n.d.	49	Machinery

Appendix D
Data Sources for Regression Analysis
(Chapter 3)

Industrial Value-Added

Value-added data in 1960 prices from appendix A are converted to 1953 prices using the general price index for industry from the Banco de México, *Informe Anual*. These data and those for per capita income are converted into 1953 U.S. dollars by a "purchasing power parity" rate from United Nations sources (United Nations, Department of Economic and Social Affairs 1963:54–55).

Per Capita Income

Sources for GNP in 1950 prices are (1) 1900–1909, Pérez López (1967); (2) 1910, 1921–1964, Nacional Financiera (1965:29); (3) 1965–1968, Banco de México, *Informe Anual 1968*, p. 51; (4) 1969–1979, Banco de México, *Informe Anual*, various issues; and (5) 1980–1982, Inter-American Development Bank, *Economic and Social Progress in Latin America*, various issues.

Population

The sources for total population are (1) 1900–1939, United Nations Economic Commission for Latin America, *Economic Survey of Latin America 1949*, pp. 408–409; (2) 1940–1962, Reynolds (1970:384); (3) 1963–1971, Dirección General de Estadística, *Anuario Estadístico 1970–71*; (4) 1972–1975, United Nations, *Demographic Yearbook*; and (5) 1976–1982, Inter-American Development Bank, *Economic and Social Progress in Latin America*.

U.S. Investment in Manufacturing

U.S. Department of Commerce, *Survey of Current Business*.

Mexican Public and Private Investment

The sources for both public and private investment are (1) 1939–1963, Goldsmith (1966:76); Secretaría de la Presidencia y Nacional Financiera (1963:43); and Fernández Hurtado (1967:55); (2) 1964–1976, Dirección General de Estadística, *Anuario Estadístico*; (3) 1977–1980, Secretaría de Programación y Presupuesto, *Información Sobre Gasto Público 1969–1978*, and *Anuario Estadístico*; and (4) 1981–1982, Banco de México, *Informe Anual*.

Appendix E
Questionnaire Mailed to Mexican and Venezuelan Industrialists, Summer 1980

GENERAL INSTRUCTIONS. Either a pen or pencil may be used to complete this questionnaire. Most of the questions may be answered by simply placing an X in the appropriate box; other questions ask for written-in answers. However, you may write in additional comments whenever you wish.

Beside each of the statements presented below, please indicate whether you Strongly Agree, Agree, are Undecided, Disagree, or Strongly Disagree.

I.   This first set of statements deals with political influence and policies.
   1. The interests of the industrial sector are well represented in the policies of the government.
   2. The industrial sector rarely acts as a unified political force.
   3. The industrial sector has been very successful since World War II in influencing government economic policy.
   4. The influence of the industrial sector depends more on a few major industrialists acting as individuals than on any industrial associations.
   5. Industrial chambers should serve only technical functions and avoid politics.
   6. Industrial chambers have been very effective in representing the interests of the industrial sector.
   7. I am an active participant in the affairs of my national industrial organization.
   8. In general, I am completely satisfied with the policies of the present government [López Portillo or Herrera Campins].
   9. In general, I was completely satisfied with the policies of the previous government [Echeverría or Andrés Pérez].

II.   This next set of statements deals with your views of different economic groups.

10.   CONCAMIN [the CIC] and CANACINTRA [FEDE-CAMARAS] are very different in their members, beliefs, and activities.

11.   The industrial sector and the agricultural sector have different and at times opposing interests.

12.   More expropriation with compensation of *latifundios* is necessary.

13.   The industrial sector and the commercial sector have different and at times opposing interests.

14.   Agricultural stagnation is a great problem in Mexico [Venezuela].

III. This next set of statements deals with your views on foreign investment.

15.   The effects of foreign investment on the Mexican [Venezuelan] economy have been generally favorable.

16.   Foreign capital should be permitted in Mexican [Venezuelan] industry only with many restrictions and in certain industries.

17.   Foreign capital in Mexico [Venezuela] is very necessary for the development of the nation.

18.   Foreign investors have too much control over the Mexican [Venezuelan] economy and Mexican [Venezuelan] industry.

IV.   This next set of statements deals with your views of the economic role of the state.

19.   The economic policies of the state play an important and positive role in the economic development of the nation.

20.   Government intervention in the economy is excessive in Mexico [Venezuela].

21.   The nationalization of enterprises is necessary in certain industries.

22.   Economic development would be best stimulated by more private initiative.

V.   This next set of statements deals with your views of labor and labor unions.

23.   The state should exercise more control over labor unions.

24. Labor leaders in Mexico [Venezuela] are only interested in increasing their own power.
25. Unequal income distribution is a major problem in Mexico [Venezuela].
26. Workers play a positive role in the industrial firm and in industrial relations.
27. Strikes have had a negative effect on economic development in Mexico [Venezuela].

VI. Which of these groups have had the most influence on government economic policy and which have had the least? Rate the groups from 1 (most influential) to 10 (least influential).

28. Bankers   33. Landowners
29. Merchants   34. Workers
30. Multinational corporations   35. Peasants
31. Large industrialists   36. Military
32. Small industrialists   37. Politicians

VII. Which of these groups have benefited the most from government economic policies and which the least? Rate the groups from 1 (most benefited) to 10 (least benefited).

38. Bankers   43. Landowners
39. Merchants   44. Workers
40. Multinational corporations   45. Peasants
41. Large industrialists   46. Military
42. Small industrialists   47. Politicians

VIII. Many government policies have affected the industrial sector.
A. Among these policies, which have favored and which have not favored the industrial sector? For each policy mark either Strongly Favored, Favored, Indifferent, Disfavored, or Strongly Disfavored.

48. Credit   51. Labor policy
49. Prices   52. Public spending
50. Protectionism   53. Taxes

B. Among these policies, which have been strongly influenced by the industrial sector and which have not been influenced by the industrial sector? For each policy mark either Strong Influence, Mild Influence, or No Influence.

54. Credit   57. Labor policy
55. Prices   58. Public spending
56. Protectionism   59. Taxes

IX.   Please mark the appropriate box in these questions on your political activity and ideology.
60.   If you want to influence a political decision or need aid in dealing with any level of government, who do you turn to?
      Trade association?
      Informal group of industrialists?
      Depend on my own contacts?
      Impossible to even try?
      Other (explain)?
61.   How do you classify your political ideology?
      Left?   Center?   Right?

X.   Please write in answers to these background questions.
62.   What has been the chief occupation of your father?
63.   When was your company founded?
64.   What is the specific branch of activity of your company (foodstuffs, machinery, etc.)?
65.   What was the value of gross production in your company in the last fiscal year [1979]?
66.   How many employees are there in your company?
67.   What is the highest level of education you have received?
68.   Were you born in Mexico [Venezuela]? If no, in what country?
69.   Was your father born in Mexico [Venezuela]? If no, in what country?
70.   Was your company established completely with private domestic capital?
71.   Does your firm depend on foreign companies for
      the purchase of parts, products, or raw materials?
      technology?
      credit or capital?

XI.   Do you think the policies of these presidential administrations were favorable or unfavorable to the industrial sector? The possible responses are Very Favorable, Somewhat Favorable, No Opinion, Somewhat Unfavorable, or Very Unfavorable.
72.   Cárdenas (1934–1940) [López Contreras (1936–1941)]
73.   Avila Camacho (1940–1946) [Medina Angarita (1941–1945)]
74.   Alemán (1946–1952) [AD Trienio (1945–1948)]
75.   Ruiz Cortines (1952–1958) [Pérez Jiménez (1948–1958)]

76. López Mateos (1958–1964) [Betancourt (1959–1964)]
77. Díaz Ordaz (1964–1970) [Leoni (1964–1969)]
78. Echeverría (1970–1976) [Caldera (1969–1974)]
79. López Portillo (1976–   ) [Andrés Pérez (1974–1978)]
80. [Herrera Campins (1979–   )]

Table A–4
Scale Items in Four Dimensions of Ideological Orientation

Sectorial Awareness
>   Item 11:   The industrial sector and the agricultural sector have different and at times opposing interests.
>   Item 13:   The industrial sector and the commercial sector have different and at times opposing interests.
>   Item 14:   Agricultural stagnation is a great problem in Mexico [Venezuela].

Perception of Foreign Investment:
>   *Item 15:   The effects of foreign investment on the Mexican [Venezuelan] economy have been generally favorable.
>   Item 16:   Foreign capital should be permitted in Mexican [Venezuelan] industry only with many restrictions and in certain industries.
>   *Item 17:   Foreign capital in Mexico [Venezuela] is very necessary for the development of the nation.
>   Item 18:   Foreign investors have too much control over the Mexican [Venezuelan] economy and Mexican [Venezuelan] industry.

Attitude toward the State Economic Role
>   Item 19:   The economic policies of the state play an important and positive role in the economic development of the nation.
>   *Item 20   Government intervention in the economy is excessive in Mexico [Venezuela].
>   Item 21:   The nationalization of enterprises is necessary in certain industries.
>   *Item 22:   Economic development would be best stimulated by more private initiative.

Opinion of Labor
>   Item 23:   The state should exercise more control over labor unions.
>   Item 24:   Labor leaders in Mexico [Venezuela] are only interested in increasing their own power.
>   *Item 26:   Workers play a positive role in the industrial firm and in industrial relations.
>   Item 27:   Strikes have had a negative effect on economic development in Mexico [Venezuela].

Notes: The possible responses were Strongly Agree, Agree, Undecided, Disagree, and Strongly Disagree.

*These items have been coded in reverse to reflect the same direction of opinion as the other items.

Acronyms

ABM	Asociación de Banqueros de México. Mexican Bankers' Association.
AD	Acción Democrática. Democratic Action Party.
AMIS	Asociación Mexicana de Instituciones de Seguros. Mexican Association of Insurance Institutions.
ANIERM	Asociación Nacional de Importadores y Exportadores de la República Mexicana. National Association of Importers and Exporters of the Republic of Mexico.
ANIQ	Asociación Nacional de la Industria Química. National Association of the Chemical Industry.
BANAMEX	Banco Nacional de México. National Bank of Mexico.
BANCOMER	Banco de Comercio. Bank of Commerce.
BANOBRAS	Banco Nacional de Obras y Servicios Públicos. National Bank of Public Works and Services.
BANPAIS	Banco del País. Bank of the Nation.
CAINTRA	Cámara de la Industria de Transformación de Nuevo León. Chamber of Manufacturing Industries of Nuevo León.
CAMCO	Cámara Americana de Comercio. American Chamber of Commerce of Mexico.
CANACINTRA	Cámara Nacional de la Industria de Transformación. National Chamber of Manufacturing Industries.
CCE	Consejo Coordinador Empresarial. Entrepreneurial Coordinating Council.
CEESP	Centro de Estudios Económicos del Sector Privado. Center of Economic Studies of the Private Sector.
CEPROFI	Certificado de Promoción Fiscal. Certificate of Fiscal Promotion.
CFE	Comisión Federal de Electricidad. Federal Electric Commission.
CIC	Cámara de Industriales de Caracas. Industrial Chamber of Caracas.
CIDE	Centro de Investigación y Docencia Económicas. Center of Economic Research and Teaching.
CMHN	Consejo Mexicano de Hombres de Negocios. Mexican Council of Businessmen.

CNE	Colegio Nacional de Economistas. National College of Economists.
CNIE	Comisión Nacional de Inversiones Extranjeras. Foreign Investment Commission.
COMERMEX	Comercial Mexicano. Mexican Commercial Bank.
CONASUPO	Compañía Nacional de Subsistencias Populares. National Staple Products Company.
CONCAMIN	Confederación de Cámaras Industriales. Confederation of Industrial Chambers.
CONCANACO	Confederación de Cámaras Nacionales de Comercio. Confederation of National Chambers of Commerce.
CONDUMEX	Conductores Mexicanos. Conduits of Mexico Company.
CONINDUSTRIA	Consejo Venezolano de la Industria. Venezuelan Council of Industry.
COPARMEX	Confederación Patronal de la República Mexicana. Mexican Employers' Confederation.
CREMI	Crédito Minero y Mercantil. Mining and Mercantile Credit Bank.
CTM	Confederación de Trabajadores Mexicanos. Mexican Labor Confederation.
CYDSA	Celulosa y Derivados. Cellulose and Derivatives Company.
DGE	Dirección General de Estadística. General Statistical Directorate.
DINA	Diesel Nacional. National Diesel Company.
FEDECAMARAS	Federación Venezolana de Cámaras y Asociaciones de Comercio y Producción. Venezuelan Federation of Chambers and Associations of Commerce and Production.
GATT	General Agreement on Tariffs and Trade.
ICA	Ingenieros Civiles Asociados. Associated Civil Engineers.
IMCE	Instituto Mexicano de Comercio Exterior. Mexican Foreign Trade Institute.
IMSA	Industrias Monterrey, S.A. Monterrey Industrial Company.
IMSS	Instituto Mexicano del Seguro Social. Mexican Social Security Institute.
INMECAFE	Instituto Mexicano de Café. Mexican Coffee Institute.
ISSSTE	Instituto de Seguridad y Servicios Sociales de los Trabajadores del Estado. Institute of Security and Social Services for State Employees.
NAFINSA	Nacional Financiera. National Development Bank.
PAN	Partido Acción Nacional. National Action party.
PDM	Partido Demócrata Mexicano. Mexican Democratic party.
PEMEX	Petróleos Mexicanos. Mexican Petroleum Company.
PGD	Plan Global de Desarrollo. Overall Development Plan.
PND	Plan Nacional de Desarrollo. National Development Plan.

PNR   Partido Nacional Revolucionario. National Revolutionary party.

PRI   Partido Revolucionario Institucional. Institutional Revolutionary party.

SAM   Sistema Alimentario Mexicano. Mexican Foodstuffs System.

SECOFIN   Secretaría de Comercio y Fomento Industrial. Secretariat of Commerce and Industrial Promotion.

SEMIP   Secretaría de Energía, Minas, e Industria Paraestatal. Secretariat of Energy, Mines, and Public Enterprises.

SEPAFIN   Secretaría de Patrimonio y Fomento Industrial. Secretariat of Resources and Industrial Promotion.

SERFIN   Servicios Financieros. Financial Services.

SICARTSA   Siderúrgica Lázaro Cárdenas - Las Truchas. Steel Mill Lázaro Cárdenas - Las Truchas.

SIDERMEX   Siderúrgicas Mexicanas. Mexican Steel Mills.

SOMEX   Sociedad Mexicana de Crédito Industrial. Mexican Society of Industrial Credit.

VAM   Vehículos Automotores Mexicanos. Mexican Automotive Vehicles Company.

VISA   Valores Industriales. Industrial Values Company.

Notes

Chapter 1. Introduction

1. See Ross (1955:3); Cockcroft (1968:61–63); Ruiz (1976:6–36); Hamilton (1977:17–26); and *Excélsior* (27 February 1983).

2. These disruptions were actually a blessing in disguise. Mexico's oil stayed in the ground until the events of the 1970s had vastly multiplied its worth.

3. Reported in Williams (1979:42–43) from Gutiérrez Santos (1977:Appendix).

4. On the relation between petroleum revenues and the National Industrial Development Plan, see FitzGerald (1980); Street (1980); and Bueno (1981). Other studies of Mexican petroleum policy and development include Grayson (1977–78, 1979, and 1981); Flores Caballero (1978); Mancke (1979); Williams (1979, 1980, and 1982); Ladman, Baldwin, and Bergman (1980); Saxe-Fernández (1980); Carrada-Bravo (1982); and Millor (1982).

5. The others are Brazil, Hong Kong, South Korea, Singapore, and Taiwan.

6. A similar political economy perspective on the part that industrialists play in the nation-building process is taken in Frits Wils's (1979) book on Peruvian industrialists.

7. The major books that touch upon this topic are those by Marco Antonio Alcázar (1970); Flavia Derossi (1971); Robert Jones Shafer (1973); Susan Kaufman Purcell (1975); and Concheiro et al. (1979). The Shafer and Alcázar books are largely descriptive, historical pieces that cover all entrepreneurial sectors. The Derossi monograph principally focuses on issues of economic development; the Purcell book analyzes a single policy issue involving industry along with other political actors; and the Concheiro research focuses on the economic and political power of the largest economic establishments.

8. Cole (1946); Hoselitz (1952); Lamb (1952, 1962); Harbison (1956); Hagen (1960–61); Papanek (1962); Brandenburg (1964:14, 24–26); Harbron (1965:43–47); Moore (1966); Cardoso (1967:100–102); and Chilcote and Edelstein (1974:51–57). For an excellent bibliography on the role of entrepreneurs, see Derossi (1971: 409–423).

9. On factors affecting the development of industrial entrepreneurs in general, see Sawyer (1962); Alexander (1967); Lipset (1967); Glade (1967); and Vogel (1979). On the failure of industrial entrepreneurs in less-developed nations (especially in Latin America) to develop fully, see Wohl (1949:37–42); Cochran (1960); Levin (1960); Papanek (1962:47); Kriesberg (1963:589); De Schweinitz (1964:10, 64–75, 239–249); Strassman (1964); Cardoso (1966:153–157; 1967:94–96, 100, 113;

and 1976:156–157); Griffin (1966); Glade (1967:253–255); Lipset (1967); Ratinoff (1967); Nun (1969:26, 30–31); Romeo (1969); Bodenheimer (1971:30); Chilcote and Edelstein (1974:51–57); Cavarozzi (1976:10–12, 31); and Amin (1977).

10. See Cole (1949:99; 1971:158–161, 206–224); Schumpeter (1949:82); Hoselitz (1952:108); Papanek (1962:46, 56); Kerr et al. (1964:22–25); Organski (1965); and Lauterbach (1966:78–115).

11. For a general discussion on the increased political participation of industrialists, see Cole (1946; 1971:79–96, 206); Schumpeter (1949:82); Wohl (1949:17–19); Gerschenkron (1953); Lamb (1962); Moore (1966:341, 349); Glade (1967:252, 256); and Chaffee (1976:56). On the political influence of industrialists in the United States, see Salamon and Siegfried (1977); and on the political participation of industrialists in Latin America, see Brandenburg (1964:15, 45–49, 75–79); Strassman (1964); and Chilcote and Edelsten (1974:51–57).

12. Sarti (1971) examines the Italian industrial association during that country's Fascist period; Ehrmann (1957) describes the political role of organized business in France; and Linz and DeMiguel (1966) analyze the monopoly of representation that the Spanish government grants to the national business associations. On the industrial and business associations as a political pressure group in West Germany, see Almond (1957); Hartmann (1959:208–254); and Braunthal (1965). Salisbury (1977) explores the political impact of business groups in the United States. In reporting on an international survey of business leaders, Bivens and Lambeth (1967:22, 34–46) emphasize the major political role of most business associations.

13. Salisbury (1977).

14. Brandenburg (1964:77), however, disagrees with this comparison.

15. Among the most important studies examining the nature and the impact of late and dependent industrialization in developing countries (especially in Latin America) are Gerschenkron (1962); Slawinski (1965:171–172); United Nations Economic Commission for Latin America (1966:18–21, 27–30, 155–226); Hirschman (1968); Glade (1969:376–529); Nun (1969:22–63); Furtado (1970:75–104); Grunwald (1970); Baer (1972); Cardoso and Faletto (1973); O'Donnell (1973:55–114; 1975); Cardoso (1974:74–130); Collier (1975); Cavarozzi (1976); Kaufman (1977); Evans (1979); Gereffi and Evans (1981); and Hewlett and Weinert (1982).

16. Also see Fitzgibbon and Johnson (1961); Cutright (1963; 1971); Neubauer (1967); Tanter (1967); Olsen (1968); and Flanigan and Fogelman (1971).

17. A voluminous literature has followed the O'Donnell piece. The most significant compilations of this research are the volumes by Malloy (1977) and Collier (1979).

18. For a comparative study that analyzes the influence of government policies and regime type on industrial growth in five Latin American nations, see Story (1980a).

19. In his book on Peru, Wils (1979:25) concludes that this "disillusionment with industrialists in Latin America is due to an important extent to an overextended set of expectations based on a good deal of ethnocentrism and neo-evolutionary, unilinear thinking."

Chapter 2. The Pattern of Industrial Growth in Mexico

1. See Kuznets (1957; 1966:86–159, 409–417); Hoffman (1958:31–38, 67–109); Hoselitz (1961); Chenery and Taylor (1968); and Grunwald (1970).

2. See United Nations, Department of Economic and Social Affairs, Statistical Office, 1958.

3. It should be noted that these classifications do not correspond to the typology used by the United Nations Economic Commission for Latin America (UNECLA) to classify import commodities by end use (consumer durable and nondurable, intermediate, capital, etc.). On the UNECLA system and its correspondence to the Standard International Trade Classification (SITC), see United Nations Economic Commission for Latin America, *Economic Bulletin for Latin America* 3, no. 2:85–86.

4. Slawinski (1965:171–172) and United Nations Economic Commission for Latin America (1966:18–21) posit four stages of industrialization in Latin America: (1) the prefactory stage; (2) the stage of traditional industries; (3) the stage of basic industries; and (4) the stage of complex forms of processing. Other studies have focused on the initiation of import-substituting industrialization in Latin America and have described two stages: (1) the substitution of consumer goods; and (2) the substitution of intermediate and capital goods (United Nations Economic Commission for Latin America 1966:27–30; Hirschman 1968; and O'Donnell 1973:55–70).

5. UNECLA defines nondurable consumer goods as those that have a "normal" life span of less than one year and that disappear at the first consumption. These primarily include the ISIC categories of foodstuffs (20), beverages (21), and tobacco (22), with some items from textiles (23), clothing (24), paper (27), and chemicals (31). Durable consumer goods are those that normally last over a year. See United Nations Economic Commission for Latin America, *Economic Bulletin for Latin America* 3, no. 2:85–86.

6. This is termed "backward-linking" ISI because it stresses the production of goods that are the inputs to the production of consumer nondurables. Thus, ISI is the continually moving "backward" through the production process.

7. See Vernon (1963:44); Rosenzweig (1965:326); Reynolds (1970:161); and Hansen (1974:18–20).

8. See Rosenzweig (1965:311) and Dirección General de Estadística, 1903.

9. The Argentine data are from Dorfman (1970:279). On early Brazilian industrial growth, see Wythe (1955:38); Baer (1965:13); United Nations Economic Commission for Latin America (1966:8); and Baer and Villela (1973:223).

10. See Dirección General de Estadística (1933).

11. The dictator Porfirio Díaz was president from 1876 to 1910, except for a brief period between 1881 and 1884. This period may be referred to as the Porfirian era, the Díaz era, or the Porfirato.

12. See Reynolds (1970:32, 206); Cinta (1972:169–182); and Villarreal (1977: 67–70).

13. Data from Villarreal (1977:72–73) also confirm these dates. Also see idem. (1976).

14. José Casar (1982) actually identifies four cycles of descent-ascent between 1950 and 1979: 1950-1960, 1960-1970, 1970-1974, and 1974-1979. According to his data, the "boom" periods of industrial growth were 1954 to 1960 (with 7.7 percent average annual growth) and 1963 to 1970 (with 9.6 percent average annual growth).

15. Data for 1980 through 1983 come from the Banco de México and the Secretaría de Programación and Presupuesto. For recent industrialization data as well as projections, also see Confederación de Cámaras Industriales 1983b, and Cámara Nacional de la Industria de Transformación, *Transformación*, March 1983.

Chapter 3. Dependent Industrialization in a Mixed Economy

(Portions of this chapter are reprinted from Story [1984], used by permission of the Regents of the University of California.)

1. Of course, state ownership or nationalization may also be motivated by purely ideological reasons. Certain areas of the economy may be seen as the natural reserve of the state.

2. The term "associated-dependent development" was first applied to Brazil by Cardoso (1976). In the case of Mexico, the collusion between foreign investors and the state is a major theme of a study by Baird and McCaughan (1979:71-92). Stallings (1972:40-41); Chilcote and Edelstein (1974:51-57); Evans (1979); and Gereffi and Evans (1981) also discuss these linkages. On the importance of state economic intervention whenever domestic entrepreneurship is weak, see Glade (1969:407).

3. On this question, also see Story (1984).

4. These policies are also discussed in terms of the industrial conflict with the traditional agroexport oligarchy in Story (1981:25-26, 56-60).

5. On this and other industrialization policies of the 1920s and 1930s, see Mosk (1950:68); Glade (1955:76-78; 1963:19-20, 45, 85); Ross and Christensen (1959: 29-31, 42-43, 187-189); Anderson (1963:123); Vernon (1963:72); Blair (1964:206-211); Shelton (1964:141-146); Aubey (1966:23-38); King (1970:10, 99); Reynolds (1970:216-218); Labastida Martín del Campo (1972:105-108); Hansen (1974:49); and Ten Kate et al. (1979:30-31).

6. For example, the 1941 law defined necessary industries as those "devoted to the manufacture or preparation of goods not produced in the country in sufficient quantity to meet the needs of domestic consumption" (Bernal-Molina 1948:81). For more detail on the 1939 decree and the 1941, 1946, and 1955 laws, see Mosk (1950:64-66); Bernal-Molina (1956:93-95); Ross and Christensen (1959:43-54, 191-240); Glade (1963:85); Strassman (1968:297-298); and King (1970:99-106).

7. On the history, purpose, and effect of NAFINSA, see Bernal-Molina (1948: 160-161); Ross and Christensen (1959:34-38); Anderson (1963:124-125); Blair (1964); Brandenburg (1964:71-72); Aubey (1966:38-52); LaCascia (1969:39-42); and King (1970:71-74).

8. The average tariff rate in the 1930s was only 16 percent *ad valorem*, which is hardly a protectionist tariff (Reynolds 1970:216-218). Also see Mosk (1950:68-69).

9. On these 1947 decrees, see Mosk (1950:74–83); Ross and Christensen (1959: 29–32); Izquierdo (1964:263–266); Strassman (1968:288–289); King (1970:32–33, 75–76); and Bueno (1971:180–182).

10. On the establishment of the Banco de México and other national banking institutions, see Glade (1963:71–74); Vernon (1963:68, 72); Shelton (1964:113–126); and King (1970:1–15).

11. For overviews of the history and functions of these and other public enterprises in Mexico, see García Ramírez (1979) and de Villarreal and Villarreal (1980).

12. Royal-Dutch Shell and Standard of New Jersey were the principal oil companies affected. They controlled over 70 percent of total Mexican production at the time. On these expropriations, see Wythe (1949:321–322); United Nations Economic Commission for Latin America (1950); Powell (1956:5–32); Wionczek (1964:60–62); Wright (1971:61–71); Meyer (1972); Rippy (1972); Baklanoff (1975: 34–62); Gordon (1975); and Mancke (1979:50–55).

13. On the history of the electrical power industry and these expropriations, see Wionczek (1964:75–106; 1967:33–165); Wright (1971:71–92); Baklanoff (1975:46–47); and Baird and McCaughan (1979:71–78).

14. Baklanoff (1975:47) says that the actual payment of compensation was far below the book value of the companies; Baird and McCaughan (1979:78) claim that the government paid an amount well above the book value; and Wionczek (1964:92–106) says that the deal was fair to both sides and, citing the 1959 Annual Report of the American Foreign Power Company, claims that the companies were satisfied.

15. See *Expansión* (various years); *Latin America Economic Report*, 8 December 1978; Centro de Información y Estudios Nacionales (1982b); and Secretaría de Programación y Presupuesto, *Boletín Mensual de Información Económica*. Only with the austere budget of 1983 did the PEMEX share of the budget shrink significantly (*Diario Oficial*, 31 December 1982).

16. In addition to *El Mercado de Valores*, I have compiled this list utilizing information from *Análisis Político* (8 November 1976); FitzGerald (1978a:10); Mann (1979:516); Centro de Información y Estudios Nacionales (1982b); *Expansión* (18 August 1982); and Secretaría de Programación y Presupuesto, *Boletín Mensual de Información Económica*. Also see Santillán López and Rosas Figueroa (1962:236–241); Anguiano Equihua (1968:10–15); Ramírez Rancaño (1974:65–69); Villarreal and de Villarreal (1977); and Bennett and Sharpe (1979a). The Office for Public Sector Studies at the Institute of Latin American Studies, University of Texas, reports that the number of public firms in Mexico actually approaches fifteen hundred, including many unregistered firms controlled by trust funds (*fideicomisos*).

17. Some analysts estimated that the bank nationalization boosted the government's share of GDP to 80 percent (*Wall Street Journal*, 7 October 1982). De la Madrid did enact legislation in December 1982 allowing one-third of the bank shares to be sold to private investors.

18. See Secretaría de Programación y Presupuesto, *Información sobre Gasto*

Público 1969–1978, pp. 133–134; FitzGerald ¿1978a:6; 1978b:273–276); and Dirección General de Estadística, *Anuario Estadístico* (various years).

19. Secretaría de Programación y Presupuesto, *Información Sobre Gasto Público 1969–1978*, p. 301. For other comparative data, see Villarreal and de Villarreal (1977:94); and FitzGerald (1978a:6).

20. Moran (1974) and Tugwell (1975b) examine government regulation of the foreign-owned extractive industries (copper and petroleum) in these two Latin American nations.

21. The value of exports rose by 600 percent in the thirty-five years of the Porfiriato, though exports became somewhat more diversified. Gold and silver declined from 79 percent of all exports in 1877 to 46 percent in 1910 (Hansen 1971:13–14).

22. On economic dependency in the Mexican automobile industry, see Jenkins (1976).

23. On the 1973 law, see Sepúlveda and Chumacero (1973:52–53); Baklanoff (1975:49); Aguilar M. et al. (1977:53–56, 75–79, 183–199); *Latin America Economic Report*, 8 April 1977; Business International Corporation (1979:20–24); Whiting (1979:15–16); and Alvarez de la Cadena (1983:84–88).

24. See *El Universal*, 18 January 1978 and 19 February 1978; and *Excélsior*, 18 February 1978.

25. See *Latin America Economic Report*, 10 March 1978, and 12 May 1978; and *New York Times*, 24 March 1979.

26. See *Proceso*, 30 May and 13 June 1983; and *Unomásuno*, 5, 24, 27 May, 9, 16, 17, 24 June 1983.

27. On U.S. investment in Mexico before 1930, see Ingalls (1922:62–65); Dunn (1926:89–107); Winkler (1928:275); Wilkins (1974:31, 55); and Whiting (1979:36).

28. See United Nations Economic Commission for Latin America (1950); Navarrete R. (1967:111); King (1970:63); and Wright (1971:61–92).

29. The figures are somewhat higher in the industrial sector, where foreign firms accounted for about 15 percent of all capital formation in the 1960s and about 30 percent of total production in the early 1970s. See Sepúlveda and Chumacero (1973:54–58, 163, 170–171); Newfarmer and Mueller (1975:56–57); Whiting (1979:42) and Peres Núñez (1982:135).

30. See Centro de Información y Estudios Nacionales (1980); and Morell (1981). The bank nationalization created tremendous problems in terms of the participation of these banks in private firms.

31. See Sepúlveda and Chumacero (1973:37, 40, 61–62); Newfarmer and Mueller (1975:68–72); Fajnzylber and Martínez Tarragó (1976:375); and Robinson and Smith (1976:82, 222). Sepúlveda and Chumacero analyzed 1,883 enterprises with greater than 5 percent foreign capital; Newfarmer and Mueller surveyed 294 U.S. manufacturing firms operating in Mexico; Fajnzylber and Martínez Tarragó examined 651 industrial enterprises with at least 15 percent foreign ownership; and Robinson and Smith questioned 239 U.S. MNCs in Mexico.

32. See Newfarmer and Mueller (1975:57). The data for industrial value-added provides similar results: MNCs in 1970 accounted for 73 percent of industrial value-added in chemical products, 65 percent in rubber, 63 percent in electrical

machinery, 36 percent in transportation equipment, and 31 percent in nonelectrical machinery (ibid.:56). Also see Sepúlveda and Chumacero (1973:54–58) and Ramírez Rancaño (1974:34).

33. See Newfarmer and Mueller (1975:60–61, 82) and Fajnzylber and Martínez Tarragó (1976:175–180).

34. See Navarrete R. (1967:105–106). His optimism is partially explained by the fact that he was deputy director of NAFINSA at the time. Also see idem (1963).

35. The first eight public enterprises are actually within the largest twenty firms. They occupy positions 1, 2, 4, 5, 12, 13, 16, and 20.

36. See Kuznets (1957; 1966:86–159, 409–417); Chenery (1960); Hoselitz (1961); United Nations, Department of Economic and Social Affairs (1963); Temin (1967); and Chenery and Taylor (1968). Some of my previous analysis has considered additional political variables as independent variables (Story 1980b).

37. The sources are described in appendix D. The logarithmic transformations correct any badly skewed distributions.

38. Actually, I have employed a form of "psuedo-GLS" estimation to transform the data, and then applied OLS to the transformed data (Hibbs 1974:282–284). I use the Cochrane-Orcutt (Ostrom 1978:39–40) approach to psuedo-GLS estimation in this analysis. Cochrane-Orcutt estimates the correlation (p) among the error terms and transforms the dependent and independent variables by the following formulas:

$$Y' = Y_t - pY_{t-1}$$

$$X' = X_t - pX_{t-1}, \text{ where } t = \text{years.}$$

Autocorrelation is no longer a problem with OLS using these transformed variaables. For an example of this same methodology with a pooling of cross-sectional and time-series data, see Hogan (1983).

Chapter 4. State-Industry Relations: Disaggregating the Authoritarian State

(This chapter, used with permission, is a revised version of Story [1980a].)

1. The most recent research substantiating this thesis is a study of the Mexican sugar industry by Susan Kaufman Purcell, who states that, "when we review the major decisions made with regard to the sugar industry, there is little evidence of business power" (Purcell 1981:229). In another case study, Bennett and Sharpe (1979b) discuss the state's regulatory powers over the automobile industry.

2. Some of the authors adopting the more authoritarian interpretation include Purcell (1973 and 1975); Stevens (1975); Grindle (1977); Reyna and Weinert (1977); and Smith (1979). Among the authors finding slightly more pluralism in the Mexican system are Scott (1964) and González Casanova (1970). In terms of the relations between entrepreneurs and the state, Kling (1961) stresses the autonomy of certain segments of the private sector, whereas Shafer (1973) and Purcell and Purcell (1977) emphasize the dominance of the state.

3. Daniel Levy (1979) explores the autonomy of higher education; Susan Purcell

and John Purcell (1980), who were in the forefront of the authoritarian interpretations of Mexico, now are refining their analysis by minimizing the importance of institutionalization in Mexico; and Rose Spalding (1981) stresses the limits of state power in shaping welfare policies. For an overview of these arguments, see Levy and Székely (1983:113–118). Nora Hamilton (1982) and James Cockcroft (1980) extend this argument by positing that state autonomy is severely constrained by powerful economic elites and their commitment to the promotion of private capital accumulation.

4. Also see chapter 7 here on these contrasts.

5. This animosity was clearly revealed to me in many interviews during the summer of 1979. Also see *Expansión* (17 October 1973); Arriola (1976); Solís (1981:98–100); Spalding (1981); and Valdés Ugalde (1982).

6. For example, see statements by entrepreneurial leaders reported in *Proceso* (7 February 1983); *Unomásuno* (17, 22, 23 February; 11, 14, 17 March 1983); and *Razones* (7–20 March 1983).

7. For discussions of business associations in the United States and Western Europe, see Ehrmann (1957); Braunthal (1965); Linz and DeMiguel (1966); McConnell (1966); Sarti (1971); and Bauer et al. (1972).

8. Linz also includes the absence of an elaborate and official ideology as a fourth characteristic, but, concurring with Purcell's concentration on the other three factors in the Mexican case, I have omitted national ideology in this analysis of state-industry relations.

9. With the bank nationalizations, the role of the ABM was essentially reduced to leading the court cases against the expropriations.

10. See Brandenburg (1958:29–35); Vernon (1963:74–76); Scott (1964:284–285); Zorrilla Gil (1964:57–68); Alcázar (1970:10–14); Labastida Martín del Campo (1972:105–108); Shafer (1973:44–49, 187–190); Purcell and Purcell (1977:194–195, 219); and Concheiro et al. (1979:272–277).

11. The initial law can be found in *Diario Oficial*, 21 August 1941, with the revisions published on 16 January 1960, 4 February 1963, 30 December 1974, and 7 January 1975.

12. This estimate is provided by the Office for Public Sector Studies, Institute of Latin American Studies, University of Texas at Austin.

13. Interview, 16 July 1979. Also see Lomnitz (1982:62) on the interpenetration of the state and private industry.

14. Some business representation, especially for the smaller enterprises, exists in the "popular sector" (middle-class segment) of the party (interview, 2 August 1979).

15. Several respondents in the summer of 1979 expressed this contentment. Also see Brandenburg (1958:36, 48–49); Vernon (1963:76); and Scott (1964:24, 285–287).

16. One could perhaps doubt the sincerity and validity of such claims. However, these same officials were surprisingly frank in criticizing the government and political leaders on a number of issues. In research on Mexican business groups in

the late 1960s, Shafer (1973:377) also reports that officials of the entrepreneurial organizations were very useful and apparently honest respondents.

17. See Anderson (1963:144–146, 164); Vernon (1963:19–20); Shafer (1973:128–146); and Van Ginneken (1980:71).

18. See Shafer (1973:54–58, 67–70, 107–112); and Purcell and Purcell (1977:194–195). Also, a few of the more conservative business leaders told me that CANACINTRA was a tool of the state. And from the Left, *Proceso* (21 February 1983) described CANACINTRA as "unofficially official."

19. See especially Shafer (1973:54–56) and various articles in Lavin et al. (1951). Medina (1978:293–296) provides a factual account of CANACINTRA's early years.

20. Some six years later the government also began to emphasize protection from foreign competition for these newer industries by creating import controls and increasing tariffs.

21. Shafer (1973:107) states that CANACINTRA "obviously always has represented the views of the political masters of Mexico."

22. The Chambers Law states that the approval of 80 percent of the industrialists in a specialized branch is required to warrant the formation of a new chamber.

23. Various respondents in 1979 and again in 1983 confirmed this preference. Also see Derossi (1971:40–41, 54).

24. The ABM did assume a higher profile during its losing battle against the bank nationalizations.

25. On CAMCO, see Delli Sante (1979); *Proceso*, 28 May 1979; and *Times of the Americas*, 2 September 1981.

26. Its "Declaración de Principios" remains one of the most significant statements on entrepreneurial ideology in Mexico. On the creation and importance of the CCE, see Saldívar (1981:172–177) and Concheiro et al. (1979:315–331).

27. See *Análisis Político*, 13 November 1978, and *Proceso*, 26 March 1979. One of the CCE's most influential arms has been the Center of Economic Studies of the Private Sector (CEESP), which issues respected economic analyses usually defending a position of the CCE.

28. See Saldaña (1965); Derossi (1971:50–58); Balán et al. (1973); Andrews (1976); Concheiro et al. (1979:51–131); Vellinga (1979); Basáñez (1982:87–92); and Nuncio (1982).

29. In a comparative analysis, Gereffi and Evans (1981:47) conclude that all large capitalists in Mexico (not just the Monterrey industrialists) are better connected with the state than are the large entrepreneurs of Brazil.

30. See *Latin America Economic Report*, 8 April 1977; and *Business Week*, 30 January 1978.

31. See *Latin America Weekly Report* (14 August, 30 November, 18 December 1981; 12 March, 7 May 1982); *Wall Street Journal* (28 April, 3 May, 19 August 1982; 24 January 1983); and *El Financiero* (18 March 1983).

32. See *Wall Street Journal* (7 November 1982); *Unomásuno* (17 March 1983); and *El Financiero* (18 March 1983).

33. These interactions were alluded to in many of my interviews in 1979 and 1983.

34. See *Proceso*, 5 November 1979; *Análisis Político*, 12 November 1979; *Comercio Exterior*, December 1979; and *Nexos*, April 1983.

35. Most of this information on the political activities of CANACINTRA comes from the chamber's annual reports (*Informe-Asamblea General Anual Ordinaria*) and its publications *20 años de lucha (1941–1961)* and *Memoria y Documentos* (del Segundo Congreso Nacional de la Industria de Transformación, 1953). This material is supplemented by Mosk (1950:22, 32–52, 76–77); Anderson (1963:124–125); Zorrilla Gil (1964:32–33, 69–96); Padgett (1966:131–132); Alcázar (1970:46–53); Shafer (1973:54–56); and Concheiro et al. (1979:294–305).

36. See Alcázar (1970:33–34); Shafer (1973:25–29); and Confederación de Cámaras Industriales, *Boletín Quincenal*, 16 January 1976, p. 28.

37. On the political activities of CONCAMIN after World War II, see Confederación de Cámaras Industriales, *Asamblea General Ordinaria* (various years); idem, *Boletín Quincenal*, 16 January 1976, p. 28: Brandenburg (1958:32–36); Shafer (1973:57); and Concheiro et al. (1979:277–294).

38. See Purcell and Purcell (1976), and *Análisis Político*, 29 March 1976 and 22 August 1977.

39. See *Decisión* (CONCANACO), December 1982; *Excélsior*, 27, 28 January 1983; *Proceso*, 31 January 1983; *Razones*, 7–20 February 1983; and *Expansión*, 2 March 1983.

40. For example, see the monthly publication of COPARMEX for February 1983 (*COPARMEX* 2, no. 5) and the February 1983 edition of CONCANACO's magazine, *Decisión*.

41. See *Proceso*, 7 February 1983; *Unomásuno*, 17 February, 2 March 1983; and *Razones*, 7–20 March 1983.

42. Also, the most recently retired president of CONCAMIN, Alfonso Pandal Graf, was allegedly very close to López Portillo. His paper mill company, Forestal de Oaxaca, received a controversial extension of a forestry concession only four days before López Portillo left office.

43. Some recent CANACINTRA presidents have achieved government posts, but these have not been at high levels. See *Proceso*, 21 February 1983.

Chapter 5. The Political Ideology and Perceptions of Industrial Elites: Mexico and Venezuela Compared

(Portions of this chapter are reprinted from Story [1983], used by permission of Sage Publications, Inc.)

1. Numerous reports in this series were published by the United Nations Economic Commission for Latin America under the general title *El Empresario Industrial en América Latina*. The case studies included Argentina (by Eduardo A. Zalduendo), Brazil (by Cardoso), Chile (by Guillermo Briones), Colombia (by Aarón Lipman), and Paraguay (by Enzo Faletto). Some of the findings are summarized in Cardoso (1967). Other cross-national surveys of Latin American entrepreneurs were done by Brandenburg (1964) and Lauterbach (1966).

2. Cardoso (1974) emphasized political variables in his comparative analysis of entrepreneurs in Argentina and Brazil. Additional case studies of industrial-elite political values have been conducted for Argentina (Freels 1970; Petras and Cook 1972); Chile (Johnson 1968–1969); and Venezuela (Jongkind 1979).

3. One exception to the interpretation of a split between economic and political power in Mexico is Cockcroft (1980), who states that large capitalists (as represented in organizations like CONCAMIN) are very close to and actually dominate the state. Also see Hamilton (1982).

4. See Blank (1973:216–217); Bond (1975:61–62, 74, 146–147, 278–282); Tugwell (1975a:4–5; 1975b:31–32); and Gil (1977:144). John Martz emphasized this point in a personal conversation with me in September 1977.

5. Story (1983) analyzes these data as well.

6. See Saldaña (1965); Derossi (1971:50–58); Balán et al. (1973); Andrews (1976); Walton (1977); Vellinga (1979); Concheiro et al. (1979:51–131); Basáñez (1982:87–92); and Nuncio (1982).

7. See Vernon (1963:19–20, 103–104, 167–174); Izquierdo (1964:279–282); Zorrilla gil (1964:97–98); Alcázar (1970:54–57, 82–83); Derossi (1971:119–125); and Shafer (1973:54, 67–68, 109–111, 120).

8. Briefly, the M-W Test involves a ranking procedure that is sensitive to any differences in medians, whereas the K-S Test compares distribution functions and is sensitive to all types of possible distributional differences, such as dispersion, skewness, and the like (Siegel 1956:119, 133; Daniel 1978:82–86, 276–279). If either sample is larger than twenty observations, the test statistic for both tests must be computed as a standardized score (Z) with a normal distribution. The null hypothesis of no difference is rejected if the significance or probability level (P) is less than 0.05. Together these two techniques provide a comprehensive test of whether significant differences exist between the CANACINTRA and CONCAMIN samples.

9. The Mexican firms here are about one hundred times as large as the average firm, according to the 1976 Mexican Industrial Census. See Secretaría de Programación y Presupuesto (1979).

10. Though even this degree of dependence on foreign inputs and foreign sources of finance can be quite problematic during a period of exchange shortage, as evidenced by the 1982 crisis.

11. In the Mexican context, Bueno states that the issue of labor relations is one of the principal problem areas of state-industry relations (1977b:69–80).

12. As examples, Gustavo Polit (1968) maintains that Argentine industrialists have been dominated by the landed elites; Dale Johnson (1968–1969) asserts that the Chilean industrial entrepreneurs have a very weak ideological base that primarily reflects industrial subordination to other economic sectors and to the state; and, as already stated, in the Mexican case, Robert Jones Shafer (1973:107) believes that the political ideology of CANACINTRA is heavily controlled by the state.

13. These coefficients demonstrate the extent to which items form a "reliable" scale, that is, how well they measure the same concept. Specifically, reliability

concerns the degree to which measurements are repeatable and is defined as the ratio of the true score variance to the measured score variance (see Nunnally [1967: 172–184]). The reliability coefficient used here is Cronbach's Alpha.

14. For a comparative study of sectorial clash between industry and other sectors in Latin America, see Story (1981).

15. Somewhat surprisingly, in a 1975 survey of U.S. multinational corporations in Mexico, Robinson and Smith (1976:96–97, 244) found that a majority did not feel that government intervention was excessive.

16. Again, the U.S. multinational firms in the Robinson and Smith survey (ibid.:265) provide a different viewpoint, as they overwhelmingly state that they enjoy excellent relations with labor unions and have not been plagued with destructive strikes.

17. A good summary of the private sector point of view regarding state intervention in the economy is Amparo Casar and Peres (1982). Also see Saldívar (1981: 73–80), and Basáñez (1982:108–111).

18. The proceedings of the conference were published by COPARMEX under the title *Seminario internacional sobre el papel de los sectores público y privado en el desarrollo socio-económico*.

19. See Consejo Coordinador Empresarial (1980:9–12). In its 1983 *Declaración de Principios* (pp. 13, 20–22), COPARMEX also stated that state economic intervention should be limited and even temporary.

20. The president seen as most favorable to industry is Miguel Alemán.

Chapter 6. A Typology of the Policy Process and a Case Study of the GATT Decision

(Portions of this chapter are reprinted from Story [1982], used by permission of the MIT Press, Cambridge, Massachusetts, and the World Peace Foundation.)

1. Purcell and Purcell (1977) also stress this in their application of Lowi's typology to Mexico. Also see Kelley (1981:5).

2. Also see chapter 3 here.

3. See *Análisis Político*, 29 August 1977, 30 January 1978, and 18 June 1979.

4. The Mexican GATT decision is also discussed as a case study of trade politics in the Third World in Story (1982).

5. Both documents as well as a statement from the secretary of commerce were published in all major Mexican daily newspapers on 5 November 1979. They are also contained in Spanish in the GATT document #L/4849.

6. *New York Times*, 9 June 1979; Malpica de Lamadrid (1979:85); and *Latin America Regional Report*, 15 February 1980.

7. In interviews with the author in the summer of 1980, many observers and participants in the GATT decision emphasized this determination of the opposition.

8. In particular, see Camp (1980 and 1981) and Levy (1980) concerning UNAM's impact on political life in Mexico.

9. For documentation, see Kelley (1981:9).

10. The interpretation of one U.S. government official working in Mexico City, as expressed to me, was that these Mexican bureaucrats represented those who favored a "small Mexico" that would never assume a leading position in the international community.

11. The secretaries of industry, finance, agriculture, labor, and foreign relations were the five "no" votes and Commerce, Interior, and Planning and Budgeting were the three "yes" votes. The director of the Banco de México was aligned with the "yes" minority but did not exercise an official vote (interview, 22 May 1980).

12. The sources for these trade data are *Comercio Exterior*, Banco de México (unpublished data), and Instituto Mexicano de Comercio Exterior (unpublished data).

13. In 1982 these fifty-six Mexican products had a combined total of exports to the U.S. of $1.7 billion, which was 15 percent of total Mexican exports to the United States and 38 percent of all Mexican nonpetroleum exports. Of course, removal from the generalized system of preferences does not eliminate those U.S. imports; it only applies to the existing import duty. Sources for this information include "Address by the Honorable John Gavin, U.S. Ambassador to Mexico, Graduate School of Management, UCLA, 28 April 1983; *Unomásuno*, 1, 5, 8 April 1983; and Instituto Mexicano de Comercio Exterior, *Boletín Mensual*.

14. Sources include Weintraub (1981) and information from the Instituto Mexicano de Comercio Exterior. Also see Truett and Truett (1980).

15. In February 1983, a group of European bankers and industrialists, who had just met with de la Madrid and his secretaries of finance, commerce, and energy, reported that "government officials" had told them that Mexico would not enter the GATT. The president of CONCANACO also stated that Mexico should not join the GATT. See *Excélsior* (27 January 1983), and *Unomásuno* (25 February and 10 April 1983).

16. These views were expressed to me in February and March of 1983 by several Mexican government officials and by leaders of Mexican trade associations. Also see *Carta de Política Exterior Mexicana*, CIDE, 3, no. 1 (January–February 1983): 5–8.

17. Some differences of opinion do exist over how much redistribution was accomplished and how much the rules of the game had changed. Even before the nationalization, some reports said the public sector controlled 85 percent of the nation's banking resources (Aguilar M. et al. 1982:55), and the bankers themselves admitted that the government had great influence over the private banks through government regulation and policy. On the other hand, the private banks controlled around 80 percent of all peso deposits in Mexico and many of the country's leading corporations. Fifty-four banks were expropriated (with 4,378 branches and almost 150,000 employees), with total resources on 30 June 1982 of about 2.4 trillion pesos. The bank nationalization even affected the Banco de México, reorganizing it as a decentralized government agency. Through interlocking directorships and investments, the private banks had close ties to other economic sectors. Thus, some

of the nation's largest private conglomerates were affected, including Alfa (through its bank, BANPAIS), Peñoles (Banco CREMI), ICA (Banco del Atlántico), VISA (Banco SERFIN), Chihuahua (Multibanco COMERMEX), and Continental (Banco Continental). The two largest private banks (BANCOMER and BANAMEX) had participation in literally hundreds of private companies. See Colmenares et al. (1982:194-196, 253-261), and Pazos (1982:45-49).

18. For example, see Aguilar M. et al. (1982:31); Colmenares et al. (1982:149-150); and *Proceso* (6 September 1982).

19. See *Wall Street Journal* (3 September 1982); *Washington Post* (12 September 1982); and *Latin America Weekly Report* (17 September 1982).

20. Most of these reactions are summarized in *Nexos*, April 1983.

Chapter 7. Industrial Development Strategies and Petroleum Policy

1. *Comercio Exterior*, January 1977.

2. Also see chapter 3 here. Tello Macías (1979) gives a generally positive interpretation of Echeverría's spending policies, and Clement and Green (1978) say that Echeverría was only trying to rectify structural weaknesses in the domestic economy. For an overall analysis of Echeverría's macroeconomic policies, see Looney (1978:61-121).

3. See *Latin America Weekly Report* (19 February, 21 March, 31 October 1980); *Proceso* (24 March, 20 October 1980); and *Análisis Político* (29 October, 26 November 1979).

4. The SAM was officially ended by de la Madrid in 1983. It had helped reduce agricultural imports in 1981 and 1982, but tremendous imports of agrarian products were expected in 1983 (*Latin America Weekly Report*, 7 January 1983).

5. For discussons of these changes and business reaction, see *Análisis Político* (17 January 1977); *Latin America Economic Report* (13 July 1979); *Proceso* (16 and 23 July 1979); *Excélsior* (24 July 1979); *Comercio Exterior de México* (February 1980); and Villarreal and de Villarreal (1981).

6. See Confederación de Cámaras Industriales, *Concamin* (December 1980); and Cámara Nacional de la Industria de Transformación, *Transformación* (October 1980) for the proposals of the respective industrial groups regarding export policy.

7. Several of these factors are analyzed in Centro de Investigación y Docencia Económicas (1982:9-21). Also, William Cline (1982-1983) discusses the international impact of Mexico's financial crisis.

8. However, as late as 19 March 1982, the *Wall Street Journal* reported that "even the most pessimistic bankers say it is unlikely that Mexico will need to restructure its loans."

9. See "Discurso de toma de posesión de Miguel de la Madrid Hurtado," *El Día*, 2 December 1982; and "Mensaje a la nación," *Comercio Exterior*, December 1982.

10. On the history of Mexican petroleum, see Flores Caballero (1978); Mancke (1979:17-91); Williams (1979:5-7); Millor (1982:15-56); and Levy and Székely (1983:221-230). For a review essay, see Grindle (1983).

11. Some of these explanations are also discussed in Williams (1979:12–15, 43–47), and *Latin America Weekly Report*, 20 June 1980.

12. Many of the negative consequences of increased petroleum dependency were also outlined in a 1981 report by the Centro de Investigación y Docencia Económicas. See *Latin America Regional Report*, 23 October 1981. Cleaves (1981:193–194) posits that petroleum dependency will even stymie political reform.

13. *Programa de Energía, Metas a 1990 y proyecciones al año 2000* (resumen y conclusiones), Secretaría de Patrimonio y Fomento Industrial, Mexico City, November 1980. On the relation between this program and the other development plans, see Salinas de Gortari (1980), and Bueno (1981).

14. See *Unomásuno* (12 February 1983), and BANAMEX (1983). The March price decrease was expected to cost Mexico about $1.3 billion in 1983.

15. Others included the National Urban Development Plan, the National Employment Plan, the National Fisheries Development Plan, and the National Tourism Plan. For a critical view of the new focus on planning, see Ceceña Cervantes et al. (1980).

16. On the history of planning in Mexico, see Solís (1975), and *Euromoney* (March 1981, supplement, pp. 11–12).

17. *Plan Nacional de Desarrollo Industrial, 1979–82*, Vols. 1 and 2, Secretaría de Patrimonio y Fomento Industrial, 1979. The plan was published in English by Graham and Trotman Limited as *Mexico: National Industrial Development Plan*. For analysis of the plan, see *Comercio Exterior de México* (June 1979); SERFIN (1979); *Transformación* (September 1979); Blair (1980); FitzGerald (1980); and Street (1980).

18. On the historical evolution of the PGD, see *Proceso* (4 February 1980 and 19 March 1979), and *Latin America Weekly Report* (23 May 1980).

19. *Plan Global de Desarrollo 1980–82*, vols. 1 and 2, Secretaría de Programación y Presupuesto, 1980. Analyses and descriptions of the PGD are found in *El Mercado de Valores* (21 April 1980, supplement); *Análisis Político* (30 April 1980); SERFIN (1980); and *Transformación* (June 1980).

20. The projections are summarized in *Plan Global de Desarrollo 1980–82*, vol. 2, pp. 109–147.

21. This commission was composed of the Secretariats of the Treasury, Planning and Budgeting, Resources and Industrial Promotion, Commerce, Agriculture, Communications and Transportation, and Public Works. The secretary of resources and industrial promotion was to preside at all meetings, and the general directors of NAFINSA and Banco Somex could attend.

22. See Article 20 of Decree Providing for the Implementation of the National Industrial Development Plan, *Diario Oficial*, 19 March 1979.

23. *Plan Nacional de Desarrollo Industrial*, vol. 1, p. 33. Also see Article 22 of Decree Providing for the Implementation of the National Development Plan, *Diario Oficial*, 19 March 1979.

24. *Plan Nacional de Desarrollo Industrial*, vol. 1, p. 33.

25. Quoted in *Euromoney*, March 1981, supplement, p. 13.

26. One of the first development programs (for the cement industry) was actually signed in 1980. See *Diario Oficial,* 1 July 1980.

27. See Goulet (1971); Packenham (1973); Berger (1974); Hewlett (1980); and Hewlett and Weinert (1982).

28. Even U.S. policy has assumed that economic growth and equality are not contradictory goals. For example, the assistant secretary of state for inter-American affairs in 1979 (Viron P. Vaky), in testimony before Congress on supplemental aid to Central America and the Caribbean (primarily Nicaragua), said one U.S. objective for the region was to achieve "economic development with equity" (U.S. State Department mimeo, "Statement in Support of Central American and Caribbean Supplemental," Testimony before the Committee on Foreign Affairs, U.S. House of Representatives, 27 November 1979). However, in a study confirming the tradeoffs involved in the "cruel dilemma," Hewlett (1980) shows that the postwar Brazilian growth-oriented strategy has exacted tremendous human costs in terms of repression, income inequality, and greater poverty.

Chapter 8. Conclusion

1. Przeworski and Teune (1970) discuss "system" variables and "country" variables. An exhaustive list of citations from both categories of research would needlessly occupy many lines here. For a few examples, one could contrast comparative research that includes Mexico in such volumes as Chilcote and Edelstein (1974) and Malloy (1977) to historical studies of Mexico such as the work by Quirk (1963) or Womack (1968). Of course, these are not suggested as "ideal types" (or the best or the worst) of either category.

2. An interesting contrast can be made between the Argentine and Mexican industrialization policies of the 1940s. Argentina's Industrial Promotion Law of 1944 granted subsidies to "industries of importance from the standpoint of national defense" (Wythe 1949:126), whereas Mexico's Law of Manufacturing Industries of 1941 granted tax exemptions to those industries "devoted to the manufacture or preparation of goods not produced in the country in sufficient quantity to meet the needs of domestic consumption" (Bernal-Molina 1948:81). Thus, the Argentine law was more to the benefit of the military, and the Mexican law was clearly designed as a boost to import-substituting industries.

3. For a more extended discussion of the sectorial clash, see Story (1981).

4. Obviously, my research does not address the issue of popular unrest. For a pessimistic evaluation from this perspective, see Cockcroft and Gandy (1981).

Appendix A. Sources of and Methods for Collecting Industrialization Data

1. This is also discussed in Randall (1976:138–139).

2. For example, one census may cover all firms with ten or more employees and the next census may cover all firms with five or more employees. This problem of which census to use as a "base year" is also addressed in Schwartz (1967:130–133 and Appendix M), and in Randall (1976:140–141).

3. The data for 1929 are from Dirección General de Estadística (1934); 1950

from United Nations, Department of Economic and Social Affairs, Statistical Office, *The Growth of World Industry*; 1970 from Dirección General de Estadística, *IX Censo Industrial 1971*; and 1975 from Secretaría de Programación y Presupuesto (1979a). Much of the industrial census data is summarized in Hernández Gutiérrez (1979).

Bibliography

Aceituno, Gerardo, and Inder J. S. Ruprah. 1982. "Déficit público e inflación." *Economía Mexicana*, no. 4, pp. 47–60.

Aguilar M., Alonso, et al. 1977. *Política mexicana sobre inversiones extranjeras.* Mexico City: Universidad Nacional Autónoma de México.

———.1982. *La nacionalización de la banca: La crisis y los monopolios.* Mexico City: Editorial Nuestro Tiempo.

Alcázar, Marco Antonio. 1970. *Las agrupaciones patronales en México.* Mexico City: El Colegio de México.

Alexander, Alec P. 1967. "The Supply of Industrial Entrepreneurship." *Explorations in Entrepreneurial History* 4, no. 2, Second Series (Winter):136–149.

Almond, Gabriel A. 1957. "The Politics of German Business." In *West German Leadership and Foreign Policy*, edited by Hans Speier and W. Phillips Davison, pp. 195–241. Evanston, Ill.: Row, Peterson.

Alvarez de la Cadena, Héctor. 1983. *Participación extranjera: Transferencia de tecnología e inversiones.* Mexico City: Editorial Diana.

Amin, Samir. 1977. "Self-Reliance and the New International Economic Order." *Monthly Review* 29, no. 3 (July–August):1–21.

Amparo Casar, Ma., and Wilson Peres. 1982. "El discurso sobre la economía mixta mexicana: Una noción, tres proyectos." Centro de Investigación y Docencia Económicas, Documentos de Trabajo no. 2, Serie Estudios Políticos. Mexico City.

Anderson, Charles W. 1963. "Bankers as Revolutionaries: Politics and Development Banking in Mexico." In *The Political Economy of Mexico*, by William P. Glade and Charles W. Anderson, pp. 103–185. Madison: University of Wisconsin Press.

Andrews, George Reid. 1976. "Toward a Re-Evaluation of the Latin American Family Firm: The Industry Executives of Monterrey." *Inter-American Economic Affairs* 30, no. 3 (Winter):23–40.

Anguiano Equihua, Roberto. 1968. *Las finanzas del sector público en México.* Mexico City: Universidad Nacional Autónoma de México.

Arriola Carlos. 1976. "Los grupos empresariales frente al estado (1973–1975)." *Foro Internacional* 16 (April–June):449–495.

Aubey, Robert T. 1966. *Nacional Financiera and Mexican Industry: A Study of the Financial Relationship between the Government and the Private Sector of Mexico.* Los Angeles: UCLA Latin American Center.

Baer, Werner. 1965. *Industrialization and Economic Development in Brazil.* Homewood, Ill.: Richard D. Irwin.

——. 1972. "Import Substitution and Industrialization in Latin America: Experiences and Interpretations." *Latin American Research Review* 7, no. 1 (Spring):95–122.

——, and Annibal V. Villela. 1973. "Industrial Growth and Industrialization: Revisions in the Stages of Brazil's Economic Development." *The Journal of Developing Areas* 7, no. 2 (January):217–234.

Baird, Peter, and Ed McCaughan. 1979. *Beyond the Border: Mexico and the U.S. Today.* New York: North American Congress on Latin America.

Baklanoff, Eric N. 1975. *Expropriation of U.S. Investments in Cuba, Mexico, and Chile.* New York: Praeger.

Balán, Jorge; Harley L. Browning; and Elizabeth Jelin. 1973. *Men in a Developing Society: Geographic and Social Mobility in Monterrey, Mexico.* Latin American Monographs, no. 30. Austin: University of Texas Press, for the Institute of Latin American Studies.

BANAMEX. 1983. *Examen de la situación económica de México*

Banco de México. *Indicadores económicos.* Various years.

——. *Indicadores del sector externo.* Various years.

——. *Informe anual.* Various years.

——. 1982a. *Actividad industrial, cuaderno 1975–1982. vol. 2, producto interno bruto.*

——. 1982b. *Serie estadísticas históricas: Inversión extranjera directa, cuaderno 1938–1979.*

Basáñez, Miguel. 1982. *La lucha por la hegemonía en México.* Mexico City: Siglo Veintiuno.

Bauer, Raymond A.; Ithiel De Sola Pool; and Lewis Anthony Dexter. 1972. *American Business and Public Policy: The Politics of Foreign Trade.* Chicago: Aldine-Atherton.

Bennett, Douglas, and Kenneth Sharpe. 1979a. "El estado como banquero y empresario: El carácter de última instancia de la intervención económica del estado mexicano, 1917–1970." *Foro Internacional* 20, no. 1 (July–September):29–72.

——. 1979b. "Agenda-Setting and Bargaining Power—The Mexican State vs. Transnational Automobile Corporations." *World Politics* 32 (October):57–89.

Berger, Peter L. 1974. *Pyramids of Sacrifice: Political Ethics and Social Change.* Garden City, N.Y.: Anchor Books.

Bernal-Molina, Julián. 1948. *A Statement of the Laws of Mexico in Matters Affecting Business in Its Various Aspects and Activities.* Washington, D.C.: Inter-American Development Commission.

——. 1956. *A Statement of the Laws of Mexico in Matters Affecting Business.* Second Edition. Pan American Union, General Legal Division, Department of Legal Affairs, Washington, D.C.

Bivens, Karen Kraus, and Helen S. Lambeth. 1967. *A World-Wide Look at Business-Government Relations: Present Problems and Future Cooperation.* New York: National Industrial Conference Board.

Blair, Calvin P. 1964. "Nacional Financiera: Entrepreneurship in a Mixed Economy." In *Public Policy and Private Enterprise in Mexico*, edited by Raymond Vernon, pp. 193-240. Cambridge, Mass.: Harvard University Press.

———. 1977. "Echeverría's Economic Policy." *Current History* 72, no. 425 (March):124-127.

———. 1980. "Economic Development Policy in Mexico: A New Penchant for Planning." Technical Papers series, no. 76. Office for Public Sector Studies, Institute of Latin American Studies, University of Texas at Austin.

Blank, David Eugene. 1973. *Politics in Venezuela: A Country Study*. Boston: Little, Brown.

Bodenheimer, Susanne J. 1971. *The Ideology of Developmentalism: The American Paradigm-Surrogate for Latin American Studies*. Beverly Hills: Sage Professional Papers in Comparative Politics, 01-015.

Bond, Robert Duane. 1975. "Business Associations and Interest Politics in Venezuela: The FEDECAMARAS and the Determination of National Economic Policies." Ph.D. dissertation, Vanderbilt University.

Bonilla, Arturo. 1980. "El fracaso histórico del GATT." *Comercio y Desarrollo* 2, no. 13 (January-March):44-50.

Brandenburg, Frank R. 1958. "Organized Business in Mexico." *Inter-American Economic Affairs* 12, no. 3 (Winter):26-50.

———. 1964. *The Development of Latin American Private Enterprise*. Washington, D.C.: National Planning Association.

Braunthal, Gerard. 1965. *The Federation of German Industry in Politics*. Ithaca, N.Y.: Cornell University Press.

Briones, Guillermo. 1963. *El empresario industrial en América Latina, 3. Chile*. United Nations Economic Commission for Latin America. E/CN.12/642/Add.3.

Bueno, Gerardo M. 1971. "The Structure of Protection in Mexico." In *The Structure of Protection in Developing Countries*, edited by Bela Balassa, pp. 169-202. Baltimore: The Johns Hopkins University Press.

———. 1977a. "Las estrategias del desarrollo estabilizador y del desarrollo compartido." In *Opciones de política económica en México después de la devaluación*, edited by Gerardo M. Bueno, pp. 21-51. Mexico City: Editorial Tecnos.

———. 1977b. "Las relaciones con el sector privado." In *Opciones de política económica en México después de la devaluación*, edited by Gerardo M. Bueno, pp. 69-80. Mexico City: Editorial Tecnos.

———. 1981. "Petróleo y planes de desarrollo en México." *Comercio Exterior* 31, no. 8 (August):831-840.

Business International Corporation. 1979. *Investment Strategies in Mexico: How to Deal with Mexicanization*. New York: Business International Corporation.

Business Week. Various issues.

Cámara Nacional de la Industria de Transformación. 1961. *20 años de lucha (1941-1961)*. Mexico City.

———. *Informe—Asamblea General Anual Ordinaria*. Mexico City. Various issues.

———. *Memoria y Documentos* (del Segundo Congreso Nacional de la Industria de Transformación, 1953). 1953. Mexico City.

———. *Transformación*. Mexico City. Various issues.

Camp, Roderic Ai. 1976. *Mexican Political Biographies, 1935-1975*. Tucson: University of Arizona Press.

———. 1980. *Mexico's Leaders: Education and Recruitment*. Tucson: University of Arizona Press.

———. 1981. "Intellectuals: Agents of Change in Mexico?" *Journal of Interamerican Studies and World Affairs* 23, no. 3 (August):297-320.

Cándano Fierro, Diego. 1980. "La influencia del proteccionismo y la estructura doméstica del mercado sobre el margen de ganancias de la industria manufacturera en México, 1970 y 1980." *Comercio y Desarrollo* 3, no. 15 (July–September):27-45.

Cardoso, Fernando H. 1963. *El empresario industrial en América Latina, 2. Brasil*. United Nations Economic Commission for Latin America. E/CN.12/642/Add.2.

———. 1966. "The Entrepreneurial Elites of Latin America." *Studies in Comparative International Development* 2, no. 10:145-159.

———. 1967. "The Industrial Elite." In *Elites in Latin America*, edited by Seymour M. Lipset and Aldo Solari, pp. 94-114. New York: Oxford University Press.

———. 1974. *Ideologías de la burguesía industrial en sociedades dependientes (Argentina y Brasil)*. Mexico City: Siglo Veintiuno.

———. 1976. "Associated-Dependent Development: Theoretical and Practical Implications." In *Authoritarian Brazil: Origins, Policies, and Future*, edited by Alfred Stepan, pp. 142-176. New Haven, Conn.: Yale University Press.

———, and Enzo Faletto. 1973. *Dependencia y desarrollo en América Latina*. Mexico City: Siglo Veintiuno.

Carrada-Bravo, Francisco. 1982. *Oil, Money, and the Mexican Economy: A Macroeconometric Analysis*. Boulder, Colo.: Westview Press.

Casar, José I. 1982. "Ciclos económicos en la industria y sustitución de importaciones: 1950-1980." *Economía Mexicana*, no. 4, pp. 77-98.

Cavarozzi, Marcelo. 1976. "El rol de los partidos gobernantes y las organizaciones públicas en la generación de políticas de industrialización." Technical Papers series, no. 2, Office for Public Sector Studies, Institute of Latin American Studies, University of Texas.

Ceceña Cervantes, José Luis, et al. 1980. *Planes sin planificación*. Mexico City: Proceso.

Central Intelligence Agency. *International Energy Statistical Review*. Washington, D.C.

Centro de Información y Estudios Nacionales. 1980. *Política de Mexicanización de Empresas Extranjeras*. E1/E-3/1980. Mexico City.

———. 1981a. *Cien empresas con inversión extranjera*. A5/E-34/1981. Mexico City.

———. 1981b. *Proceso de mexicanización de empresas extranjeras*. E9/E-44/October, 1981. Mexico City.

———. 1982a. *El comercio en México y el rol de la inversión extranjera*. E13/ E-57/March 1982. Mexico City.

———. 1982b. *Las empresas estatales*. E14/E-59/March 1982. Mexico City.

Centro de Investigación y Docencia Económicas. *Carta de política exterior mexicana*. Mexico City. Various issues.

———. 1982. "Evolución reciente y perspectiva de la economía mexicana." *Economía Mexicana*, no. 4, pp. 9–24.

Chaffee, Wilber A., Jr. 1976. "Entrepreneurs and Economic Behavior: A New Approach to the Study of Latin American Politics." *Latin American Research Review* 11, no. 3:55–67.

Chenery, Hollis B. 1960. "Patterns of Industrial Growth." *American Economic Review* 50:624–654.

———, and Lance Taylor. 1968. "Development Patterns: Among Countries and Over Time." *The Review of Economics and Statistics* 50 (November):391–416.

Chilocote, Ronald, and Joel Edelstein, eds. 1974. *Latin America: The Struggle with Dependency and Beyond*. New York: Halsted Press.

Cinta G., Ricardo. 1972. "Burguesía nacional y desarrollo." In *El perfil de México en 1980, Vol. 3*, by Jorge Martínez Ríos et al., pp. 165–199. Mexico City: Siglo Veintiuno.

Cleaves, Peter S. 1981. "Mexican Politics: An End to the Crisis?" *Latin American Research Review* 16, no. 2:191–202.

Clement, Norris, and Louis Green. 1978. "The Political Economy of Devaluation in Mexico." *Inter-American Economic Affairs* 32, no. 3 (Winter):47–75.

Cline, William R. 1982–83. "Mexico's Crisis, The World's Peril." *Foreign Policy* 49 (Winter):107–118.

——— et al. 1978. *Trade Negotiations in the Tokyo Round: A Quantitative Assessment*. Washington, D.C.: The Brookings Institution.

Cochran, Thomas C. 1960. "Cultural Factors in Economic Development." *Journal of Economic History* 20, no. 4 (December):515–530.

Cockcroft, James D. 1968. *Intellectual Precursors of the Mexican Revolution, 1900–1913*. Latin American Monographs, no. 14. Austin: University of Texas Press, for the Institute of Latin American Studies.

———. 1980. *El imperialismo, la lucha de clases y el estado en México*. Mexico City: Editorial Nuestro Tiempo.

———, and Ross Gandy. 1981. "The Mexican Volcano." *Monthly Review* 33, no. 11 (May):32–44.

Cole, Arthur H. 1946. "An Approach to the Study of Entrepreneurship." *Journal of Economic History* 6, Supplement:1–15.

———. 1949. "Entrepreneurship and Entrepreneurial History: The Institutional Setting." In *Change and the Entrepreneur: Postulates and Patterns for Entrepreneurial History*, edited by Richard Wohl, pp. 85–107. Cambridge, Mass.: Research Center in Entrepreneurial History, Harvard University.

———. 1971. *Business Enterprise in its Social Setting*. Cambridge, Mass.: Harvard University Press.

Colegio Nacional de Economistas. *El Economista Mexicano*. Mexico City.

Collier, David. 1975. "Timing of Economic Growth and Regime Characteristics in Latin America." *Comparative Politics* 7, no. 3 (April):331–359.

———, ed. 1979. *The New Authoritarianism in Latin America*. Princeton, N.J.: Princeton University Press.

Collier, Ruth Berins, and David Collier. 1979. "Inducements versus Constraints: Disaggregating 'Corporatism'." *American Political Science Review* 73, no. 4 (December):967–986.

Colmenares, David; Luis Angeles; and Carlos Ramírez. 1982. *La nacionalización de la banca*. Mexico City: Editorial Terra Nova.

Comercio Exterior. Various issues.

Comercio Exterior de México. Various issues.

Concheiro, Elvira; Antonio Gutiérrez; and Juan Manuel Fragaso, 1979. *El poder de la gran burguesía*. Mexico City: Ediciones de Cultura Popular.

Confederación de Cámaras Industriales. *Asamblea General Ordinaria*. Mexico City.

———. *Boletín Quincenal*. Various issues.

———. *Concamin*. Various issues.

———. 1983a. *Integración, funciones, organización, objetivos*. Mexico City.

———. 1983b. *La industria mexicana*. Mexico City.

Confederación de Cámaras Nacionales de Comercio. *Decisión*. Various issues.

———. 1983. *Declaración de principios*. Mexico City.

Confederación Patronal de la República Mexicana. *COPARMEX*. Mexico City. Various issues.

———. 1971. *Seminario internacional sobre el papel de los sectores público y privado en el desarrollo socio-económico*. Mexico City.

———. 1983. *Declaración de principios: Nuestra doctrina social*. Mexico City.

Consejo Coordinador Empresarial. 1980. *Ideario del Consejo Coordinador Empresarial*. Mexico City.

Consejo Venezolano de la Industria. *Producción*. Various issues.

Corredor Esnaola, Jaime. 1981. "El significado económico del petróleo en México." *Comercio Exterior* 31, no. 11 (November):1311–1323.

Cosío Villegas, Daniel. 1965. *Historia moderna de México: 7. El Porfiriato—Vida económica*. Mexico City: Editorial Hermes.

Cutright, Phillips. 1963. "National Political Development: Measurement and Analysis." *American Sociological Review* 28, no. 2 (April):253–264.

———. 1971. "Political Structure, Economic Development, and National Social Security Programs." In *Macro-Quantitative Analysis*, edited by John V. Gillespie and Betty A. Nesvold, pp. 539–555. Beverly Hills: Sage Publications.

Dahl, Robert A. 1959. "Business and Politics: A Critical Appraisal of Political Science." *American Political Science Review* 53, no. 1 (March):1–34.

Dallas Times Herald. Various issues.

Daniel, Wayne W. 1978. *Applied Nonparametric Statistics*. Boston: Houghton Mifflin.

De la Peña, Moisés T. 1945. "La industrialización de México y la política arance-
laria." *El Trimestre Económico* 12, no. 2 (July–September):187–218.

Delli Sante, Angela M. 1979. "The Private Sector, Business Organizations, and
International Influence: A Case Study of Mexico." In *Capitalism and the State
in U.S.-Latin American Relations*, edited by Richard R. Fagen, pp. 337–381.
Stanford: Stanford University Press.

Derossi, Flavia, 1971. *The Mexican Entrepreneur*. Paris: Development Centre of
the Organisation for Economic Co-operation and Development.

De Schweinitz, Karl. 1964. *Industrialization and Democracy: Economic Necessities
and Political Possibilities*. New York: Free Press.

El Día. Various issues.

Diario Oficial. Various issues.

Dirección General de Estadística. 1903. *Estadística industrial formada por la Dirección General de Estadística a cargo del Dr. Antonio Peñafiel*. Mexico City:
Oficina Tip. de la Secretaría de Fomento.

——. 1933. *Primer censo industrial de 1930*.

——. 1936. *Segundo censo industrial de 1935*.

——. *Sexto censo industrial 1956*.

——. *IX censo industrial 1971*.

——. *Anuario estadístico*. Various years.

——. *Anuario estadístico del comercio exterior*. Various years.

——. *Compendio estadístico*. Various issues.

Dirección General de Inversiones Extranjeras y Transferencia de Tecnología.
Anuario estadístico. Various years.

Domínguez, Jorge I. 1982. "International Reverberations of a Dynamic Political
Economy." In *Mexico's Political Economy: Challenges at Home and Abroad*,
edited by Jorge I. Domínguez. Beverly Hills: Sage Publications.

Dorfman, Adolfo. 1970. *Historia de la industria argentina*. Buenos Aires: Ediciones Solar.

Dos Santos, Theotonio. 1968. *La crisis de la teoría del desarrollo y las relaciones de
dependencia en América Latina*. Boletín de Centro de Estudios Socio-Econó-
micos, no. 3.

Dunn, Robert W. 1926. *American Foreign Investment*. New York: B. W. Huebsch
and the Viking Press.

Economist. Various issues.

Ehrmann, Henry W. 1957. *Organized Business in France*. Princeton, N.J.: Princeton University Press.

Euromoney. Various issues.

Evans, Peter. 1979. *Dependent Development: The Alliance of Multinational, State
and Local Capital in Brazil*. Princeton, N.J.: Princeton University Press.

Excélsior. Various issues.

Expansión. Various issues.

Fajnzylber, Fernando, and Trinidad Martínez Tarragó. 1976. *Las empresas trans-
nacionales: Expansión a nivel mundial y proyección en la industria mexicana*.
Mexico City: Fondo de Cultura Económica.

Faletto, Enzo. 1963. *El empresario industrial en América Latina, 5. Paraguay*. United Nations Economic Commission for Latin America. E/CN.12/642/Add.5.

Fernández Hurtado, Ernesto. 1967. "Private Enterprise and Government in Mexican Development." In *Mexico's Recent Economic Growth*, edited by Tom E. Davis, pp. 45–68. Austin: University of Texas Press.

El Financiero. Various issues.

FitzGerald, E. V. K. 1978a. "Patterns of Public Sector Income and Expenditure in Mexico." Technical Papers series, no. 17. Office for Public Sector Studies, Institute of Latin American Studies, University of Texas.

———. 1978b. "The State and Capital Accumulation in Mexico." *Journal of Latin American Studies* 10, no. 2 (November):263–282.

———. 1980. "Oil and Mexico's Industrial Development Plan." *Texas Business Review* 54, no. 3 (May–June):133–137.

Fitzgibbon, Russell H., and Kenneth F. Johnson. 1961. "Measurement of Latin American Political Change." *American Political Science Review* 55, no. 3 (September):515–526.

Flanigan, William, and Edwin Fogelman. 1971. "Patterns of Political Development and Democratization: A Quantitative Analysis." In *Macro-Quantitative Analysis*, edited by John V. Gillespie and Betty A. Nesvold, pp. 441–473. Beverly Hills: Sage Publications.

Flores Caballero, Romeo. 1978. "El petróleo: Una alternativa para el desarrollo de México." Technical Papers series, no. 19. Office for Public Sector Studies, Institute of Latin American Studies, University of Texas.

Freels, John. 1970. *El sector industrial en la política nacional*. Buenos Aires: Editorial Universitaria de Buenos Aires.

Furtado, Celso. 1970. *Economic Development of Latin America: A Survey from Colonial Times to the Cuban Revolution*. London: Cambridge University Press.

García Ramírez, Sergio. 1979. "Panorama sobre la empresa pública en México." Paper prepared for the Seminario Internacional sobre Regulación de la Empresa Pública, Mexico City, 14–16 November 1979.

Gereffi, Gary, and Peter Evans. 1981. "Transnational Corporations, Dependent Development, and State Policy in the Semiperiphery: A Comparison of Brazil and Mexico." *Latin American Research Review* 16, no. 3:31–64.

Gerschenkron, Alexander. 1953. "Social Attitudes, Entrepreneurship, and Economic Development." *Explorations in Entrepreneurial History* 6, no. 1, Old Series (October):1–19.

———. 1962. *Economic Backwardness in Historical Perspective: A Book of Essays*. Cambridge, Mass.: Harvard University Press.

Gil, José Antonio. 1977. "Entrepreneurs and Regime Consolidation." In *Venezuela: The Democratic Experience*, edited by John D. Martz and David J. Myers, pp. 134–157. New York: Praeger.

Glade, William P. 1955. "The Role of Government Enterprise in the Economic Development of Underdeveloped Regions: Mexico, a Case Study." Ph.D. dissertation, The University of Texas.

———. 1963. "Revolution and Economic Development: A Mexican Reprise." In *The Political Economy of Mexico*, by William P. Glade and Charles W. Anderson, pp. 3–101. Madison: University of Wisconsin Press.

———. 1967. "Approaches to a Theory of Entrepreneurial Formation." *Explorations in Entrepreneurial History* 4, no. 3, Second Series (Spring/Summer): 245–259.

———. 1969. *The Latin American Economies: A Study of Their Institutional Evolution.* New York: American Book Company.

———. 1980. "Mexico and GATT: An Evolving Relationship." Paper presented at Seminar for Instituto Mexicano de Ejecutivos de Finanzas, Saltillo, Mexico, 28 February 1980.

Goldsmith, Raymond W. 1966. *The Financial Development of Mexico.* Paris: Development Centre of the Organisation for Economic Co-operation and Development.

González Casanova, Pablo. 1970. *Democracy in Mexico.* London: Oxford University Press.

Gordon, Wendell C. 1975. *The Expropriation of Foreign-Owned Property in Mexico.* Westport, Conn.: Greenwood Press.

Goulet, Denis. 1971. *The Cruel Choice: A New Concept in the Theory of Development.* New York: Atheneum.

Grayson, George W. 1977–78. "Mexico's Opportunity: The Oil Boom." *Foreign Policy*, no. 29 (Winter), pp. 65–89.

———. 1979. "Oil and U.S.-Mexican Relations." *Journal of Interamerican Studies and World Affairs* 21, no. 4 (November):427–456.

———. 1981. *The Politics of Mexican Oil.* Pittsburgh: University of Pittsburgh Press.

Griffin, Keith B. 1966. "Reflections on Latin American Development." *Oxford Economic Papers* 18, no. 1 (March):1–18.

Grindle, Merilee S. 1977. "Policy Change in an Authoritarian Regime: Mexico under Echeverría." *Journal of Interamerican Studies and World Affairs* 19, no. 4 (November):523–555.

———. 1983. "Black Gold in Mexico and in U.S.-Mexican Relations." *Latin American Research Review* 18, no. 2:230–239.

Grunwald, Joseph. 1970. "Some Reflections on Latin American Industrialization Policy." *Journal of Political Economy* 78, no. 4 (July–August):826–856.

Gutiérrez Santos, Luis E. 1977. "Algunas reflecciones sobre los criterios de exportación a corto plazo." Mimeograph, Mexico City.

Hagen, Everett E. 1960–61. "The Entrepreneur as Rebel against Traditional Society." *Human Organization* 19, no. 4 (Winter):185–187.

Hamilton, Nora. 1977. "The State and Class Formation in Post-Revolutionary Mexico." Paper presented at joint national meeting of the Latin American Studies Association and the African Studies Association, Houston, Texas.

———. 1982. *The Limits of State Autonomy: Post-Revolutionary Mexico.* Princeton, N.J.: Princeton University Press.

Hansen, Roger D. 1971. *Mexican Economic Development: The Roots of Rapid Growth.* Studies in Development Progress, no. 2. Washington, D.C.: National Planning Association.

———. 1974. *The Politics of Mexican Development.* Baltimore: The Johns Hopkins University Press.

Harbison, Frederick. 1956. "Entreprenerial Organization as a Factor in Economic Development." *Quarterly Journal of Economics* 70, no. 3 (August):364–379.

Harbron, John D. 1965. "The Dilemma of an Elite Group: The Industrialist in Latin America." *Inter-American Economic Affairs* 19, no. 2 (Fall):43–62.

Hartmann, Heinz. 1959. *Authority and Organization in German Management.* Princeton, N.J.: Princeton University Press.

Hayes, Michael T. 1978. "The Semi-Sovereign Pressure Groups: A Critique of Current Theory and an Alternative Typology." *The Journal of Politics* 40, no. 1 (February):134–161.

Hernández Gutiérrez, Ignacio. 1979. *Estadísticas históricas industriales.* Mexico City: Instituto de Investigaciones Económicas, Universidad Nacional Autónoma de México.

Hewlett, Sylvia Ann. 1980. *The Cruel Dilemmas of Development: Twentieth Century Brazil.* New York: Basic Books.

———, and Richard S. Weinert, eds. 1982. *Brazil and Mexico: Patterns in Late Development.* Philadelphia: Institute for the Study of Human Issues.

Hibbs, Douglas A., Jr. 1974. "Problems of Statistical Estimation and Causal Inference in Time-Series Regression Models." In *Sociological Methodology, 1973-1974,* edited by Herbert L. Costner, pp. 252–308. San Francisco: Jossey-Bass.

Hirschman, Albert O. 1968. "The Political Economy of Import-Substituting Industrialization in Latin America." *The Quarterly Journal of Economics* 82, no. 1 (February):1–32.

Hoffman, W. G. 1958. *The Growth of Industrial Economics.* Manchester, England: Manchester University Press.

Hogan, Timothy D. 1983. "Estimating the Urban Family Budget with a Pooled Cross-Section/Time-Series Model." *Social Science Quarterly* 64, no. 2 (June): 412–416.

Holt, Robert T., and John E. Turner. 1966. *The Political Basis of Economic Development: An Exploration in Comparative Political Analysis.* Princeton, N.J.: D. Van Nostrand.

Hoselitz, Bert F. 1952. "Entrepreneurship and Economic Growth." *American Journal of Economics and Sociology* 12, no. 1 (October):97–110.

———. 1961. "Some Problems in the Quantitative Study of Industrialization." *Economic Development and Cultural Change* 9, no. 3 (April):537–549.

Industridata 1980–81. Mexico City: Mercamétrica Editores.

Ingalls, Walter R. 1922. *Wealth and Income of the American People.* York, Penn.: G. H. Merlin.

Instituto de Estudios Políticos, Económicos y Sociales, Partido Revolucionario Institucional. 1981. *Plan básico 1982-1988 y plataforma electoral.* Mexico City.

Instituto Mexicano de Comercio Exterior. *Boletín Mensual.* Various issues.

Inter-American Development Bank. *Economic and Social Progress in Latin America.* Various years.

International Monetary Fund. *International Financial Statistics.* Various years.

Izquierdo, Rafael. 1964. "Protectionism in Mexico." In *Public Policy and Private Enterprise in Mexico,* edited by Raymond Vernon, pp. 243–289. Cambridge, Mass.: Harvard University Press.

Jacobs, Eduardo. 1982. "La evolución reciente de los grupos de capital privado nacional." *Economía Mexicana,* no. 3, pp. 23–44.

Jenkins, Rhys Owen. 1976. *Dependent Industrialization in Latin America: The Automotive Industry in Argentina, Chile, and Mexico.* New York: Praeger.

Johnson, Dale L. 1968–69. "The National and Progressive Bourgeoisie in Chile." *Studies in Comparative International Development* 4, no. 4:63–86.

Johnston, J. 1972. *Econometric Methods.* New York: McGraw-Hill.

Jongkind, Fred. 1979. "Industrialists and the State: Private Views on the Public Role in the Industrialization of Venezuela." Paper presented at the Latin American Studies Association Meeting, 5–8 April, Pittsburgh, Penn.

Kaufman, Robert R. 1977. "Mexico and Latin American Authoritarianism." In *Authoritarianism in Mexico,* edited by José Luis Reyna and Richard S. Weinert, pp. 193–232. Philadelphia: Institute for the Study of Human Issues.

Kelley, Guillermo. 1981. "Politics and Administration in Mexico: Recruitment and Promotion of the Politico-Administrative Class." Technical Papers series, no. 33. Office for Public Sector Studies, Institute of Latin American Studies, University of Texas.

Kerr, Clark, et al. 1964. *Industrialism and Industrial Man.* New York: Oxford University Press.

King, Timothy. 1970. *Mexico: Industrialization and Trade Policies since 1940.* London: Oxford University Press.

Kling, Merle. 1961. *A Mexican Interest Group in Action.* Englewood Cliffs, N.J.: Prentice-Hall.

Kriesberg, Louis. 1963. "Entrepreneurs in Latin America and the Role of Cultural and Situational Processes." *International Social Science Journal* 15, no. 4: 581–594.

Kuznets, Simon. 1957. "Quantitative Aspects of the Economic Growth of Nations: II, Industrial Distribution of National Product and Labor Force." *Economic Development and Cultural Change* 5, no. 4 (July):supplement.

———. 1966. *Modern Economic Growth: Rate, Structure, and Spread.* New Haven, Conn.: Yale University Press.

Labastida Martín del Campo, Julio. 1972. "Los grupos dominantes frente a las alternativas de cambio." In *El Perfil de México en 1980, Vol. 3,* by Jorge Martínez Rios et al. pp. 99–164. Mexico City: Siglo Veintiuno.

LaCascia, Joseph S. 1969. *Capital Formation and Economic Development in Mexico.* New York: Praeger.

Ladman, Jerry R.; Deborah J. Baldwin; and Elihu Bergman. 1980. *United States–Mexico Energy Relationships.* Boulder, Colo.: Westview Press.

Lamb, Robert K. 1952. "Political Elites and the Process of Economic Development." In *The Progress of Underdeveloped Areas*, edited by Bert F. Hoselitz, pp. 30–53. Chicago: University of Chicago Press.

——. 1962. "The Entrepreneur and the Community." In *Men in Business: Essays on the Historical Role of the Entrepreneur*, edited by William Miller, pp. 99–119. New York: Harper and Row.

Latin America Economic Report. Various issues.

Latin America Political Report. Various issues.

Latin America Regional Report. Various issues.

Latin America Weekly Report. Various issues.

Lauterbach, Albert. 1966. *Enterprise in Latin America: Business Attitudes in a Developing Economy*. Ithaca, N.Y.: Cornell University Press.

Lavin, José Domingo et al. 1951. "Comentarios al estudio de Sanford Mosk: La revolución industrial en México." *Problemas Agrícolas e Industriales de México* (April–June), pp. 237–296.

Levin, Jonathan V. 1960. *The Export Economies: Their Pattern of Development in Historical Perspective*. Cambridge, Mass.: Harvard University Press.

Levy, Daniel. 1979. "University Autonomy in Mexico: Implications for Regime Authoritarianism." *Latin American Research Review* 14, no. 3:129–152.

——. 1980. *University and Government in Mexico: Autonomy in an Authoritarian System*. New York: Praeger.

——, and Gabriel Székely. 1983. *Mexico: Paradoxes of Stability and Change*. Boulder, Colo.: Westview Press.

Linz, Juan J. 1970. "An Authoritarian Regime: The Case of Spain." In *Mass Politics: Studies in Political Sociology*, edited by Erik Allardt and Stein Rokkan, pp. 251–283. New York: Free Press.

——, and Amando DeMiguel. 1966. *Los empresarios ante el poder público*. Madrid: Instituto de Estudios Políticos.

Lipman, Aarón. 1963. *El empresario industrial en América Latina, 4. Colombia*. United Nations Economic Commission for Latin America. E/CN.12/642/Add.4.

Lipset, Seymour M. 1959. "Some Social Requisites of Democracy: Economic Development and Political Legitimacy." *American Political Science Review* 53, no. 1 (March):69–105.

——. 1967. "Values, Education, and Entrepreneurship." In *Elites in Latin America*, edited by Seymour M. Lipset and Aldo Solari, pp. 3–60. New York: Oxford University Press.

Lomnitz, Larissa. 1982. "Horizontal and Vertical Relations and the Social Structure of Urban Mexico." *Latin American Research Review* 17, no. 2:51–74.

Looney, Robert E. 1978. *Mexico's Economy: A Policy Analysis with Forecasts to 1990*. Boulder, Colo.: Westview Press.

Lowi, Theodore J. 1964. "American Business, Public Policy, Case-Studies, and Political Theory." *World Politics* 16, no. 4 (July):677–715.

Malloy, James M., ed. 1977. *Authoritarianism and Corporatism in Latin America*. Pittsburgh: University of Pittsburgh Press.

Mancke, Richard B. 1979. *Mexican Oil and Natural Gas: Political, Strategic, and Economic Implications.* New York: Praeger.

Mann, Arthur J. 1979. "The Evolution of Mexico's Public Expenditure Structure, 1895–1975." *Bulletin for International Fiscal Documentation* 33:514–523.

Martínez de la Vega, Francisco. 1976. "¿Crisis del sistema mexicano?" *Cuadernos Americanos* 208, 5 (September–October):29–35.

Mathieson, John A. 1979. *The Advanced Developing Countries: Emerging Actors in the World Economy.* Washington, D.C.: Overseas Development Council.

McConnell, Grant. 1966. *Private Power and American Democracy.* New York: Alfred A. Knopf.

Medina, Luis. 1978. *Historia de la Revolución Mexicana, período 1940–1952, del cardenismo al avilacamachismo.* Mexico City: El Colegio de México.

Mexico: National Industrial Development Plan. 1979. London: Graham and Trotman.

Meyer, Lorenzo. 1972. *México y los Estados Unidos en el conflicto petrolero (1917–1942).* Mexico City: El Colegio de México.

Millor, Manuel R. 1982. *Mexico's Oil: Catalyst for a New Relationship with the U.S.?* Boulder, Colo.: Westview Press.

Moore, Wilbert E. 1966. "Industrialization and Social Change." In *Industrialization and Society*, edited by Bert F. Hoselitz and Wilbert E. Moore, pp. 299–370. New York: UNESCO.

Moran, Theodore H. 1974. *Multinational Corporations and the Politics of Dependence: Copper in Chile.* Princeton, N.J.: Princeton University Press.

Morell, Nilda. 1981. *Inversión extranjera en México.* Mexico City: Editorial Expansión.

Mosk, Sanford A. 1950. *Industrial Revolution in Mexico.* Berkeley and Los Angeles: University of California Press.

Muñoz, Oscar. 1971. *Crecimiento industrial de Chile, 1914–1965.* Santiago: Universidad de Chile, Instituto de Economía y Planificación.

Nacional Financiera. 1965. *La economía mexicana en cifras.* Mexico City.

———. 1981. *1981 Annual Report.*

———. 1981. *La economía mexicana en cifras.* Mexico City.

———. *El Mercado de Valores.* Various issues.

Navarrete R., Alfredo. 1963. "El desarrollo industrial de México: Situación y perspectivas." *El Trimestre Económico* 30, no. 120 (October–December): 574–587.

———. 1967. "The Financing of Economic Development." In *Mexico's Recent Economic Growth*, by Enrique Pérez López et al., pp. 105–130. Austin: University of Texas Press.

Neubauer, Deane E. 1967. "Some Conditions of Democracy." *American Political Science Review* 56, no. 4 (December):1002–1009.

Newfarmer, Richard S., and Willard F. Mueller. 1975. *Multinational Corporations in Brazil and Mexico: Structural Sources of Economic and Noneconomic Power.* Report to the Subcommittee on Multinational Corporations of the Committee on Foreign Relations, United States Senate, August.

New York Times. Various issues.

Nexos. Various issues.

Nun, José. 1969. *Latin America: The Hegemonic Crisis and the Military Coup.* Politics of Modernization Series, no. 7. Berkeley: Institute of International Studies, University of California, Berkeley.

Nuncio, Abraham. 1982. *El grupo Monterrey*. Mexico City: Editorial Nueva Imagen.

Nunnally, Jim C. 1967. *Psychometric Theory*. New York: McGraw-Hill.

O'Donnell, Guillermo. 1973. *Modernization and Bureaucratic-Authoritarianism: Studies in South American Politics*. Politics of Modernization Series, no. 9. Berkeley: Institute of International Studies, University of California, Berkeley.

———. 1975. *Reflexiones sobre las tendencias generales de cambio en el estado burocrático-autoritario*. Buenos Aires: Centro de Estudios de Estado y Sociedad.

Oficina de Asesores del C. Presidente de la República. 1978. *Encuesta sobre actividad económica empresarial 1978*. Mexico City.

Olsen, Marvin E. 1968. "Multivariate Analysis of National Political Development." *American Sociological Review* 33, no. 5 (October):699–712.

Organski, A. F. K. 1965. *The Stages of Political Development*. New York: Alfred A. Knopf.

Ostrom, Charles W. 1978. *Time-Series Analysis: Regression Techniques*. Sage University Paper Series on Quantitative Applications in the Social Sciences. Beverly Hills: Sage Publications.

Packenham, Robert A. 1973. *Liberal America and the Third World*. Princeton, N.J.: Princeton University Press.

Padgett, L. Vincent. 1966. *The Mexican Political System*. Boston: Houghton Mifflin.

Papanek, Gustav F. 1962. "The Development of Entrepreneurship." *American Economic Review* 52, no. 2 (May):46–58.

Pazos, Luis. 1982. *La estatización de la banca*. Mexico City: Editorial Diana.

Peres Núñez, Wilson. 1982. "La estructura de la industria estatal, 1965–1975." *Economía Mexicana*, no. 4, pp. 115–136.

Pérez López, Enrique. 1967. "The National Product of Mexico: 1895 to 1964." In *Mexico's Recent Economic Growth*, by Enrique Pérez López et al., pp. 23–44. Austin: University of Texas Press.

Petras, James F., and Thomas C. Cook. 1972. "Componentes de la acción política: El ejecutivo industrial argentino." *Desarrollo Económico* 12, no. 46 (July–September):387–396.

Petróleos Mexicanos. *Anuario estadístico*. Various years.

———. *Informe del director general de Petróleos Mexicanos*. Various years.

———. *Memoria de labores*. Various issues.

Polit, Gustavo. 1968. "The Argentine Industrialists." In *Latin America: Reform or Revolution?* edited by James Petras and Maurice Zeitlin, pp. 399–430. Greenwich, Conn.: Fawcett.

Powell, J. Richard. 1956. *The Mexican Petroleum Industry: 1938-1950*. Berkeley and Los Angeles: University of California Press.

Proceso. Various issues.

Przeworski, Adam, and Henry Teune. 1970. *The Logic of Comparative Social Inquiry*. New York: Wiley-Interscience.

Purcell, Susan Kaufman. 1973. "Decision-Making in an Authoritarian Regime: Theoretical Implications from a Mexican Case Study." *World Politics* 26, no. 1 (October):28-54.

———. 1975. *The Mexican Profit-Sharing Decision: Politics in an Authoritarian Regime*. Berkeley and Los Angeles: University of California Press.

———. 1981. "Business-Government Relations in Mexico: The Case of the Sugar Industry." *Comparative Politics* 13, no. 2 (January):211-233.

Purcell, John F. H., and Susan Kaufman Purcell. 1976. "El estado y la empresa privada." *Nueva Política* 1, no. 2:229-250.

———. 1977. "Mexican Business and Public Policy." In *Authoritarianism and Corporatism in Latin America*, edited by James M. Malloy, pp. 191-226. Pittsburgh: University of Pittsburgh Press.

Purcell, Susan Kaufman, and John F. H. Purcell. 1980. "State and Society in Mexico: Must a Stable Polity Be Institutionalized?" *World Politics* 32, no. 2 (January):194-227.

Quijano, José Manuel, ed. 1983. *La banca: Pasado y presente (Problemas financieros mexicanos)*. Mexico City: Centro de Investigación y Docencia Económicas.

Quirk, Robert E. 1963. *The Mexican Revolution, 1914-1915: The Convention of Aguascalientes*. New York: Citadel Press.

Ramírez Rancaño, Mario. 1974. *La burguesía industrial: Revelaciones de una encuesta*. Mexico City: Editorial Nuestro Tiempo.

Ramos Garza, Oscar. 1972. *México ante la inversión extranjera: Legislación, políticas, y prácticas*. Mexico City: Docal.

Randall, Laura. 1976. "Lies, Damn Lies, and Argentine GDP." *Latin American Research Review* 11, no. 1:137-158.

Ratinoff, Luis. 1967. "The New Urban Groups: The Middle Classes." In *Elites in Latin America*, edited by Seymour M. Lipset and Aldo Solari, pp. 61-93. New York: Oxford University Press.

Razones. Various issues.

Reyna, José Luis, and Richard S. Weinert, eds. 1977. *Authoritarianism in Mexico*. Philadelphia: Institute for the Study of Human Issues.

Reynolds, Clark. 1970. *The Mexican Economy: Twentieth-Century Structure and Growth*. New Haven, Conn.: Yale University Press.

———. 1971. "Public Finance in Postrevolutionary Mexico." In *Government and Economic Development*, edited by Gustav Ranis, pp. 332-372. New Haven, Conn.: Yale University Press.

Rippy, Merrill. 1972. *Oil and the Mexican Revolution*. Leiden, Netherlands: E. J. Brill.

Robinson, Harry J., and Timothy G. Smith. 1976. *El impacto de la inversión privada extranjera en la economía mexicana*. Menlo Park, Cal.: Stanford Research Institute.

Romeo, Carlos. 1969. "Revolutionary Practice and Theory in Latin America." In *Latin American Radicalism*, edited by Irving Louis Horowitz, Josué de Castro, and John Gerassi, pp. 580–606. New York: Vintage Books.

Rosenzweig, Fernando. 1965. "La Industria." In *Historia Moderna de México*, Vol. 7, Pt. 1, *El Porfiriato, La Vida Económica*, by Daniel Cosío Villegas, pp. 311–481. Mexico City: Editorial Hermes.

Ross, Stanford G., and John B. Christensen. 1959. *Tax Incentives for Industry in Mexico*. Cambridge, Mass.: Law School, Harvard University.

Ross, Stanley R. 1955. *Francisco Madero: Apostle of Mexican Democracy*. New York: Columbia University Press.

Ruiz, Ramón Eduardo. 1976. *Labor and the Ambivalent Revolutionaries: Mexico, 1911–1923*. Baltimore: The Johns Hopkins University Press.

Salamon, Lester M., and John J. Siegfried. 1977. "Economic Power and Political Influence: The Impact of Industry Structure on Public Policy." *American Political Science Review* 71, no. 3 (September):1026–1043.

Saldaña, José D. 1965. *Apuntes históricos sobre la industrialización de Monterrey*. Monterrey: Centro Patronal de Nuevo León.

Saldívar, Américo. 1981. *Ideología y política del estado mexicano (1970–1976)*. Mexico City: Siglo Veintiuno.

Salinas de Gortari, Carlos. 1980. "Los excedentes del petróleo y la planeación en México." *Comercio y Desarrollo* 3, no. 16 (October–December):22–32.

Salisbury, Robert H. 1977. "Peak Associations and the Tensions of Interest Intermediation." Paper presented at the 1977 Annual Meeting of the American Political Science Association, Washington, D.C.

Santillán López, Roberto, and Aniceto Rosas Figueroa. 1962. *Teoría general de las finanzas públicas y el caso de México*. Mexico City: Universidad Nacional Autónoma de México.

Sarti, Roland. 1971. *Fascism and the Industrial Leadership in Italy, 1919–1940*. Berkeley and Los Angeles: University of California Press.

Sawyer, John E. 1962. "The Entrepreneur and the Social Order: France and the United States." In *Men in Business: Essays on the Historical Role of the Entrepreneur*, edited by William Miller, pp. 7–22. New York: Harper and Row.

Saxe-Fernández, John. 1980. *Petróleo y estrategia: México y Estados Unidos en el contexto de la política global*. Mexico City: Siglo Veintiuno.

Schatán, Claudia. 1981. "Efectos de la liberalización del comercio exterior en México." *Economía Mexicana*, no. 3, pp. 79–108.

Schattschneider, E. E. 1935. *Politics, Pressures, and the Tariff*. New York: Atherton.

Schumpeter, Joseph A. 1949. "Economic Theory and Entrepreneurial History." In *Change and the Entrepreneur: Postulates and Patterns for Entrepreneurial History*, edited by Richard Wohl, pp. 63–84. Cambridge, Mass.: Research Center in Entrepreneurial History, Harvard University.

Schwartz, Hugh H. 1967. "The Argentine Experience with Industrial Credit and Protection Incentives 1943-1958." Ph.D. dissertation, Yale University.

Scott, Robert E. 1964. *Mexican Government in Transition*. Urbana: University of Illinois Press.

Secretaría de Comercio. 1974. *Empresas con inversión extranjera mayor de 24.99%*. Mexico City.

Secretaría de Economía, Dirección General de Estudios Económicos. 1948. "La industrialización de México." *Trimestre de Barometros Económicos* 8 (March): 36-57.

Secretaría de Industria y Comercio. 1975. *La empresa: Empresas industriales del país (datos económicos)*. Mexico City.

Secretaría del Patrimonio y Fomento Industrial. 1979. *Plan nacional de desarrollo industrial, 1979-82*, Volumes 1 and 2. Mexico City.

———. *Programa de energía, metas a 1990 y proyecciones el año 2000* (resumen y conclusiones). 1980. Mexico City.

Secretaría de la Presidencia and Nacional Financiera. 1963. *50 años de Revolución Mexicana en Cifras*. Mexico City.

Secretaría de Programación y Presupuesto. *Anuario estadístico*. Various years.

———. *Boletín Mensual de Información Económica*. Various issues.

———. 1979a. *X censo industrial 1976. Resumen general*. Mexico City.

———. 1979b. *X censo industrial 1976. Empresas de participación estatal y organismos descentralizados*. Mexico City.

———. 1980a. *Características de la industria de transformación en México*. Mexico City.

———. 1980b. *X censo industrial 1976. Industrias de extracción y refinación de petróleo y petroquímica básica e industria de generación, transmisión y distribución de energía eléctrica para servicio público*. Mexico City.

———. 1980c. *Plan global de desarrollo 1980-82*, Volumes 1 and 2. Mexico City.

———. 1980d. *Información sobre gasto público 1969-1978*.

———. 1983. *Plan nacional de desarrollo, 1983-1988*. Mexico City.

Sepúlveda, Bernardo, and Antonio Chumacero. 1973. *La inversión extranjera en México*. Mexico City: Fondo de Cultura Económica.

SERFIN. 1979. "The National Industrial Development Plan: Its Objectives, Mechanisms, and Limitations." *Economy and Finance* 8, no. 4 (November).

Shafer, Robert Jones. 1973. *Mexican Business Organizations: History and Analysis*. Syracuse, N.Y.: Syracuse University Press.

Shelton, David H. 1964. "The Banking System: Money and the Goal of Growth." In *Public Policy and Private Enterprise in Mexico*, edited by Raymond Vernon, pp. 113-189. Cambridge, Mass.: Harvard University Press.

Siegel, Sidney. 1956. *Nonparametric Statistics for the Behavioral Sciences*. New York: McGraw-Hill.

Slawinski, Zygmundt. 1965. "Structural Changes in Employment within the Context of Latin America's Economic Development." *Economic Bulletin for Latin America* 10, no. 2 (October):163-187.

Smith, Peter. 1977. "Does Mexico Have a Power Elite?" In *Authoritarianism in Mexico*, edited by José Luis Reyna and Richard S. Weinert, pp. 129–151. Philadelphia: Institute for the Study of Human Issues.

———. 1979. *Labyrinths of Power: Political Recruitment in Twentieth-Century Mexico*. Princeton, N.J.: Princeton University Press.

Smith, T. Alexander. 1969. "Toward a Comparative Theory of the Policy Process." *Comparative Politics* 1, no. 4 (July):498–515.

Solís M., Leopoldo. 1975. *Planes de desarrollo económico y social en México*. Mexico City: Secretaría de Educación Pública.

———. 1981. *Economic Policy Reform in Mexico: A Case Study for Developing Countries*. New York: Pergamon Press.

Spalding, Rose J. 1981. "State Power and Its Limits: Corporatism in Mexico." *Comparative Political Studies* 14, no. 2 (July):139–161.

Stallings, Barbara. 1972. *Economic Dependency in Africa and Latin America*. Beverly Hills: Sage Professional Papers in Comparative Politics.

Stevens, Evelyn P. 1975. "Protest Movement in an Authoritarian Regime: The Mexican Case." *Comparative Politics* 7, no. 3 (April):361–382.

Story, Dale. 1978. "Industrialization and Political Change: The Political Role of Industrial Entrepreneurs in Five Latin American Countries." Ph.D. dissertation, Indiana University.

———. 1980a. "Entrepreneurs and the State in Mexico: Examining the Authoritarian Thesis." Technical Papers series, no. 30. Office for Public Sector Studies, Institute of Latin American Studies, University of Texas.

———. 1980b. "Time-Series Analysis of Industrial Growth in Latin America: Political and Economic Factors." *Social Sciences Quarterly* 61, no. 2 (September):293–307.

———. 1981. *Sectoral Clash and Industrialization in Latin America*. Syracuse, N.Y.: Maxwell School Press, Syracuse University.

———. 1982. "Trade Politics in the Third World: A Case Study of the Mexican GATT Decision." *International Organization* 36, no. 4 (Autumn):767–794.

———. 1983. "Industrial Elites in Mexico: Political Ideology and Influence." *Journal of Interamerican Studies and World Affairs* 25, no. 3 (August):351–376.

———. 1984. "Sources of Investment Capital in Twentieth-Century Mexico." In *Statistical Abstract of Latin America*, Volume 23, edited by James W. Wilkie and Adam Perkal, pp. 837–856. Los Angeles: UCLA Latin American Center Publications.

Strassman, W. Paul. 1964. "The Industrialist." In *Continuity and Change in Latin America*, edited by John J. Johnson, pp. 161–185. Stanford, Cal.: Stanford University Press.

———. 1968. *Technological Change and Economic Development: The Manufacturing Experience in Mexico and Puerto Rico*. Ithaca, N.Y.: Cornell University Press.

Street, James H. 1980. "Prospects for Mexico's Industrial Development Plan in the 1980s." *Texas Business Review* 54, no. 3 (May–June):125–131.

Tanter, Raymond. 1967. "Toward a Theory of Political Development." *Midwest Journal of Political Science* 11, no. 2 (May):145–172.

Tello Macías, Carlos. 1979. *La política económica en México 1970–1976.* Mexico City: Siglo Veintiuno.

Tello, Carlos, and Rolando Cordera. 1981. *México: La disputa por la nacion; perspectivas y opciones del desarrollo.* Mexico City: Siglo Veintiuno.

Temin, Peter. 1967. "A Time-Series Test of Patterns of Industrial Growth." *Economic Development and Cultural Change* 15, no. 2, pt. 1 (January):174–182.

Ten Kate, Adriaan, et al. 1979. *La política de protección en el desarrollo económico de México.* Mexico City: Fondo de Cultura Económica.

Times of the Americas. Various issues.

Truett, Dale B., and Lila Flory Truett. 1980. "Mexico and GSP: Problems and Prospects." *Inter-American Economic Affairs* 34, no. 2 (Autumn):67–85.

Tugwell, Franklin. 1975a. "Brief Report on Research Project on the Venezuelan Private Sector." Prepared for the Conference on the State and Public Policy in Latin America, Buenos Aires, Argentina.

———. 1975b. *The Politics of Oil in Venezuela.* Stanford, Cal.: Stanford University Press.

United Nations. *Demographic Yearbook.* Various years.

———, Department of Economic and Social Affairs. 1963. *A Study of Industrial Growth.* ST/ECA/74.

———, Statistical Office. 1958. *International Standard Industrial Classification of All Economic Activities.* Series M, No. 4, Rev. 1. ST/STAT/SER.M/4/Rev.1.

———. *The Growth of World Industry.* Various years.

United Nations Economic Commission for Latin America. 1950. *Legal and Economic Status of Foreign Investments in Selected Countries of Latin America: Foreign Investment in Mexico.* E/CN.12/166/Add.8.

———. 1957. *External Disequilibrium in the Economic Development of Latin America: The Case of Mexico.* E/CN.12/428.

———. 1966. *The Process of Industrial Development in Latin America.* E/CN.12/716/Rev.1.

———. *Economic Bulletin for Latin America.* Various issues.

———. *Economic Survey of Latin America.* Various issues.

———. *Statistical Bulletin for Latin America.* Various issues.

United States Department of Commerce. *Survey of Current Business.* Various issues.

United States Energy Information Administration. *Weekly Petroleum Status Report.* Various issues.

El Universal. Various issues.

Unomásuno. Various issues.

Valdés Ugalde, Francisco. 1982. "Una aproximación al análisis de las relaciones entre empresarios y gobierno en México, 1970–1976." Mimeo. Mexico City: Centro de Investigación y Docencia Económicas.

Van Ginneken, Wouter. 1980. *Socio-Economic Groups and Income Distribution in Mexico.* New York: St. Martin's Press.

Vellinga, Menno. 1979. *Economic Development and the Dynamics of Class: Industrialization, Power and Control in Monterrey, Mexico*. The Netherlands: Van Gorcum Assen.

Vernon, Raymond. 1963. *The Dilemma of Mexico's Development*. Cambridge, Mass.: Harvard University Press.

————, ed. 1964. *Public Policy and Private Enterprise in Mexico*. Cambridge, Mass.: Harvard University Press.

Villarreal, René. 1976. *El desequilibrio externo en la industrialización de México (1929-1975): Un enfoque estructuralista*. Mexico City: Fondo de Cultura Económica.

————. 1977. "The Policy of Import-Substituting Industrialization, 1929-1975." In *Authoritarianism in Mexico*, edited by José Luis Reyna and Richard S. Weinert, pp. 67-107. Philadelphia: Institute for the Study of Human Issues.

Villarreal, Norma Rocío de, and René Villarreal. 1980. "Public Enterprises in Mexican Development Under the Oil Perspective in the 1980s." Mimeo.

Villarreal, René, and Norma Rocío de Villarreal. 1977. "La empresa pública." In *Opciones de política económica en México después de la devaluación*, edited by Gerardo M. Bueno, pp. 81-112. Mexico City: Editorial Tecnos.

————. 1981. "Mexico's Development Strategy." In *Mexico-United States Relations*, edited by Susan Kaufman Purcell, pp. 97-103. New York: Academy of Political Science.

Vogel, David. 1979. *Lobbying the Corporation: Citizen Challenges to Business Authority*. New York: Basic Books.

Wall Street Journal. Various issues.

Walton, John. 1977. *Elites and Economic Development: Comparative Studies on the Political Economy of Latin American Cities*. Latin American Monographs, no. 41. Austin: Institute of Latin American Studies, University of Texas.

Washington Post. Various issues.

Weinert, Richard S. 1977. "The State and Foreign Capital." In *Authoritarianism in Mexico*, edited by José Luis Reyna and Richard S. Weinert, pp. 109-128. Philadelphia: Institute for the Study of Human Issues.

Weintraub, Sidney. 1981. "Mexican Subsidies and U.S. Law: Potential Collision Course." *The Mexican Forum* 1, no. 2 (April):7-9.

Whiting, Van R., Jr. 1979. "International Aspects of National Regulation: Transnationals and the State in Mexico, 1970-1978." Paper presented at the Annual Convention of the International Studies Association, Toronto, March 23.

Wilkie, James W. 1970. *The Mexican Revolution: Federal Expenditure and Social Change Since 1910*. Berkeley and Los Angeles: University of California Press.

Wilkins, Mira. 1974. *The Maturing of the Multinational Enterprise: American Business Abroad from 1914 to 1970*. Cambridge, Mass.: Harvard University Press.

Williams, Edward J. 1979. *The Rebirth of the Mexican Petroleum Industry*. Lexington, Mass.: Lexington Books.

——. 1980. "Petroleum Policy and Mexican Domestic Politics: Left Opposition, Regional Dissidence, and Official Apostasy." *The Energy Journal* 1, no. 3:75–96.

——. 1982. "Petroleum and Political Change." In *Mexico's Political Economy: Challenges at Home and Abroad*, edited by Jorge I. Domínguez, pp. 23–77. Beverly Hills: Sage Publications.

Wils, Frits. 1979. *Industrialization, Industrialists, and the Nation-State in Peru.* Research Series, no. 41. Berkeley: Institute of International Studies, University of California, Berkeley.

Winkler, Max. 1928. *Investments of United States Capital in Latin America.* World Peace Foundation Pamphlets, vol. 11, no. 6.

Wionczek, Miguel S. 1964. "Electric Power: The Uneasy Partnership." In *Public Policy and Private Enterprise in Mexico*, edited by Raymond Vernon, pp. 21–110. Cambridge, Mass.: Harvard University Press.

——. 1967. *El nacionalismo mexicano y la inversión extranjera.* Mexico City: Siglo Veintiuno.

——. 1971. "Foreign-Owned Export-Oriented Enclave in a Rapidly Industrializing Economy: Sulphur Mining in Mexico." In *Foreign Investment in the Petroleum and Mineral Industries*, by Raymond F. Mikesell et al., pp. 264–311. Baltimore: The Johns Hopkins University Press.

Wohl, Richard, ed. 1949. *Change and the Entrepreneur: Postulates and Patterns for Entrepreneurial History.* Cambridge, Mass.: Research Center in Entrepreneurial History, Harvard University.

Womack, John, Jr. 1968. *Zapata and the Mexican Revolution.* New York: Vintage Books.

World Bank. *World Development Report.* Washington, D.C. Various issues.

Wright, Harry K. 1971. *Foreign Enterprise in Mexico: Laws and Policies.* Chapel Hill: University of North Carolina Press.

Wythe, George. 1949. *Industry in Latin America.* New York: Columbia University Press.

——. 1955. "Brazil: Trends in Industrial Development." In *Economic Growth: Brazil, India, Japan*, edited by Simon Kuznets, Wilbert E. Moore, and Joseph J. Spengler, pp. 29–77. Durham, N.C.: Duke University Press.

Yúnez Naude, Antonio. 1979. "Política petrolera y perspectivas de desarrollo de la economía mexicana." In *Las perspectivas del petróleo mexicano*, pp. 203–225. Mexico City: El Colegio de México, Centro de Estudios Internacionales.

Zalduendo, Eduardo A. 1963. *El empresario industrial en América Latina, 1. Argentina.* United Nations Economic Commission for Latin America. E/CN. 12/642/Add.1.

Zorrilla Gil, José. 1964. "La Cámara Nacional de la Industria de Transformación en el desarrollo industrial del país." M.A. thesis, Universidad Nacional Autónoma de México.

Index